QUEERING THE MIDWEST

Queering the Midwest

Forging LGBTQ Community

Clare Forstie

NEW YORK UNIVERSITY PRESS

New York

NEW YORK UNIVERSITY PRESS
New York
www.nyupress.org

References to Internet websites (URLs) were accurate at the time of writing. Neither the author nor New York University Press is responsible for URLs that may have expired or changed since the manuscript was prepared.

Library of Congress Cataloging-in-Publication Data
Names: Forstie, Clare, author.
Title: Queering the midwest : forging LGBTQ community / Clare Forstie.
Description: New York : New York University Press, [2022] |
Includes bibliographical references and index.
Identifiers: LCCN 2021062397 | ISBN 9781479801862 (hardback) |
ISBN 9781479801879 (paperback) | ISBN 9781479801886 (ebook) |
ISBN 9781479801893 (ebook other)
Subjects: LCSH: Sexual minority community—Middle West. | Sexual minorities—
Middle West—Social conditions.
Classification: LCC HQ73.3.U62 M5446 2022 | DDC 306.760977—dc23/eng/20220127
LC record available at https://lccn.loc.gov/2021062397

New York University Press books are printed on acid-free paper, and their binding materials are chosen for strength and durability. We strive to use environmentally responsible suppliers and materials to the greatest extent possible in publishing our books.

Manufactured in the United States of America

10 9 8 7 6 5 4 3 2 1

Also available as an ebook

There is much to be learned from wanting something both ways.
—Maggie Nelson, *The Argonauts*

CONTENTS

Introduction

Kai and I are perched with a small Christmas tree between us in the crowded back office of a nonprofit. Beyond our closed door, people who clearly know each other well are milling about, drinking coffee, and chatting with each other as they offer mutual support. Sitting close together causes Kai and me to joke about our different heights; I am proudly six feet tall and Kai is equally proudly somewhat less than that. We pick up a conversation we began at a nearby coffee shop, and I ask them about LGBTQ community in River City, the small Midwestern city where their family lives and where they decided to make a permanent home.[1] Like a number of my participants, Kai describes LGBTQ community as "cliquey," although they explain that, unlike more urban LGBTQ communities, River City's has come a long way in a short period of time.

Kai is well attuned to the ways LGBTQ people's lives both have and have not changed over the past two decades in River City, a postindustrial small city of between 50,000 and 60,000. In some ways, Kai's demographic profile, like that of a majority of River Citizens, would place them squarely in the category of working-class, white people who were Trump's primary demographic in the 2016 and 2020 election (Cramer 2017). Politically, however, Kai refuses this categorization, and they employ a complex frame when thinking about River City LGBTQ community, reflecting on their experiences and those of their friends along the way. On the one hand, they see River City as pretty safe, noting that there aren't many places where they feel unsafe. Yet, when I ask them about whether they'd describe River City as post-gay, or entering a time when gay identities are less central to LGBTQ lives, they respond, "We're kind of in a post-gay thing, but that's for white, cisgender gay men. You know, when we're talking about, like, LGBT overall, you know, transgender women of color are getting brutally murdered at a ridiculous rate, and, you know, it's still not necessarily OK to be a lesbian, or God forbid bisexual."

Drawing from their own experiences as an activist and community member with family in River City, Kai describes "the hierarchy of the alphabet soup" of LGBTQ identities, locating transgender people at the bottom of that hierarchy relative to cisgender lesbians (higher) and gay men (higher still) even as they are not as far behind as outsiders like me might think. In framing this social hierarchy, Kai's reflections echo research on LGBTQ communities, research that has historically prioritized the experiences of white gay men in large cities (Eaves 2017; Stone 2018). Researchers and community members have challenged this research trajectory in recent decades, for example, in research prioritizing the experiences of queer women of color, of LGBTQ youth in rural communities, and of transgender men in rural places (Abelson 2019; Gray et al. 2016; Moore 2011). And, still, in the popular imagination, and in the imaginations of my participants, LGBTQ communities in small cities remain largely invisible, the "little brother" to the other, more visible, and larger communities in cities like Chicago and New York, as Karen, another participant, explained.

After living in a distant state, Kai made a conscious choice to build a future in River City, but this choice came with painful personal costs. Later in our conversation, Kai becomes emotional when we talk about their dating prospects and the intentional trade-off they've made between what they describe as their "calling" to support progressive social change in River City and the emotional, ephemeral, and practical reasons why they want to find a partner. After describing their feeling about the choice to stay as a "bitter pill," given how much work they've done to support LGBTQ community, they shared why they felt emotional: "In my case, you know . . . I wanna have a family and stuff, and also, um . . . those things that other people kinda have taken for granted, like, you know, when my parents are gone, that's it. It's like, I have some really cool friends, and stuff, but it's not the same, plus, it's like, relationships are nice! You know?"

And evidence that Kai is working hard to generate social change abounds. During my research, Kai was arguably the most active of my participants in generating relationships and among the most knowledgeable about the landscape and history of LGBTQ community in River City. Kai is a force unto themself in creating community, coordinating with nonprofits and individual friends and family to show up at

LGBTQ community events, even as they were often on the physical and metaphoric periphery of these events. If an LGBTQ event is happening in River City, Kai is almost always there, either in an official capacity through their work or as themself, a friendly introvert, excited to share their experience and knowledge and strategize about social change. And they are rarely the center of attention, preferring to play the role of educator and occasionally quipping quietly that lesbians are the ones that get things done. Unlike more visible LGBTQ organizations (Ghaziani 2014a), Kai is quietly doing the work of community building, even as this "calling" limits their own life in sometimes painful ways.

I begin with Kai's experience because they are the kind of person who, we might imagine, would flee to a larger city (Weston 1995) to escape the presumed hostility of a Midwestern small city like River City. And, yet, there are a number of pulls keeping Kai in River City: family, friendships, a familiar cultural landscape, and the possibility of making change. LGBTQ people in River City often face the "stay or go" choice, sometimes repeatedly across a lifetime, and many of my participants express an array of ambivalences about this choice. Some are strongly motivated to stay, drawn by relationships and the accessible amenities this small city has to offer, while others find little sense of community and leave for opportunities elsewhere (sometimes in other small cities). Some leave for work, for communities more aligned with their identities, and when they do, community institutions shift and sometimes disappear. Kai's story suggests the ways that LGBTQ communities in small, rural cities play out in individuals' lives, and the ways those lives inform what I'm calling ambivalent communities. It's a story of racialized sexualities and genders, of community contexts informing collective and individual affects and decision making, and of assimilation alongside differentiation. The broader racial, classed, and gendered contexts of communities in cities like River City inform how individuals navigate ambivalences they feel and, in turn, affect the shape these communities take.

In this book, my aim is to identify what constitutes LGBTQ communities in smaller cities like River City, where LGBTQ organizations and events occur occasionally but are generally not grounded in long-standing LGBTQ institutions (Ghaziani 2014a). A second aim is to assess what *kind* of LGBTQ community exists in River City, given existing frameworks for understanding such communities in a moment of shifting identities. The case of River City offers conflicting evidence of visible, out gay community alongside hidden pockets of friends who form their own miniature community clusters (Ghaziani 2019). A final aim is to examine the role that non-LGBTQ allies play in forming, and possibly dissolving, LGBTQ communities in communities like River City, as LGBTQ community events require the involvement of allies to be sustainable in the longer term.[2] Given the form of ambivalent community in River City, I consider whether close relationships like friendships and family networks constitute, supplement, or substitute for LGBTQ community.

In what follows, I draw on Kai's story to propose the concept of "ambivalent communities" as a way to recognize the contradictions evident in River City's LGBTQ community and in the choices people make within them. While individuals feel ambivalence about their lives, ambivalence is evident in relationships and institutions, too, all components of LGBTQ community in River City. Kai's ambivalence can be traced through these three dimensions of ambivalent communities (individual, relationship, and institutional): visible, first, in their eyes as they speak about their decision to stay in River City; second, the role their LGBTQ friends and non-LGBTQ family play in their lives; and, third, institutionally in the ways organizations and events wax and wane. I develop these three components of ambivalence by discussing research focused on LGBTQ communities and their historic changes, especially in the shift toward assimilation, at least in urban communities. I propose ambivalent communities as a practical intervention in this research and as particularly useful as progress narratives in the United States continue to be challenged politically and socially. I then frame ambivalence in relationships by identifying an absence in sociological approaches to LGBTQ community: the role of friendship as a necessary ingredient in community formation. While friendship is often referenced obliquely in LGBTQ community research, its contours remain unexplored, leaving significant gaps in our knowledge about these communities and how communities are formed and organized. Finally, I briefly describe the context of River City itself, discuss my research methods, and outline the chapters of the book.

I argue that River City's LGBTQ community does not follow the linear narrative of progress suggested by researchers of urban, gay neighborhoods. A close examination of key components of LGBTQ community (institutions, friendships, and allies) reveals that multiple "phases" of LGBTQ community development (Ghaziani 2014b) exist simultaneously within the same context. LGBTQ community members express hopes that LGBTQ institutions might no longer be needed while they also long for affirming spaces and relationships, as Kai does. Shared-identity friendships both do and do not "matter" for LGBTQ participants. Allies benefit from their relationships with LGBTQ people and institutions even as they work to sustain them. These findings shift LGBTQ community theory making from a linear to an ambivalent model and challenge assumptions about how LGBTQ communities grow and change.

LGBTQ Progress and Community Ambivalence

It is not an exaggeration to suggest that the early 2020s is a time of deep ambivalence in the United States, and ambivalence about social change in particular is likely to persist in future years. Indicators of progress in terms of LGBTQ identities seem in decline, and claims like "it gets better" ring a bit hollow, given attention to the dual pandemics of COVID-19 and systemic racism, both of which have affected, and sometimes ended, LGBTQ lives. The moment I am writing is a different one from the moment I began my research, where hope seemed possible, even as tragedies within LGBTQ communities abounded, like the massacre at the Pulse nightclub on Latinx night in 2016.[3] Ambivalence is highly relevant to this moment, especially as a framework to understand our past, present, and future. While we may, as individuals, feel a sense of ambivalence, what might it mean to think about ambivalence more broadly from a sociological perspective, particularly with respect to communities?

First, a note about what "community" means in the context of this book. Colloquially, community might mean any sense of shared identity, or perhaps the spaces in which those identities are recognized and supported, like the community space of a gay bar. However, research on the contested boundaries of those community spaces and identities, as well as an expansion of the kinds of communities that "count" (Ghaziani 2014a, 2019; Gray 2009; Greene 2021; Mattson 2020; Moussawi and Vidal-Ortiz

2020; Stone 2018), requires a more specific definition. In this project, I use Albert Hunter's (1974, 1975, 2006) tripartite framework of community as ecological (across space and time dimensions), social structural (including interpersonal networks and institutional density), and symbolic (composed of identity and culture). LGBTQ communities, then, require a bounded place located in time, identifiable institutions, personal relationships that link individuals, and a sense of shared identity and culture. LGBTQ community research has historically addressed each of these elements of community. For example, early LGBTQ community research identified the spatial as well as temporal dimensions of gay community formation, focusing on gay institutions that emerged in cities like New York, San Francisco, and Chicago (Chauncey 1995; D'Emilio 1998; Ghaziani 2014a; Levine 1979). Others have considered the symbolic centrality of the foundational LGBTQ community story: the raid on the Stonewall Inn in New York City (Armstrong and Crage 2006; Ghaziani 2014a). Still others have analyzed the personal relationships that form LGBTQ community, like Kath Weston's "chosen family" (1991) and gay men's and lesbians' friendships (Nardi 1999; Weinstock and Rothblum 1996). As I will show below, River City's LGBTQ community contains each of these three dimensions; however, my focus in this book is largely on the social structural dimension of LGBTQ community specifically. Within this dimension, I analyze LGBTQ community through its institutions (even when they disappear) and friendships (even when they draw LGBTQ people away from those institutions).

Researchers of LGBTQ community have long argued that "gay community," and, later, LGBTQ and queer community, encapsulate an array of disparate experiences under one identitarian roof—the "same umbrella, different raindrops" that a participant, Colby, will mention.[4] Elizabeth Armstrong (2002), for example, highlights the process by which San Francisco's gay community unified a set of conflicting identities under a single organizational umbrella that also managed to acknowledge the differences within, while Amin Ghaziani (2009) describes the "resinous condition" under which communities on the opposite coast solidify their identitarian boundaries (if temporarily). More recently, researchers have identified the processes by which LGBTQ social movements coalesce (Ghaziani, Taylor, and Stone 2016), suggesting the ongoing relevance of an imagined (Weston 1995), if perpetually fractured, LGBTQ community.

And some challenge the usefulness of "community" itself as a frame, highlighting the ways communities fundamentally exclude even as they coalesce (Joseph 2002). While there are a range of identities and experiences within LGBTQ community, tensions around the boundaries of LGBTQ communities are certainly not new (Weiss 2003).

To what extent can we speak of LGBTQ community in River City, specifically? Despite an array of everyday experiences that vary across gender, sexual, racial, and class identities, the evidence is strong. River City's LGBTQ community is limited spatially and temporally (as discussed in the first few chapters of this book), includes LGBTQ-specific and broadly inclusive institutions like youth groups and "queer bars," is composed of social networks of varying density, and references national and local LGBTQ identities and iconography, like rainbow flags, Pride events, shared jokes, and identity-specific terminology. Institutions and symbols like these are clear markers of LGBTQ community (Ghaziani 2014a). Other researchers have analyzed the organizational logics of LGBTQ communities (Armstrong 2002), which are also evident in River City. One clear, powerful example of what Armstrong (2002) calls the "interest group" logic of LGBTQ community might be seen in the rapid organization of the vigil following the 2016 mass murder of LGBTQ people in Orlando, attended by participants of *several* LGBTQ identities, described in chapter 1. If anything, LGBTQ community might be *more* coherent in River City than in larger, urban contexts where organization under different identities might be possible and, some argue, necessary (P. Doan 2007).

Despite its persistence, River City's LGBTQ community has experienced the same kinds of shifts noted in communities across the United States: growing acceptance among friends, family, and communities alongside persistent hostility, discrimination, and inequality (Ghaziani 2014a). Researchers have grappled with the meaning of these changes and have marked the most recent decades as ones of declining gay identity relevance (Brown-Saracino 2011; Ghaziani 2011, 2014b), at least among urban and "friendly" community contexts. The overall focus of this literature has typically been on white, urban gay contexts (Chauncey 1995; D'Emilio 1998; Gray 2009; Greene 2021; Weston 1995), and much of the thinking about gay community has emerged from research focused on gay communities in large, often gay-friendly cities. More recent research on rural (Gray 2009; Gray, Johnson, and Gilley 2016; C. Johnson 2013) and suburban (Brekhus 2003; Kirkey and Forsyth 2001; Tongson 2011) LGBTQ communities has challenged some of this thinking, suggesting multiple forms of LGBTQ communities that depend on their local community contexts and possibilities for LGBTQ identity expression (Brown-Saracino 2017). Still, the theoretical division between urban and rural remains squarely mapped onto friendly and hostile, post-gay and closet, and progressive and conservative binaries, even as researchers continually challenge this framework (Gray et al. 2016).

Noting a shift from an era of gay activism in the 1980s and 1990s, pop cultural critiques of gay community beginning in the 1990s (Collard 1998) suggested that urban gay communities were evolving toward a post-gay era (Ghaziani 2011), a time marked by declining and disappearing gay institutions like gay bars and increasing equivocation about gay identity. Among lesbians, similar themes involving the downplay of differences relative to straight people have emerged (Brown-Saracino 2011; Stein 2010). Same-sex marriage might have been considered a threshold for communities' evolving toward a post-gay and perhaps post-lesbian era (Forstie 2018; McNaron 2007). Following the logic of a post-gay framework, we might expect to find communities across the United States developing familiar gay institutions that thrive during a coming-out era, only to disappear as a national narrative of assimilation, multiculturalism, and emphasis on sameness permeates these contexts. Within River City, the cyclical rise, fall, and rise (again) of gay bars and LGBTQ community organizations, popular drag shows, and LGBTQ-friendly social activities suggests a mix of identities and spaces that challenge such linear narratives of progress centered in urban, gay communities.

Furthermore, shifting our lens from LGBTQ communities in large cities to those in smaller cities and rural towns suggests an attendant shift in how we think about community change. For example, while LGBTQ institutions anchor communities in large cities (Ghaziani 2014a), *people* anchor communities (and sometimes LGBTQ institutions) in smaller cities like River City. As people migrate to and from these communities, relationships, institutions, and events rise and fall, as in the "pooping-out" phenomenon that the participant Karen will describe. As a result, the innovative "queer pop-up" events becoming more common in large cities (Stillwagon and Ghaziani 2019) have been present—indeed, necessary—in smaller cities and even smaller rural towns. As Mary Gray noted in her 2009 research with rural LGBTQ young people, LGBTQ community has been *necessarily* temporary in contexts where institutions cannot be sustained.

A focus on small cities also challenges who, truly, is "included" in LGBTQ community. LGBTQ community has long been subsumed under the umbrella term "gay community," and some participants used the language of "gay community" to describe community that includes a range of gender and sexual identities. I use the term "LGBTQ community" to highlight the disparate identities of participants who might not be visible under the term "gay community" (see appendix B for a discussion of terminology). While some suggest that LGBTQ community might not unify such a broad range of gender and sexual identities, I argue that LGBTQ as a unified category is already embedded in the local and national cultural imagination. Some local examples are the "LGBTQ+" support groups available at a multicultural center in River City, as well as the language of a municipal proclamation designating June as "Lesbian, Gay, Bisexual, and Transgender (LGBT) Pride Month." Recall, though, that LGBTQ communities are not necessarily universally welcoming. LGBTQ communities remain contested and hostile, particularly to Black, Indigenous, and People of Color (BIPOC), young people, nonbinary and trans people, and specifically to cisgender and trans women (Abelson 2019; Battle et al. 2017; Eaves 2017; Greene 2018, 2021; Hulko and Hovanes 2018; Joseph 2002; Thorpe 1996). As Kai notes above, "LGBTQ communities" is sometimes seen as code for white, middle-class, gay communities, and the experiences of BIPOC participants, LGBTQ and ally alike, bear this out. The local community contexts organized around race and gender matter for this "stay or go" decision, one felt acutely by River City's BIPOC LGBTQ participants.

Researchers have examined LGBTQ communities beyond gay, urban contexts, and these approaches have yielded alternative models of LGBTQ community, some of which resonate with ambivalent communities. For instance, Japonica Brown-Saracino's discussion of "ambient community" (2011:362) suggests that, for lesbians and queer women in especially friendly communities, being part of a lesbian-specific community is less central to lesbian and queer women's lives. "Ambient" communities centered around shared leisure activities and interests have largely replaced traditional lesbian institutions and organizations. As Kai's comments suggest, however, this is not necessarily the case in communities that might be seen as less friendly, even as rural LGBTQ communities make space for white lesbians (C. Johnson 2013; Kazyak 2012).

Furthermore, researchers have found that rural LGBTQ communities exist but are temporary, contingent, and technology-based as few visible gay institutions endure in these spaces (Bell and Valentine 1995; Browne 2009; Gray 2009). And suburban and rural spaces seem marked by the possibilities of comfort, mobility, and urban gay tourism (Brekhus 2003; Greene 2014). For example, Wayne Brekhus's research describes "tunnel and bridge gays" (2003:99), or "lifestylers" (2003:33), who live in the suburbs but commute to the city to attend gay community institutions and events. Similarly, Theo Greene suggests that suburban and rural gay citizens may engage in gay community "vicariously" by traveling to well-known urban gay contexts (2014:99). Post-gay theorists acknowledge that the picture of gay community is complex (Ghaziani 2014b) and shifting, but a tension exists in the literature between the declining relevance of LGBTQ communities and their ongoing importance as a touchstone, if a temporary one (Ghaziani 2019; Stillwagon and Ghaziani 2019).

My research in this book draws on this key tension in discussions of LGBTQ communities, a tension that is reflected in my participants' mixed feelings of local LGBTQ community and narratives of identity, sometimes painfully articulated in their decisions to stay or go. In the simplest terms, LGBTQ communities are persistently ambivalent and not easily located along a trajectory toward assimilation or progress (two different possible endpoints theorized currently in the literature) (Love 2009). The contours of each community's specific ambivalences may be found by examining three dimensions of community: institutions, as sociologists have traditionally examined; relationships; and individuals squarely located in social contexts, each of which I discuss briefly below. As should be apparent, the temporal dimension is critical here. Understanding how each of these change over time helps us to think about the shape of things to come. Finally, the spatial context matters, too; in the case of River City, consider the local context of the city itself alongside the state, regional, national, and global contexts. These temporal, spatial dimensions are the social structural stuff underpinning the possibilities of agency in individuals and relationships.

Social Contexts of Ambivalence

We might begin by understanding ambivalence as an individual feeling, one that has had a relatively recent history, originating as a psychological concept in 1910 (Merton and Barber 1963; Smelser 1998). In my research, participants often described mixed feelings and the desire to hold them in tension, the "both/and" framing Jack offered. As Smelser explains, "The nature of ambivalence is to hold *opposing affective orientations* [emphasis in original] toward the same person, object, or symbol. [And] with some exceptions, preferences are regarded as relatively stable; ambivalence tends to be unstable, expressing itself in different and sometimes contradictory ways as actors attempt to cope with it" (1998:5). Individual experiences of ambivalence highlight its nature as fundamentally unstable, always in process, and a characteristic of changing circumstances. As an individual-level concept, ambivalence is uniquely suited to understanding LGBTQ people's lives.

Thinking beyond individuals' experiences, though, sociologists argue that ambivalence stems from and informs our social contexts. Sociological ambivalence, although not always named explicitly in this way, has existed conceptually in the discipline for more than a century, and some of this research predates the concept of ambivalence (Gould 2001). Consider W. E. B. Du Bois's "double consciousness," which describes the sensation of "two-ness" Black Americans experience, arising from the structural source of white supremacy. Writing many years later, ambivalence is threaded through feminist analyses of inequality and identity, some within sociology and some within adjacent, critical theoretical fields. Patricia Hill Collins's "outsider within" framework identifying the theory-making possibilities emerging from the specific experiences of Black women in academia may not be focusing specifically on communities, but she describes the benefits of an approach that takes into account the mixed feelings arising from one's social context. Similarly, Kimberlé Crenshaw's foundational theorizing of the concept of intersectionality (1995) also addresses the historical and institutional contexts in which Black women's lives and experiences are embedded. As she later explains, "political intersectionality highlights the fact that women of color are situated within at least two subordinated groups that frequently pursue conflicting political agendas" (1995:360). This is also true of communities more broadly, which are at times organized around conflicting political goals.

Even more explicitly, feminist theorist Gloria Anzaldúa writes about "a new *mestiza* consciousness, *una conciencia de mujer* . . . a consciousness of the Borderlands" (Anzaldúa 1999:77). Drawing from her own life as a Chicana from the Borderlands between Mexico and the United States, she adds, "The ambivalence from the clash of voices results in mental and emotional states of perplexity. Internal strife results in insecurity and indecisiveness. The mestiza's dual or multiple personality is plagued by psychic restlessness. In a constant state of mental nepantilism, an Aztec word meaning torn between ways, *la mestiza* is a product of the transfer of the cultural and spiritual values of one group to another" (1999:78). Anzaldúa notes that *la mestiza*, or more specifically, the "new mestiza consciousness," represents the future, a way of thinking that dismantles dualistic thinking. Although most of my participants do not draw from the same cultural contexts as Anzaldúa, ambivalence as a response to the dual pressures of assimilation and differentiation offers a similar "third way."

How individuals navigate feelings of ambivalence are well studied in sociology; for example, social psychological research identifies ambivalence as central to institutional maintenance (Merton 1976; Smelser 1998). Ambivalence's primary purchase in sociology has been in the case of families, as, for example, older family members express intergenerational ambivalence as they navigate between solidarity and conflict with younger generations (Lüscher 2002; Lüscher and Hoff 2013; Lüscher and Pillemer 1998). In their foundational piece, Ingrid Connidis and Julie Ann McMullin explain that "we formulate a conceptualization of ambivalence as structurally created contradictions that are experienced by individuals in their interaction with others" (2002:559). Furthermore, feminist and gender scholars have explored ambivalence as a conceptual tool useful in theory making (Bondi 2004; Butler 2002) but have not applied this concept empirically to social life. Applying ambivalence to identity-based communities is a logical next step, given its utility as a concept in families and status systems in transition (Coser 1966). Indeed, we see calls for more ambivalent approaches to processes of assimilation in research focused on communities of color grappling with assimilation (Garcia 2016). Given its rich theoretical roots in sociology, it is time to apply the concept of ambivalence to LGBTQ identity and community change.

Importantly, scholars who examine ambivalence in communities highlight the ways communities are always incoherent, always in flux, and necessarily exclusionary (Joseph 2002). Puar's analysis of "assemblage theory" (Puar 2007, 2020), an approach that challenges the firmness of identities and, by extension, communities organized around them, does some of this work. Deborah Gould's research on LGBTQ community conflict names ambivalence explicitly and describes community as "a useful fiction that is always in process, a becoming rather than a being, and one that is always unsettled" (2001:155). In this book, and in line with Ghaziani (2014a), I am arguing that the unsettledness of communities varies and is specific to each community's contours and histories.

Focusing on LGBTQ communities, most recently, scholars have explored how communities maintain the dual tensions between assimilation and marginalization. Most well known in this field is Ghaziani's (2011, 2014b) post-gay theory, which describes a trajectory through which urban gay communities typically pass: from closeted, to coming out, to post-gay, when gay identities are less central to gay lives. While the presumed normative outcome of this framework has been challenged (Kampler and Connell 2018), it reflects a national progress narrative that my participants vehemently disputed *and* desired, and, in any case, clearly understood. And, yet, retaining a focus on race and nationality at the center of analyses of LGBTQ communities (Manalansan et al. 2014; Moussawi and Vidal-Ortiz 2020), as ambivalence research suggests, challenges the notion that we will ever fully arrive in a post-gay moment, despite the claims of urban, white gay men. As Ghassan Moussawi and Salvador Vidal-Ortiz note, we need to no longer ignore "multiple genealogies of queer theory—particularly women of color feminisms, Black feminist thought, and the queer of color critique" (2020:1274). Their roadmap for transforming queer sociology aligns with my project in developing a theory of ambivalent communities, and central to that process is a shift from presumed, stable identities rooted in white, Western cultural norms toward understanding the lived realities of LGBTQ people rooted in histories of white and American supremacy.

We can look to empirical research to arrive at the kind of specificity that probably feels lacking at this point. What, precisely, does ambivalent community *look* and *feel like*, given local community histories? Two examples suffice in this moment, and what follows is a project that seeks to add to this growing chorus. First, Juan Battle and coauthors (2017) use a national sample of LGBT people of color to explore feelings of connectedness among Black LGBT respondents to white LGBT communities. As the Battle study found, Black LGBT people often feel a stronger sense of connection to Black communities (as is true of my BIPOC participants, more generally, who traveled to other cities to reconnect with families and BIPOC communities), where perhaps ambivalence in home communities feels more manageable. While the local and national context matters for feelings of belonging, returning to the specificity of local, small-city contexts, LaToya Eaves (2017) writes about a participant, Rebeca, who was managing ambivalence as a Black, queer woman in a small city in the South. Noting that race and sexuality are co-constituted (2017:87), Eaves describes the ways queer geography, similar to sociology, has focused on fixed places (institutions, neighborhoods) and populations (density, for example) and argues that,

> put differently, queer and sexual geographies can frequently rely on singular node of analysis, such as the negotiations of public spaces or the structure of home life. Queer Black geographic research, as a project of a Black Geographies framework, pressingly calls attention to overlapping dialectics that link institutions, power, and knowledge. Central to advancing Black geographies in Southern studies is the deconstruction of queer sexual identities, spatial productions, and sociospatial interactions. (2017:87)

Eaves's findings echo other scholars' research documenting Black communities in larger cities (Hunter and Robinson 2018; Thorpe 1996). While no project focused on Black geographies in the Midwestern small city exists, as far as I know, Eaves's participant Rebeca shares a sense of ambivalence with Charlie, a Black, queer woman and one of my River City participants.

As we will see, the ambivalent community formation is location-specific, enabled in particular community contexts, especially those that do not fit neatly into narratives of urban gay progress. Ambivalent community reflects a sense of both/and—a sense of both the need and lack of need for LGBTQ community. And it draws from the perspectives of a range of identities: gay, lesbian, genderqueer, transgender, and other identities that have been traditionally, and academically, lumped under the gay or LGBTQ umbrella (P. Doan 2007; Easterbrook et al. 2013). Drawing from the concept of the post-gay community, which encapsulates assimilative changes in gay identities, spaces, and lives, ambivalent community does not suggest a linear narrative of progress but retains attention on the desire for LGBTQ community alongside a desire for its absence, even as full community acceptance may not be possible, particularly for LGBTQ people of color in places like River City. Similar to the concept of ambient community (Brown-Saracino 2011), ambivalent community demonstrates the ways that LGBTQ community is embedded in broader community contexts in relation to their degree of acceptance; array of local norms; landscape of white, settler colonialism; conservative and liberal political frameworks; and community "friendliness," for example.

Ambivalent community may well be specific to small cities like River City, a typical case of the kinds of places that are not fully urban, not fully rural, and not traditionally suburban or proximate to large cities.[5] Ambivalent community suggests an emphatic interest and need for LGBTQ community institutions and symbols, and this need is demonstrated in well-attended community events; at the same time, ambivalent community presents a desire for the declining relevance of LGBTQ identity, for sameness and assimilation reminiscent of post-gay narratives. In other words, ambivalent community encapsulates the desires for LGBTQ community alongside a wish for its absence. We might think of ambivalent community as post-gay with "gay" bolded, as ambient community with an emphasis on the longing for lesbian community, and as vicarious citizenship (Greene 2014, 2018) with a memory of one's home always in mind.

The Missing Friendships in LGBTQ Community Research

Critically, for LGBTQ communities, LGBTQ *relationships* are shifting as acceptance of LGBTQ people grows, even in places like River City. While some scholars have investigated the changing context of LGBTQ romantic relationships (Bernstein and Taylor 2013; Ocobock 2013), there remains a surprising dearth of research about the ways LGBTQ friendships have changed. Yet the shifting landscape of LGBTQ friendships is central to post-gay claims. As Ghaziani notes, "Those who consider themselves post-gay profess that their sexual orientation does not form the core of how they define themselves, and they prefer to hang out with their straight friends as much as with those who are gay" (2014b:3). Indeed, some research demonstrates how friendships that cross lines of sexual identity both challenge and reinforce gender and sexual norms (Muraco 2012), but it remains unclear how friendships benefit or limit community formation. My research aims to fill the gap left by discussions of friendship that do not show *how* friendship may, in fact, hold LGBTQ institutions together or constitute communities after such institutions have faded away. This research is especially critical in contexts beyond large cities, in places like River City, where, as I show, relationships anchor LGBTQ community events.

Research on LGBTQ friendships is not new; for example, long-standing research on "chosen families" (Weston 1991) argues that close relationships among LGBTQ people are critical to LGBTQ individuals' and communities' survival. However, in a post-gay era, researchers have not continued to examine close friendships in communities and how those friendships may or may not contribute to community continuity. A political focus in the United States on same-sex marriage has placed LGBTQ romantic relationships more squarely at the center of research about LGBTQ people, with some exceptions. Perhaps the assumption is that LGBTQ-specific friendships are less necessary for LGBTQ people in a post-gay, post-marriage era, a perspective that reinforces the normative, nuclear family as the most critical relationship form newly available to LGBTQ people.

Two notable exceptions are worth mentioning. Jason Orne (2017) explores the ongoing negotiation of gay spaces and the queer radical histories and possible futures of "sexy communities," community formations that prioritize erotic connections in space. Orne describes the centrality of sex to interpersonal relationships and a broader sense of community in Boystown, Chicago's historic gay neighborhood and a community undergoing a process of assimilation. In another example, recent research explores the "intersectional friendships" between LGBTQ people and allies, as in the case of gay men and straight women and lesbians and straight men (Muraco 2012). In both of these examples, the urban contexts of Chicago and San Francisco affect the kinds of relationships LGBTQ people have available to them, as well as the effect those relationships have on community institutions.

A limitation of this research on LGBTQ communities and friendships, however, is that it tends to be disconnected from an analysis of community context, and it is unclear whether findings about LGBTQ friendships in urban settings apply to processes of community and identity in suburban and rural contexts (Fischer 1982a). Friendships formed in San Francisco and Chicago encounter an array of LGBTQ institutions, organizations, and events not available to LGBTQ people in smaller places—for instance, in Midwestern cities like River City. It is hard to imagine the kinds of social events Orne and Muraco describe taking place in River City, even as my research suggests that smaller-scale, temporary "sexy communities" imagined and supported primarily by queer women may be more common in these contexts. Furthermore, in research on LGBTQ friendships more generally, friendship is often referenced as an aspect of community and broadly related to identity, although without a clear explanation of how friendship relates to community, a topic that remains largely underexplored. Community-based research on LGBTQ friendships beyond urban, gay enclaves offers a helpful corrective to theory making focused on these contexts. In other words, might LGBTQ friendships offer a way into understanding changes in LGBTQ communities more broadly?

One challenge with friendship research is the range of relationships that fall under a "friendship" umbrella. Sociologists of friendship agree that definitions continue to evolve (Allan 2009; Fischer 1982b), and this process is especially relevant for changing LGBTQ communities as relationship terminology changes rapidly. Most relevant to my research, researchers have sought to describe the variation of friendships present in the lives of lesbians and gay men (Gillespie et al. 2015; Nardi 1999;

Weinstock and Rothblum 1996). Fruitful research on friendship emerges at the boundaries between friendship and other types of close relationships. The changing boundary between kinship and friendship, for example, suggests changing norms and marks shifts in expectations about relationships (Allan 2008). Weston's (1991) groundbreaking work on "chosen families" of lesbians and gays challenged the boundary between kinship and friendship in San Francisco. Similarly, Peter Nardi's edited volume on gay men's friendships (1999) highlights the overlap and tension between friendships, family, and romantic relationships. Following this earlier work, researchers probed the boundaries between close relationships: between friendships, family, and romantic relationships (Monsour 2002), particularly for lesbians and gay men (Stacey 2004; Weeks, Heaphy, and Donovan 2001; Weinstock and Rothblum 1996). Beyond a focus on gays and lesbians, however, research about friendships in transgender and queer lives is limited (Galupo et al. 2014). Definitions of friendship as it relates to other close relationships also remain in flux, although a growing research field at the boundaries of friendship, around kinship (Tillmann 2014; Wilkinson 2014) and romantic relationships (Cronin 2015), shows promise. Debate about these definitional boundaries continues, as friendships are folded into the language of kinship and, more recently, some have argued that family members are folded into the language of friendship, a phenomenon Liz Spencer and Raymond Pahl (2006) describe as "suffusion."

These studies of friendship focused on definitional debates, some of which were clearly located in specific communities, missed community determinants of friendship. In a second friendship literature theme, friendship researchers have focused on the *causes* of friendship with limited attention to friendship definitions, with some notable exceptions. Early sociological approaches to friendship have responded to causal questions of choice, making strong assertions that friendships are partially determined by institutional and community contexts (Adams and Allan 1999; Allan 1979, 1990; Bell and Boat 1957; Blatterer 2015; Eve 2002). And researchers of LGBTQ friendships argue that membership in LGBTQ communities generates, logically, LGBTQ friends, while these friendships then sustain LGBTQ in what Nardi calls an "ongoing dialectic" between friendship and community (1999:172). This "ongoing dialectic" depends in part on shared identities, a theme explored in LGBTQ friendship literature, although, again, these analyses are removed from community contexts. LGBTQ friendship researchers have explored, for example, within-identity friendships (Goins 2011; Hall and Fine 2005) and have sought to explain how cross-identity friendships are possible (Korgen 2002; Monsour 2002; Muraco 2012). Yet researchers have little to say about how these friendships relate to community.

For LGBTQ people, the rise in cross-identity friendships has been seen as evidence of the declining relevance of at least gay and lesbian identities (Ghaziani 2014b:9), even as researchers have found that these cross-identity friendships reinforce heteronormative gender and sexual norms (Galupo et al. 2014; Muraco 2012; Ueno and Gentile 2015a). In Muraco's study of straight men and women's friendships with lesbians and gay men, these "intersectional friendships" (a term used to describe friendships that cross lines of gender and sexuality, for example, between lesbians and straight men and between gay men and straight women) both challenge and re-create expectations about gender expression and behavior. In Muraco's research, and in research on LGBTQ friendships more generally, an understanding of the community context of these friendships is missing or beyond the scope of the project. For LGBTQ people, while friendship networks limited exclusively to within-identity contacts are rare (Muraco 2012), researchers still assume that the majority of LGBTQ friendships are with people who share a sexual or gender identity. Given changing LGBTQ identities and communities, friendship in the context of these changes is a barometer of LGBTQ community and requires in-depth analysis.

We can no longer assume that LGBTQ friendships generate a sense of LGBTQ community, or that LGBTQ community institutions generate LGBTQ friendships. And yet the LGBTQ community landscape is partially determined by friendships, as clusters of people who clearly know each other gather at LGBTQ events, in LGBTQ-friendly spaces, and in places that are *not* marked as especially welcoming for LGBTQ people. But what *kinds* of friendships generate LGBTQ community? Two dimensions of friendship remain underexplored in the literature on LGBTQ friendships and communities: friendship *closeness* and friends' *identities*. In other words, are close friends more likely to create LGBTQ community? And given growing acceptance of LGBTQ in straight and cisgender families and communities, do cross-identity friendships generate LGBTQ community, too?[6] What might it mean if LGBTQ people's friendships with straight and cisgender people *centrally* sustain LGBTQ communities? I respond to these questions using the case of River City, where LGBTQ community is small but observable.

The Research Setting and Methods

I am a native New Englander, so River City initially felt to me like a postindustrial city similar to those that surrounded my hometown, cities like Fall River and Lawrence, Massachusetts. Those who grew up in Fall River might feel a little bit at home with River City's architecture, and, conversely, River Citizens might feel a little bit at home in Fall River. While River City shares some characteristics of these kinds of small cities on the East Coast, its distinct history, geographic context, and racial and cultural demographic shifts make it important to understand it on its own terms, a task I attempt in chapter 1. Overall, River City is an ideal location for understanding LGBTQ community and friendship processes, as it simultaneously demonstrates characteristics of smaller towns and larger cities. River City is a small, Midwestern, postindustrial city surrounded by green hills and farmland and bordered on one side by a large, commercially active river. Its population of between 50,000 and 60,000 has declined since its peak in the 1980s (US Census Bureau 2010), and the nearest midsized city (with a population greater than 250,000) is more than an hour away by car. Quantitative and qualitative measures (further discussed in chapter 1) suggest that River City is a small city bordered by farmland, one that is distinct from more distant large cities; for example, River City County is a Metropolitan Statistical Area, bordered by one metropolitan county, one micropolitan county, and four other counties, the populations of which are too small to be designated either metropolitan or micropolitan. Indeed, none of my participants reported regularly commuting to nearby larger cities for work.

River City operates as a hub for several small towns in the region, drawing nearby residents who come to River City to shop, connect with family, visit local parks, or see a movie at one of the city's multiplexes. River City's downtown streets are active in the summertime with festivals and public music performances, as well as a sprawling weekend farmers' market. The city contains three primary neighborhoods divided sharply by class and race, as well as outlying communities connected directly to the downtown area via a series of four-lane highways. River City is home to three small, religiously affiliated four-year colleges; a community college satellite office; and at least two other higher education institutions run by religious groups. All three of River City's four-year colleges hosted small LGBTQ student groups at the time of my research. These LGBTQ student groups generally operated as social and support groups and were not organizing politically within the broader River City community; for example, none of these groups were involved in supporting, or tabling at, River City's Pride picnic or other LGBTQ events, although individual LGBTQ students, staff, and faculty attended many of these events.

Despite its sometimes-urban feel, River City might also be characterized as a small town, as information about neighborhoods, businesses, churches, and other community institutions is communicated primarily by word of mouth (not, notably, through online services popular in larger cities, like the restaurant-rating app Yelp). Yet anonymous dating apps and websites are popular, especially for gay men, and these provide a measure of protection for LGBTQ people who may not wish to "be out." Regular LGBTQ social events are increasing in popularity, although no visible gay or lesbian bars existed in River City at the time of my research. For those seeking LGBTQ community beyond River City, options within a two-hour drive of River City include a metropolitan cluster of several small cities, a known-to-be-liberal city of about 250,000, and smaller cities of about 125,000 and 70,000. River City's population is about 90% white (not Hispanic or Latino), 4% Black, 2% Hispanic or Latino, and 4% Asian, American Indian, Alaska Native, Native Hawaiian, Pacific Islander, or two or more races, and the median household income is about $47,500 (US Census Bureau 2010).

To assess LGBTQ identities, friendships, and community, I used a number of recruitment strategies in locating participants. My aim was to analyze River City as a "case" (Small 2009), a small city that contains an LGBTQ community that is small enough to observe yet large enough to contain visible community events. I initially posted calls for interviews on craigslist, local LGBTQ Facebook groups, and a BDSM/fetish social network, and I contacted LGBTQ community leaders directly by email, phone, and Facebook message. I attended LGBTQ community events and asked participants if they would be interested in being interviewed. Some LGBTQ River Citizens enthusiastically responded to my call for interviews, actively shared my advertisements with their networks, and put me in touch with friends and acquaintances I "really should" interview. Additional participants were recruited through snowball sampling and follow-up postings on social media. And while I posted flyers at local bars, coffee shops, grocery stores, and retail establishments, it is worth noting that none of my contacts responded to my flyers. As interviews proceeded, I remained attentive to the mix of identities included in my sample, aiming to interview a range of participants across class, race, gender, age, and sexual identities, as well as partnership status, residential history, and connection to LGBTQ networks. In other words, I sought interviews with people who were from River City *and* were recent River City transplants, those who were single *and* partnered in various configurations, and those who were leaders in LGBTQ communities *and* kept their distance from LGBTQ community events.

This recruitment strategy yielded 52 interviews with 54 participants (two couples were interviewed together). Participants reflect the range of LGBTQ community members in River City. In terms of sexuality, participants identified as gay men (14); lesbians (10); queer, fluid, and "whatever" (8); bisexual or pansexual (6); asexual (1); straight or heteroflexible (15); and polyamorous (2). In terms of gender, participants identified as cisgender women (27), cisgender men (16), nonbinary and genderqueer people (5), trans women (4), and trans men (2).[7] A discussion of terminology is included in appendix B, and participants' descriptive statistics may be found in appendix C. Participants also include non-LGBTQ allies (13, including 10 women and 3 men), community members who participate in LGBTQ events and have LGBTQ friends, but who do not necessarily identify as LGBTQ. Furthermore, the line between ally and LGBTQ community member is fuzzy at best, as especially bisexual participants' discourse about LGBTQ community suggested a self-understanding more in line with ally than community member identities. Most my participants were white (46), some were BIPOC (8), and participants' implicit and explicit discussions of race suggested that they understand LGBTQ community in River City as limited to white LGBTQ people. Participants ranged in age from 19 to 59, with 20 participants who were under 30, and 34 participants between 30 and 59.

More than half of participants (31) reported an annual salary of $40,000 or less (9 participants reported an annual salary of $10,000 or less, 8 between $10,000 and $20,000, 8 between $20,000 and $30,000, and 6 between $30,000 and $40,000). Thirteen participants reported that their annual salary was between $40,000 and $75,000 (3 reported a salary between $40,000 and $50,000, and 10 between $50,000 and $75,000), solidly middle class for River City. Three participants indicated that they made $75,000 a year or more, and 7 declined to respond to this portion of the demographic survey. Most participants were employed (46), about half were partnered (28), and most had at least a college degree (34) and had lived in River City for more than six years (34). Interviews were audio-recorded and transcribed verbatim, and I analyzed transcripts using Excel (La Pelle 2004), a simple and intuitive tool for coding.

In each interview, I asked participants to complete a brief demographic survey and an open-ended friendship map (Fischer 1982a), which helped me understand participants' understanding of their identities, friendships, and friendship networks and offered a visual network of LGBTQ friends throughout River City. Participants were instructed to draw a map of their friends and connections between their friends, with themselves at the center, and they indicated as few as 4 and as many as 50 individual friends on these maps. I did not define "friendship" for participants, even when pressed, and some participants included partners and family members on their maps. Some friendship maps substantially overlapped, for example, when I interviewed close friends. Other friendship maps were wholly distinct and included no friendships with any other participants. Some participants grouped their friends into subcategories, like friendships from college, from work, or from community organizations. Others drew their maps like spokes on a wheel, a network of relatively disconnected individuals (McCabe 2016).

I also conducted ethnographic observations at 36 community meetings, events, and locations. Community events included LGBTQ-specific events (like Pride picnics, panels, and workshops), events that are not LGBTQ-specific but likely to attract LGBTQ people (like screenings of the *Rocky Horror Picture Show*, film festivals, and public storytelling events), and some events one might think would not welcome LGBTQ people (like a mixed martial arts event). Whenever possible, I took notes on my cell phone during these events, and I recorded and developed my field notes immediately upon returning home. This broad-based approach enabled me to observe friendship networks indicated on participants' maps in action and yielded surprising insights about the landscape of LGBTQ community in River City, demonstrating, for example, the "cliquey" social structure of LGBTQ community and bubbles of friends as mini-communities surrounding LGBTQ participants. Furthermore, being a known LGBTQ community member who lives in River City gave me access to events that featured identifiable groups of LGBTQ friends and other clusters of queer kinship (Ghaziani 2019), patterns that would not have been visible to me had I focused on interviews and friendship mapping alone.

Where We're Headed: Chapter Outline

This book is roughly organized into sections addressing ambivalence in individuals, institutions, and relationships. Chapter 1 introduces us to River City, locating this small Midwestern city within the broader research and geographic landscape of small cities and LGBTQ lives within them. In chapter 2, I analyze LGBTQ participants' discussions of LGBTQ community in River City, which appear mixed. A closer examination of participants' discussions revealed the presence of ambivalent community, as LGBTQ participants felt safe as long as they were not visible; identified disappointing cycles of LGBTQ events and organizations; and described the "cliquey" social structure of LGBTQ community.

In chapter 3, I address the dimension of community that has traditionally been the focus of LGBTQ community research: institutions. I examine LGBTQ events and organizations in River City, highlighting the ambivalences of "gay-friendly" (but not visibly gay) organizations, ally involvement in LGBTQ institutions, and the cyclical nature of LGBTQ organizations. I offer an example of one kind of event catalyzed by national events, local organizations, and relationships among LGBTQ and ally community members as one way in which ambivalent community is resolved, at least temporarily.

In chapter 4, I turn to friendships, analyzing the ways that LGBTQ participants ambivalently explained that shared-identity friendships both *did* and *did not matter* to them. Participants minimized identity differences and explained that shared identities were insufficient to generate a friendship. Participants also explained that shared-identity friendships offered affirmation and a shared sense of LGBTQ culture. I conclude this chapter with a discussion of the loneliest LGBTQ participants, connecting friendships to relationship norms embedded in family-oriented River City.

I discuss ally participants' involvement in LGBTQ community and friendships in chapter 5. I outline the ways that allies offered "diversity resources" to their LGBTQ friends and to LGBTQ community institutions, even as they consumed such resources from friends and community. I demonstrate the ways that LGBTQ community cannot be understood fully without analyzing the contributions of allies, but how these allies drew on LGBTQ communities for their own benefit must simultaneously be recognized.

In chapter 6, I consider whether and how friendships create community, and I identify two ways that the friendship-community connection should be unpacked. First, I examine friendship closeness, as close friends and acquaintances offered differing connections to LGBTQ community for LGBTQ and ally community members. Second, participants' roles in LGBTQ community also affected how they connected, through friends, to community institutions. I also highlight participants' challenges to simplistic definitions of friendship, as some, for example, identified their friends as their community, while others included families of origin alongside chosen families on their friendship maps.

In chapter 7, I analyze participants' responses to an interview question that asked them to consider whether River City's LGBTQ community might be considered post-gay. Participants offered three types of responses, suggesting their approaches to LGBTQ community. I call these three responses inclusive, progressive, and exclusive, and they represent a range of perspectives on whether and how LGBTQ people should assimilate into River City's normative mainstream culture. These three responses demonstrate dimensions of ambivalent community that might be explored in future research and hint at the kinds of futures envisioned, and possible, for LGBTQ and ally River Citizens.

In the conclusion, I return to the overarching concepts of ambivalence and friendship as essential elements of LGBTQ community analyses. I challenge linear narratives of community progress centered in urban LGBTQ communities, and I highlight the ways that friendships may themselves constitute the future of LGBTQ community, for better or worse. Finally, I identify several ongoing changes for River City's LGBTQ community and for my participants. These shifts suggest a way forward in understanding how identity-based communities coalesce and disperse. These processes will continue to involve ambivalence among community insiders and outsiders and will require analyses of friendships as a key social institution.

1

River City

LGBTQ Life in a Small City

Driving into River City from the Northeast, you drive smack through the middle of what looks like an enormous, geologic layer cake, millions of years stacked visibly on either side of you as you descend onto the river bridge. You cross the river and cruise smoothly around downtown, likely coasting over the ghosts of working-class families' homes razed to build the highway in the 1970s. You might be driving to River City from one of the nearby small towns in order to shop at a local supermarket chain, or to spend the evening at a local bar, or, perhaps, to find a sense of community among like-minded queers. In 2014, when I began my research in River City, you would have been hard-pressed to find visible manifestations of queer community, visible, at least, to outsiders like me. Even online, you might struggle to find a gay bar that is still open in your extensive Google searching (but you might find hook-up possibilities via craigslist or apps like Grindr and Scruff). As with many small communities (Gray 2009; Gray et al. 2016), you need to ask; word of mouth remains the primary way information about LGBTQ community is conveyed. When you ask, you might hear about Brews, or gay-owned Barney's. You might hear about spaces where LGBTQ people might gather with friends and partners, sources of queer nightlife (Adeyemi, Khubchandani, and Rivera-Servera 2021) like newly explosive drag performances, or places dedicated to supporting young queer and trans community members, nonprofits that support a vast array of marginalized kids alongside the "friendly" individual people in their lives.

This landscape of shifting LGBTQ community institutions is in the Midwest, but not in Chicago, the Twin Cities, St. Louis, Milwaukee, or Omaha. This is River City, a picturesque, postindustrial, small city of between 50,000 and 60,000, a regional hub for the many small towns and townships spread out across the nearby landscape. While I would hesitate to call River City itself "rural" due to its population size and density, some of my participants do, and their understandings affect how they interpret their lives.[1]

By a number of metrics, River City resides at the increasingly fuzzy boundary (Lichter and Brown 2011) between rural and urban contexts. Its designation as the urban center of a Metropolitan Statistical Area indicates that River City isn't clearly "rural." On the other hand, several measures suggest that it isn't "urban" in the same way Chicago or the Twin Cities are. For example, River City County receives the smallest urban designation according to two key measures of rurality (helpfully summarized in Vanderboom and Madigan 2007). Four of its six neighboring counties are designated by the Office of Management and Budget as "nonmetropolitan" (one is micropolitan and one is metropolitan), a term that's used as shorthand for "rural."

And beyond quantitative measures of rurality, symbolic measures matter, too. Popular descriptions of the city depict it as an isolated small town, and its connection to rural life through local events and the presence of more than one "farm and fleet" store is beyond dispute.[2] In coverage of the 2016 US presidential campaign, for example, a news comedy show featured a Southern ranch owner whose comments about River City suggested his understanding of the city as an isolated haven of small-minded, uncritical Americans. Simultaneously, a 2016 episode of a popular, traveling reality TV show presented River City as a quaint, "cute" small town but one that is unwelcoming, particularly to LGBTQ people. In a national imagined community (Anderson 2006), River City represents the kind of "flyover country" celebrated as the Midwestern heart of American culture and simultaneously decried as its seat of ignorance.

In the popular press, River City acts as a foil to more sophisticated urban contexts across the country. My participants contrast River City with "real" cities in the region and on the coasts, like Chicago, San Francisco, and Minneapolis. In one example, Karen, a white, transgender activist working to build LGBTQ community, summarized River City's status by describing cities like Chicago and Minneapolis as the "big boys," who were "all 14 and 18 and you're, like, 11." Karen's comment suggests the possibility that River City might one day grow to compete with larger cities, at least, in her eyes, in terms of local amenities. Despite these comparisons, River City represents a kind of urban formation that is both *more* common than we might imagine and *less* well understood, given research on communities in general and research on LGBTQ community specifically.

Small Cities

"Metronormativity" (Halberstam 2005) describes the assumption that large cities represent the most desirable urban form, especially for LGBTQ people, and this assumption is deeply embedded in research on communities and in the popular imagination (Manalansan et al. 2014). However, research from geographers and sociologists suggests that small cities are actually the most common urban form (Forstie 2020), especially for LGBTQ people (Gates 2013). Small, or "ordinary," cities (Robinson 2006; Stone 2018) are where most of us live our lives, and they share a number of characteristics, beyond being generally undervalued in the literature. In small cities, for example, relationships matter, communities may be temporary (Gray 2009), and allies are central to sustaining LGBTQ community institutions (Mattson 2020).

And, yet, the local and historic contexts of small cities also differentiate them, and these differences matter for the lives of their residents. For example, their proximity to larger cities or location within urban agglomerations affects what kinds of community institutions residents can access. Some small cities offer connections to institutions like colleges, small museums, libraries, and commercial opportunities not available in the surrounding rural towns, while others operate as connectors between, or suburbs of, larger cities nearby. Consider another Midwestern small city, Evanston, Illinois, compared to River City, for example. While Evanston is slightly larger, its adjacency to Chicago and shared public transit routes mean that Evanstonians can travel with relative ease to amenities available in the city. River City, however, offers a different set of amenities, less accessible via public transit: think hiking opportunities rather than the Field Museum. Other considerations affect the local community culture of small cities, too. Histories of colonization, including dynamics of religion, globalization, industry, and location along transit routes, make small cities located in the same region in the United States similar in some ways, distinct in others. Thinking globally, national contexts matter in the lives of small-city residents, as what "small" means varies widely.

Small cities offer benefits and drawbacks for LGBTQ people specifically, complicated by gender, race, class, and religion in local, regional, national, and transnational contexts (Abelson 2019; Allen 2020; Forstie 2020; Myrdahl 2013). Small-city LGBTQ institutions like gay bars, for example, require the support of straight allies (Mattson 2020) even as they offer cosmopolitan amenities to all patrons in spaces beyond large cities. And, yet, these amenities are not equally available to all LGBTQ people; looking beyond bars, community organizations and events specifically for LGBTQ people are often most accessible to *white* LGBTQ people (Eaves 2017). Understanding how these dynamics play out in the "case" of River City (Small 2009) offers one potential roadmap for thinking through how LGBTQ communities are shaped by, and shape, their small-city contexts (Brown-Saracino 2017).

LGBTQ Lives in River City

With respect to LGBTQ people's lives, River City, according to Census data, has historically had one of the lowest proportions of gay men (technically gay male couples) in the nation (Baumle, Compton, and Poston 2009), is quite religious (especially Catholic) and largely white, and contains a growing Black community with a number of active, youth-focused institutions. Despite this growing Black community, persistent racism and a rise of backlash against these community-building efforts are evident across an array of social and print media, in addition to racist incidents like a cross burning, set ablaze in River City's predominantly Black neighborhood in recent years. To outside appearances, River City is hostile toward L, G, and B, and especially T and Q people and people of color.

Indeed, a number of metrics suggest that River City is not an obvious, welcoming community for LGBTQ people. In the 2010 Census year, according to the Williams Institute (2016), River City County's proportion of male same-sex couples is listed as zero, suggesting that gay male couples may not be willing to be "out" in Census documents or aware that their households are counted. Despite progress toward LGBTQ equality, the proportion of gay male couples in River City remains low, relative to other cities in the region (Williams Institute 2016). Like in populations of other small cities and rural towns (Brown-Saracino 2017; C. Johnson 2013; Kazyak 2012), same-sex female couples outnumber male couples, although Census data indicate fewer than three same-sex female couples per 1,000 households at the county level (Williams Institute 2016). The proportion of same-sex couples in River City County, furthermore, is disproportionately lower than its population would suggest; in other words, other smaller counties within the state contain higher proportions of same-sex couples. Counties that are half, a quarter, and a fifth of the size of River City County contain proportionately more same-sex couples. At the state level, despite legal protections for lesbian, gay, and transgender people, River City's home state remains in the lower third of states by LGBT proportion of the population. Given the position of River City County within the state, the proportion of LGBT individuals within the county is also likely to be low. I describe participants' perspectives on River City's ecological, symbolic, and social structural landscape (A. Hunter 2006) in more detail in chapter 2.

And, yet, analyzing the numbers, the proportion of LGBTQ people in River City doesn't tell us the whole story. In one of my earliest interviews, I sat with Peter, a participant who is well connected to River City's gay community, and we "did the math," trying to calculate the number of LGBTQ people in the city, producing a guess of about 250 people.[3] Research participants described LGBTQ community in River City as disconnected, dispersed, difficult to find, and "cliquey." And while some LGBTQ institutions seem to be growing, others are declining, and still others remain invisible to community members. A brief genealogy of River City's gay bars illustrates these shifts. For example, Next Level, a gay bar open for nearly a decade, closed in 2007, while Barney's operated on a well-traveled downtown street for a scant few years as an unmarked gay-friendly, or, as one participant explained, "queer," bar. Barney's, everyone knew, was gay-owned, but visitors to River City would see no indication that Barney's is gay-friendly. No rainbow flags or stickers marked its façade, even as participants identified Barney's by name when asked whether there are any gay bars in town.

In the spring of 2017, Barney's announced that it, too, was being sold to new owners, thus losing its "gay-owned" reputation, just as a new, purportedly gay bar, Underground, was opening down the street. The

Underground, too, is not marked as gay, except perhaps by the colorful lights behind the bar and the more visibly gay bartenders, young men whose masculinity fits with a more urban hipster aesthetic than is common among their straight River City peers. Two "pop-up" queer-bar events were hosted at the Underground during my time in River City, attended largely by a small cluster of queer women and trans men, the "introverts" of the LGBTQ community in River City, as one participant explained. These queer and trans River Citizens carved out a small space within the not-obviously-gay gay bar.

So, what is going on here? Is River City the rural vanguard of overlapping queer and gay communities, its closeted past, or its performative present? How do we make sense of highly visible and popular drag shows alongside gay spaces that remain committed to invisibility, and queer spaces meant to be inclusive of a range of LGBTQ identities nested within gay spaces? How can LGBTQ institutions be growing with such a small, divided, and often invisible community? And why are some institutions explosively popular (like drag shows) while others struggle to survive (like gay bars)?

I begin this story with the complicated picture of LGBTQ life in small cities because it is important to understand small cities on their own terms, with their painful histories, joyful moments of connection, and mundane routines. If we imagine LGBTQ communities as composed of institutions, relationships, and allies, it becomes important to imagine the ways small-city LGBTQ communities might be generalizable alongside the limitations of generalizable thinking. Small cities may be uniquely ambivalent among community forms; indeed, the term "small cities" contains a kind of internal ambivalence, a pressure between the small(ish) scale of a community and the cosmopolitan elements it contains (Mattson 2020). How participants understand River City—in particular, what *kind* of small city it is—helps us set the stage for understanding ambivalent communities through institutions like bars and events like drag shows, and it is to this task that I now turn.

2

Should I Stay or Should I Go?

Social Contexts of Ambivalent Experiences

When I first arrived in River City to conduct focus groups about LGBTQ community, Brews was the first LGBTQ-friendly space a participant suggested. It is neither gay-owned nor visibly gay-friendly, but it is known among queer and progressive locals as a space that welcomes River City's misfits, from liberal college professors to hippies and local activists to college students seeking a slightly crunchy vibe. A coffee shop and pub, Brews is perched just above street level in the heart of River City's tourist-centered downtown, and its dark interior includes an array of cozy nooks for coffee and beer consumption and conversation. Brews as a community space shifts neatly from coffee (and beer) consumption during the day to beer (and coffee) consumption at night, when regional bands flail at small but energetic crowds in the bar's lower level. I met Derek and his partner, Sean, both white gay men in their 20s and employed in the healthcare industry, at Brews one late spring afternoon. Perched at a tall table surrounded by encroaching plants, Derek shared a story of his experience with employment discrimination in a nearby town, one that I sense could have been challenged legally. Despite these experiences, Derek held a surprising view of River City. He explained, "I view [River City] as a progressive city. It's pretty progressive, compared to what's around us."

Examining 2010 Census data suggests an absence of partnered gay men in River City (Williams Institute 2016); indeed, River City is among the cities with the lowest proportion of gay men in the nation by this admittedly imperfect measure. We might imagine that a low proportion of gay men signals a conservative context, but that is not necessarily the perception of my participants (and, indeed, some were quite politically conservative). Derek was not the only gay participant who described River City as "progressive" and "liberal." But not everyone agreed. At a different downtown coffee shop, I talked with white, gay, partnered participant Kyle, who offered a contrasting perspective, describing River City as "conservative" and not a place where he and his husband would choose to live in the long term. On the surface, Kyle and his partner are similar to Derek and Sean: young, partnered, upwardly mobile gay men making their homes in River City. And, yet, their perspectives about River City, and their engagement with gay community, differed significantly. While Derek and Sean generally did not attend LGBTQ community events, they viewed River City as progressive. Kyle, however, understood River City to be conservative, yet he was highly involved as a leader in the LGBTQ youth group and in other community events and organizations. Their differing perspectives on River City and of LGBTQ people highlight a paradox in perspectives on LGBTQ communities: perception of a "progressive" context is associated with less LGBTQ community engagement, while perception of a "conservative" context is related to more LGBTQ community involvement. These two perspectives also demonstrate a challenge in LGBTQ community research: how to interpret sometimes opposing perspectives on community acceptance and the ongoing need for LGBTQ community spaces.

In this chapter, we take a closer look at individual LGBTQ and ally perspectives on River City as an LGBTQ-friendly place (or not). Given River City's cultural, geographic, and historical context, it might (still) be surprising that LGBTQ people can make a comfortable home in River City, let alone see it as "progressive" (Allen 2020). I am certainly not the first, though, to examine LGBTQ lives in places that seem hostile to those who live in large coastal cities (Gray et al. 2016). And, yet, examining LGBTQ people's perspectives on River City specifically reveals a more complicated picture: some find it welcoming, while others do not. This complicated picture is interesting not simply because it is complicated; it reveals the local dynamics that enable some to find a home in River City while isolating, and excluding, others. Here, it becomes clear that ambivalence has real effects on LGBTQ lives: some manage to navigate ambivalent communities while others leave for more manageably ambivalent homes.

In this chapter, I share seemingly conflicting views of LGBTQ community in River City, a context that participants describe as politically progressive for some, conservative for others, and personally isolating for many. I begin by describing River City from the perspectives of participants, some of whom grew up in River City and its surrounding towns, and others who were not "from" River City. Their perspectives suggest that, by some metrics, River City is hostile and unfriendly toward LGBTQ people. I then offer contradictory evidence from participants that suggests that River City is a post-gay LGBTQ community in some ways quite similar to what Amin Ghaziani observed in gay neighborhoods in larger, more urban cities. I argue that LGBTQ perspectives on their communities in small cities such as River City may be better understood as cases of ambivalent communities, which require LGBTQ people to manage perceptions of community as both inclusive and exclusive. In contrast to a linear narrative of progress, River City's LGBTQ community suggests that progress and pressures to stay closeted persist simultaneously. At the end of the day, communities are shaped by and shape the contexts of their participants (Brown-Saracino 2017).

Closet River City: A "Closed-Door Type of Town"

As I discussed previously, an urban, gay outsider's perspective on River City suggests a closet-era community hostile to LGBTQ people, and such messages are conveyed through mainstream media and through indicators of LGBTQ acceptance. In one example, participants' descriptions of River City reflect an understanding that the city is *seen* as Catholic, *ergo* conservative, even as research suggests that Catholics' support for LGBTQ policy initiatives is mixed (Greenberg et al. 2019). Participants who migrated to River City after living in other communities described River City's hostile conservatism most strongly and were least interested in staying in River City in the longer term. For example, Zara, a white, transgender woman who moved to River City from a distant Midwestern state, described River City as an "intolerant closed-minded group of people." Kyle, a gay, Southern newcomer to River City, expressed hesitation about staying, stating "I know that I couldn't live there forever—partially being the cold, partially being the conservatism. Especially the Catholic. It's very Catholic." Kyle moved to River City with his husband, who was relocated for work. Once there, Kyle quickly became involved in the local LGBTQ youth group, as well as other community-based initiatives. Kyle's description of River City as simultaneously "friendly" and "closed-minded" captures a sense of surface-level Midwestern friendliness that other participants noted. As Fia, a white, transgender participant who had returned to River City following years living throughout the Midwest, explained, "They're very restricted and reserved, if they don't know you. And it's like you're talking to a closed door. That's, that's very much how I describe [River City], it's a closed-door type of town." Participants who migrated *from* River City and now live in other communities made similar observations. Kit, a young, white lesbian born and raised in River City but attending college at a nearby university, explained that River City is religious, as well as "conservative not in the sense of political views but conservative in the sense of just, mindset, ideas, social interactions, that kind of thing." To some, River City's Catholicism was seen as an indicator of social conservatism, one that is, at least implicitly, not open and accepting of LGBTQ people.

Participants also spoke broadly about River City's hostility, overlapping discussions of race with discussions of gender and sexuality and referencing former and recent cross burnings—including one in 2016—alongside descriptions of River City's religiosity. River City, like other small cities (Abelson 2019), might also be described as a "closed-door type of town" in terms of race, perhaps more than gender and sexuality. While overwhelmingly white, segregation by race is very visible, as growing Black community organizations and public events are held largely in one neighborhood. White River Citizens demonstrate the kind of "colorblind" racism that has characterized American discourse about race in recent years (Bonilla-Silva 2006), and euphemistic terms for people of color (such as "people from Chicago") dominate local discussions about crime.[1] Despite the efforts of local business leaders and River City employees, it seems that little progress has been made.

And white community newcomers are warned away especially from River City's main Black neighborhood. Both work colleagues and acquaintances suggested I (a white, nonbinary person) avoid renting a home within this "downtown" neighborhood because they described it as "unsafe." While there is little evidence to suggest that River City's downtown, or any neighborhood, is less safe than any other, or is less safe today than in the past, white River Citizens publicly lamented that they are afraid to walk downtown streets even in broad daylight. Despite this implicit and sometimes explicitly hostile context, organizations sup-porting Black and Pacific Islander communities are increasingly visible, drawing resources and volunteers from River City and nearby towns.

River City's LGBTQ community, too, remains largely segregated by race, as similar implicitly racist rhetoric emerges in group discus-sions, for example, and one-on-one conversations. LGBTQ participants of color explained that they left River City to travel to nearby cities in which they could engage with communities of color, while white LGBTQ participants could access LGBTQ events and organizations *either* within River City *or* in these nearby cities. Participants reported some evidence of segregation by class, too, as working-class LGBTQ people also tended to gravitate to organizations that were largely composed of working-class people and were not necessarily LGBTQ-friendly. In one exam-ple, working-class LGBTQ participants noted a local substance-abuse recovery organization as a primary source of community. Given the cen-trality of relationships to community, especially in small cities and rural towns, similar-identity friendships—or friendship homophily (McPher-son, Smith-Lovin, and Cook 2001)—deeply affected perceptions of com-munity, leaving multiply marginalized LGBTQ people (Crenshaw 1995) feeling the effects of multiple closed doors.

Given the various indicators I have discussed, it would be tempting for urban outsiders to lump River City with presumed rural, hostile cit-ies where LGBTQ people are forced to remain "in the closet," or perhaps just beginning to enter a "coming out" era, following more progressive cities. Evidence of post-gay community would thus be surprising. While I do not wish to contribute to this narrative of surprise (Brown-Saracino 2017), it is important to remain attentive to *who* feels River City is "safe" and "comfortable" and why. We have already heard from two partici-pants who shared this perspective; let us hear from a few more.

Post-Gay River City: "More Progressive Than Anywhere Else"

In contrast to evidence suggesting River City's hostility toward LGBTQ community members, several participants described River City as accepting, liberal, and friendly toward LGBTQ people. In their narra-tives of inclusion and safety, participants who made these claims were especially careful to compare River City to two community contexts:

other imagined regions (like "the South"), and River City in the past (typically two decades ago). Some gay, lesbian, and transgender participants (notably, all white) described River City as explicitly "progressive." Robin, a white, lesbian, partnered participant, is a key example of such a perspective.

While Robin is not a River City native, she and her partner worked hard to develop ties to an array of River City community organizations, and, together with their children, they have clearly made River City their home. Exuberant and effusive, Robin describes herself as a "hugger," and her love and enthusiasm for River City's Catholic culture are evident in her support for a relationship-based approach to community. She is no longer active in the Catholic Church, although she described herself as "culturally Catholic," and her complex views of Catholicism as a source of community echo the complex views of other LGBQ Catholics (García et al. 2008; Fuist 2017; Izienicki 2017; Wedow et al. 2017). She explained that the "spirit of Catholicism" present in River City represented Catholicism "not as a religion but just as a way of life. That people really value people and relationships and community and kindness." Robin noted that she has "always loved [River City]," because "I feel like it's a lot more liberal and progressive, you know?" Robin's cultural Catholicism echoes that of a specific liberal, progressive, even feminist community in River City: nuns. While a focus on nuns' significant role in progressive circles in River City is beyond the scope of this chapter, their role in creating overlapping progressive community in River City was meaningful to more than one of my participants.

However, Robin's statement about "liberal and progressive" River City leaves an implicit, comparative context unnamed. As Robin's comment indicates, participants stressed River City's progressiveness *in relation to* two other contexts: River City in the past, and River City compared to other towns and regions. For example, participants stressed River City's "progress" relative to specific timelines, typically 20 years. As Peter, a gay man with a long-term partner, noted, "Thinking about where it's come from the last 20 years when I first was dealing with my [coming out], I think it's significantly come a lot further, and I think that's even just from a societal perspective has really happened."

Non-LGBTQ allies also described River City's progressiveness, compared to the past. Shelley, a longtime and well-known LGBTQ community ally who has performed more than 30 weddings with LGBTQ couples in River City and neighboring towns, offered her feelings about River City: "This is certainly as much home to us as any place, and we love the people, it's a lovely city now, and lovely livable place, very livable and has been progressive and in a lot of things now, very different than when we came here originally." Paul, a straight man, drag queen, and active community ally who described his oft-mistaken-as-gay identity as "gay adjacent," offered a similar perspective: "If you were to come here 20 years ago, you would have wanted to leave right away. . . . Seriously, very homophobic, very racist, very close-minded, very backwards, a lot more conservative. . . . Now, I believe [River City] is actually fairly LGBT-friendly." Compared with nearby towns and River City's more conservative past, River City, according to participants, demonstrated a more inclusive community for LGBTQ people, or, at least, for white LGBTQ people.

Participants sometimes explicitly named the "anywhere else," comparing River City to "the South" or to other small towns in the area or to seemingly more dangerous larger cities like Chicago. In other words, "anywhere else" could include small towns or large cities. Greg, in an interview with his partner, Steve, observed, "I mean, for the most part, I feel safe here. [River City] has its ups and downs, but that's anywhere, but I think it's more progressive than anywhere else."

Some participants who migrated from nearby cities described River City's Catholic context as necessarily conservative but did not see this reputation as a barrier to staying in the longer term. For married couple Steve and Greg, active membership in a local Protestant church helped them feel more accepted in the larger River City community. Steve, discussing the benefits of his and his husband's church, explained that "a lot of people come to [River City], they see that it's heavy Roman Catholic, and they kinda go, ehhhh, this is a really conservative small town, I don't know." Steve had moved to River City from the Chicago suburbs to attend a local college, met his husband through a gay social networking website, and he and his husband have no interest in leaving. Both men are deeply engaged in River City's larger community organizations, and they appreciate River City's affordability and short commute time, *especially* relative to their friends' experiences in Chicago. They see River City's conservative culture as largely avoidable, through choice. Finding more, as he described them, "liberal" and "accepting" groups "requires you as the participant to seek that out. If you choose not to, you're not gonna find it," according to Steve.

Participants also explained that they felt relatively comfortable and safe in River City, especially compared to other urban communities. Notably, when white participants identified areas of River City in which they did not feel safe, those narratives at times aligned with implicit assumptions about race, rather than gender or sexuality. White LGBTQ participants euphemistically referred to racially segregated "downtown" (Maddy) or "gang-related activity" (Jack) as making them feel unsafe. On the other hand, some white participants were explicitly critical of such framing. Paul, for example, described the specific neighborhood that others identified as unsafe, noting, "Of course, it happens to be more Black populated but, you know, when I drive by there like all I see is they're just sitting out on their porches watching. What, you know, pfft, big deal. I don't know if people just get like, 'Oh my God, you know, they're like gangs' and I'm like, 'No.'"

Few participants identified specific places where they would not be comfortable, or places in River City that they would avoid due to their gender or sexual identities. Safety, to white participants, in particular, meant freedom from public harassment and physical violence. This was especially true among young participants (in their 20s and 30s) like Teagan, Charlie, and Leah. Teagan, a white, cisgender woman who identified as "bisexual or something," explained, "I've lived in [River City] literally all my life. . . . I've lived here for a long time, I have heard a lot of people say a lot of things about it, but I really, really like it here. I think it's for me, it's always been a really comfortable, happy kind of place to be." Charlie, a queer woman of color, noted that her sense of physical safety in River City rivaled that of her small, paragon-of-liberal-arts college, compared to other places she had lived, particularly in the South. For white, queer and genderqueer Leah, openly religious places felt less comfortable, but "other than that, I haven't really found any places that I'm not comfortable going." She felt that her "bulky" stature as a rugby player made her "intimidating," and her comments about River City suggested a less-welcoming comparative context. She observed, "I think just [River City] being an open and accepting community has really made it easy for me to live. I know in other areas, people don't always get that luxury but . . . for me in [River City], I haven't really found any areas where you know I go there and I'm holding my partner's hand and somebody says something to me about it."

For some participants, safety included something beyond invisibility and freedom from harassment; for participants like Janine, safety meant a sense of *recognition*, for example. Janine, a white, transgender, pansexual woman whose gender identity fluctuates between feminine and masculine expression, explained that she "feel[s] pretty safe" in River City, then offered the following story:

> I was at a corner at a stop light, and basically this woman comes out, and to the corner, she looks at me, like once or twice, she's like "You're the one that goes, has gone down to McDonalds all dressed up in that black dress, that real nice black dress." I'm like "Yeah, um, that was me." I mean, had a real nice short conversation, right there on the spot at the corner, and you know, she said she actually talked about how she really liked it and all that, you know, the way I am, [that] I don't care, I'm willing to do that, go to some place like that all dressed up and she said I looked really good, as to say "well, thanks so much." And it's like, we went our way. I mean, just briefly, but it made me feel really good, too.

Janine's sense of safety was bolstered by the affirmation she received by strangers in the community. Specifically, for Janine, explicit recognition based on her gender expression—that she "looked really good"—facilitated a feeling of safety in River City. This kind of public recognition by a stranger was remarkable in River City, for Janine.

While Janine's sense of safety could be traced to a specific type of interaction, for others, comfort in River City was present but more nebulous. Speaking about a particular downtown coffee shop, Colby explained, "I get this sense that they're LGBT-friendly. It's not that they have done something specifically to make me think that way or, you know, not think that way. It's just like I feel comfortable there and I think they would be [friendly]." Safety for participants was multidimensional: it included freedom from harassment and a sense of at least potential affirmation and recognition, if not (yet) fully realized.

These narratives of comfort and progressiveness demonstrate a post-gay understanding of River City, a sense that most places in River City were safe and comfortable for LGBTQ people, who did not need to sequester themselves in LGBTQ spaces. Unlike a "coming-out" phase in which LGBTQ people connect through LGBTQ institutions, or a "closet" phase in which LGBTQ people must hide their identities (Ghaziani 2014b), some participants agreed that River City as a whole was liberal and progressive, providing a safe place to hold their partner's hand or express their gender identity in public spaces.

However, reading these perspectives of evidence that River City has arrived in a post-gay era limits our understanding of LGBTQ communities and the ways LGBTQ people navigate their lives in small cities like River City (Abelson 2019; Kampler and Connell 2018). Informed by their identities, biographies, and the racialized and classed context of River City, participants expressed ambivalence about River City, about River City's LGBTQ community specifically, and about their feelings of belonging in the place they lived.

Ambivalent LGBTQ Community: "It's Both *And*"

As I argued in the introduction, ambivalent community acknowledges the complexity of individuals' sense of connection to LGBTQ community. Jack exemplified this sense of complexity when he acknowledged his desire to both be himself, as a white, transgender man and graduate student, and to feel recognition for his identity. Jack's assertion that LGBTQ community in River City is "both *and*" captures this simultaneous desire for LGBTQ community and for a time when such community is not needed. In participants' discussion of LGBTQ community, they frequently juxtapose closet, coming-out, and post-gay frameworks (Ghaziani 2014b), and in their comments we see that community is never fully realized *and* never fully absent.

Discourses of safety and comfort in River City were often coupled with caveats. Colby, a young, white transgender man and college student, offered an explanation of safety in stealth *and* his greater fear in contexts where he was "out" as a trans man.[2] He stated, "I only feel safe because most people in [River City] don't know [that I'm trans]. Like [my university] community knows and I actually feel less safe with everyone knowing almost. Like I know there's people I don't feel, I don't know, I'm always scared that somebody's gonna decide to act out or get violent towards me." Colby's unrelentingly positive approach to life and vast friendship network (including 35 named friends on his friendship map) belied his fears about violence toward transgender people, fears he felt could be realized in River City. Remaining invisible as a member of the LGBTQ community was key to other participants' sense of safety, too. Some participants located their sense of safety in contrast to more visibly flamboyant LGBTQ community members. Explaining why he and his husband felt comfortable in River City, Steve explained, "I mean maybe it's because, I mean in talking in like LGBT terminology, him and I can both pass, in the sense that we're not, you know, flamboyantly, rah-rah-shish-koom-bah gay, you know? So we can pass, so we, I don't look at it, I don't feel the need to have to be in a queer community type of area." While trans participants going "stealth" (Beauchamp 2018) and gay participants "passing" as straight are not equivalent strategies (Schilt 2011), both suggest a fear of being visible as LGBTQ people in River City.

Mark, a gay, single man who was planning to leave River City, was critical of this approach, and his comments challenge the level of safety even for normatively gendered LGBT people. He reflected that

> I even wonder for those folks who are able to, who are gay or lesbian and fit the stereotypical roles and physical features of those sexes. I wonder how many of them have actually had real conversations with the people they surround themselves with would find affirming answers when they would ask the question of, "what if your son or daughter was gay or would you want to have a son or daughter that's gay?" I think that there is a perception that there is more acceptance then there really is. And I don't think that's the case.

Participants' comments suggest a comparative context in which safety both is and is not possible: passing, being stealth, or generally being perceived as normative provides some protection (probably), while being "out" and identifiable as LGBTQ may make for uncomfortable conversations, risks of violence, and, as Leah suggested, a loss of a job, especially in a religious context. River City's home state provides some legal protection from discrimination based on sexual orientation and gender identity. While some federal protections for LGBTQ people exist as of this writing, local contexts and political fluctuations make the realization of these protections uncertain, and many LGBTQ people fear that the rise of religious exemptions will affect their future employment.

As these comments suggest, post-gay and closet community phases become nearly indistinguishable, as safety is contingent on invisibility and normativity (Thomsen 2021). One symbol of lesbian and gay identities that participants used to describe this line was holding hands with a partner. Some participants shared narratives of hand-holding with a partner as a marker of a sense of safety, as Leah's comments in the above section indicate. Participants also stated that holding hands in public was becoming newly possible. For Shelley, a strong LGBT ally, "I'm actually now seeing on the streets people holding hands, which is something, when you talk to the couples who've been together, even those who've gotten married, they would never show public affection, same-sex couples, but that's beginning to happen, and I'm glad for that." Others explained that they would not hold their partner's hand, or that others had shared fears about hand-holding. Callie, speaking about Keith, one of Barney's owners, explained:

> Part of the reason he even opened the bar was that once the gay bar closed, he and his boyfriend had no place to go that they felt comfortable. So they opened their own bar. Like that was absolutely part of the reason that they did that, because they would go to other places, and they would hear people saying things, or whatever, and they just didn't feel like they could be in public, and be themselves, or like hold hands, or like you know, any of that kind of stuff, and like feel safe.

Callie further described the contexts where same-sex couples might not feel safe expressing affection through hand-holding or kissing, like the dog park or "just going for a walk." Colby recalled holding hands with his girlfriend at the local fair, "and like people were like scoffing, like, agh, lesbians." Hand-holding, a simple gesture between partners, operated as an ambivalent marker of *both* safe *and* unsafe community for LGBTQ and ally participants. In these narratives of safety holding hands in public, we see evidence that some participants felt safe being visible LGBTQ people in River City, while others experienced marginalization. Being able to "pass" or be "intimidating" (in Leah's case) seemed key to staying free at least from public harassment, although the depth of acceptance, as Mark suggests, remains an open question.

Reflecting on their sense of community, LGBTQ participants noted that their community felt fractured and "cliquey." Fia described the LGBTQ community in River City as "sparse," also asserting that "there definitely is a community here. It's kind of slightly disjointed. And it doesn't seem like, with many people, the LGBT community is their primary concern." Steve and Greg echoed each other's descriptions of gay community in River City, describing it as "terribly fractured." For Mark, at the time of our interview, he asserted, "There is no gay community here. There is but it's cliquey in a way, and there is not unified like let's all come with our differences and look at the whole and see where we can leverage our diversity to help improve the life of a gay and lesbian, transgendered, queer person living in this city." Paul, an LGBTQ ally and straight drag queen, also described the "cliques" he saw in River City: "Even within the LGBT community, there's strife. I see kind of cliques with different groups and it's, you know, too bad. You know, I just want to say, you guys gotta all just get along, come on. But, you know, I mean everyone is like that so is it fair to say that they shouldn't do it just because they're an LGBT community, maybe not." Participants' comments about the cliquey-ness of River City resonate with the kinds of cultural clustering described in larger cities (Ghaziani 2019) and are not new, although the effects of this kind of "fractured" community are different in a small city (and are discussed in more detail in chapter 3).

Describing the "larger cultural force at play" in River City that keeps the LGBTQ community disconnected, Robin noted that "the ingredients for the recipe are not here, I don't even know what the ingredients are. But the recipe is not intact." Robin's comments suggest that individual people, even small-group "ingredients" of LGBTQ community exist in River City, while the chemistry needed to bring these groups together through a holistic "recipe" was missing. The role of city size matters here; as Robin suggested, "In a larger city you're going to have a much easier time finding the subgroup that you connect with, and in River City that doesn't exist, you know?" It is unclear whether a larger city would produce a less cliquey LGBTQ community, however. For these LGBTQ community leaders, most with extensive knowledge of LGBTQ community history in River City, the community felt disconnected and not unified.

And, yet, even as participants described the disjointed landscape of LGBTQ community, they also expressed a desire for some kind of coming together. Participants' desire for some sense of LGBTQ community suggests ambivalence about the reality of LGBTQ community and its necessity, or possibility (Pidduck 2009). Colby explained, "I just feel like there's people out there who would be a part of something if they knew it was there, and if it was open and I feel like there are like little groups, like kind of spotted throughout that would come together if they had something to pull them together." Maddy's desire for community was not necessarily limited to LGBTQ-specific events, but she hoped for shared spaces with LGBTQ people. After stating that she "wish[ed] there was more of a community where I could meet other people," she explained the need for such a community:

> Just so you don't feel so alone and so isolated and like, there is definitely something to say of people sharing a common experience, and going through similar things, even if these groups or hangouts don't revolve around specified LGBT issues just knowing that this other person has gone through similar things or shares a similar worldview to you, to some respect, you already know you have this common ground, and just to meet new people . . . I think it's important to have other people that identify that way in some respect as well so you can talk if you need to talk and they will know and have experienced similar things to you.

Robin, too, wanted a sense of community, stating, "And so it's like, yeah, we really need each other for support and just to know we're there and to not feel alone. Just to increase our sense of safety and belonging." Finally, Mark's speculation about his unmet need for LGBTQ community again suggests an approach to community that could be read as post-gay *and* closeted. He explained that he

> would want us to better collectively understand the lived experience of the folks . . . but we don't. And so maybe there isn't a need. I know they've tried to start two gay clubs and they closed. Now is that because there's safety issues and people don't feel proud or safe to come and support

those establishments? Or is it because people here are more interested in drag queens? But I guess they have that, so I don't know. I just . . . Maybe people feel that the collective thing is not necessary. Because nobody is being killed, nobody is being murdered. You know they think about these worst-case scenarios but what about like just your quality of life?

Mark's reflections suggested ambivalence about LGBTQ community through the example of gay clubs, a well-known source of gay community and collective identity (Armstrong 2002). Ultimately, for him, and for other young, single LGBTQ people in River City, this sense of fractured community led him to make plans to leave River City in search of a more unified, accessible community. However, Mark's comments predated the 2016 mass murder of 49 people at Pulse, a gay nightclub in Orlando, on Latinx night, an example of a "worst-case scenario" that generated a sense of community, discussed below.

Conclusion: From Ambivalent Individuals to Ambivalent Community

In this chapter, I shared some of the conflicting perspectives on River City's LGBTQ friendliness and participants' sense of LGBTQ community. Some felt safe in River City in most places, but their safety depended on their ability to blend in, to be read as normative, in brief, to be *invisible*. And while few reported feeling especially unsafe themselves, *what safety meant* was somewhat narrow: freedom from harassment and violence. As Mark's comments suggest, safety from violence is not the same as acceptance, and River City's Midwestern cultural context suggests a veneer of niceness that may not extend to full acceptance and recognition, for example, of LGBTQ, and especially trans, youth. Reflecting upon LGBTQ community, participants' near universal understanding of River City's community as "cliquey" persists alongside desires for a feeling of shared identity. Participants were ambivalent in their individual feelings about River City's LGBTQ friendliness and about the form of LGBTQ community, in other words.

Examining this ambivalence sociologically, though, requires attention to the community context of River City itself and to take seriously the array of perspectives about community (Abelson 2019; Brown-Saracino

2017). What determines these perspectives? Context, migration, and biography matter; for example, if you're "from" River City, or you fit within its local, racialized, gendered, and partnered norms, you're more likely to feel safe. If you have a local connection to family, perhaps the "cliquey" feeling of LGBTQ community is easier to tolerate. These social contexts inform the ambivalent experiences of individuals and how they manage those feelings and affect the actions people take—mainly, whether to stay or go.

Is individual ambivalence the same as an ambivalent community? These perspectives are a piece of the puzzle. As research has recently shown (Battle et al. 2017; Brown-Saracino 2017), community context informs individuals' senses of community, which then inform the shape community takes. Participants' contradictory approaches to LGBTQ community highlight the limitations of applying a linear, post-gay framework to LGBTQ community. In sum, participants shared conflicting perspectives about their sense of safety in River City and their sense of LGBTQ community. LGBTQ community members in River City demonstrate post-gay, coming-out, and closet community characteristics (Ghaziani 2014b) that are better understood through the concept of an ambivalent community. Ambivalent community includes, in the case of River City, senses of comfort and safety alongside desires to remain invisible and "cliquey," isolating social landscapes alongside desires for a more coherent feeling of community. A post-gay analysis of River City makes a singular LGBTQ community difficult to analyze; ambivalent community helps us understand the specific, if contradictory experiences of LGBTQ people.

3

Out, but Not Too Out

The Line between Inclusion and Invisibility

It is a late winter weekend evening in River City, and I am passing through a smoke-filled casino floor, heading toward a drag show at a popular local bar and performance venue tucked away in the corner of the building.[1] To be honest, I am expecting a sparse crowd because I suspect that this small community's capacity for drag performance has reached its limit. This is not the first drag show I have seen, and previous shows have been so full of people that it's hard to find enough elbow room to drink your beer, let alone get a clear view of the stage. When I arrive, though, the bar is packed, tables are full, and I quickly grab a seat up in the mezzanine level for a clear view of the show. Performances are as raunchy and campy as drag shows anywhere tend to be, except with perhaps a slightly higher-than-average emphasis on country music and, interestingly, also Disney songs. Two drag queens offer an homage to *The Little Mermaid*'s "Poor Unfortunate Souls," featuring a fabulous Ursula-like costume and an Ariel who sports a flouncy tail and wheeled sneakers, allowing her to zoom around the stage as though she is underwater.

The "Queen of River City," a drag queen who has performed locally since the early 1980s, executes a particularly clever number about a drilling dentist accompanied by a large, black dildo as a prop, notable given River City's predominantly white population. In the audience, I spot several of my lesbian-, gay-, and queer-identified research participants, but I see none of my trans participants. My initial estimates of the crowd suggest that at least 300 people are in attendance, but a post on the local group's Facebook page later suggests that more than 400 people decided to spend their weekend evening—and money—watching a drag show. Interestingly, two weeks later, a second, newly created drag group hosts its first show at a different local bar. When I arrive just three minutes after the scheduled start of the show, one of my participants informs me that they are turning people away at the door. The bar is at capacity, and they are worried about breaking the fire code.

While drag shows are indeed a booming business in River City, they are not the only indicator of what I observed over the course of my research in a growing LGBTQ community. A well-attended, biweekly LGBTQ youth group meets at a local community center, a new *weekly* LGBTQ adult support group has been meeting at the same location, each of the local high schools supports an active gay-straight alliance (GSA), alongside college LGBTQ groups, and local organizations—notably healthcare-specific—have sought LGBTQ competency training for their staff. No commercial establishments advertise themselves explicitly as gay venues, and some of my participants mourn the loss of now-closed gay bars in River City. However, "everyone knows" about the local gay-owned bar and which establishments are owned by lesbians and lesbian couples, identified exclusively through word of mouth, a key way information about LGBTQ community circulated in River City, as a participant, Kai, noted. In fact, at the time of our interview, Kai was working on compiling a resource list of local LGBTQ and "known" friendly LGBTQ organizations and businesses to help convey that word-of-mouth knowledge to a broader audience.

If we're thinking about finding LGBTQ community, researchers often begin (and sometimes end) with LGBTQ institutions like gay bars (Ghaziani 2014a, 2014b; Mattson 2020). They use institutions as a measure of LGBTQ community, noting their rise and fall as an indicator of LGBTQ people's growing relevance and, alarmingly, decline. These researchers agree that bars are one component of a broader community landscape, and they have the benefit of being visible and measurable, outlined in documents like the Damron Guide and taking up physical space in the largely urban landscapes under study.

Even as visible LGBTQ institutions like bars and nonprofits were few and far between, there is enough of a critical mass of them in River City to say something about the shape of LGBTQ community from these perspectives. Indeed, LGBTQ communities of all kinds face the simultaneous pressures of differentiation and assimilation. For some communities, the pressures of assimilation have resulted in LGBTQ institutions closing, as (some) LGBTQ people feel at least nominally comfortable accessing other kinds of spaces, and, perhaps, LGBTQ spaces are no longer needed. In other communities, visible, differentiated LGBTQ institutions are new, or temporary (Gray 2009), and seen as very much needed. These dual pressures are highly contextual, and those who research ambivalence sociologically begin with this key insight: local context determines how ambivalence is expressed and managed (Gould 2001; Merton and Barber 1963). In River City, the shapes that LGBTQ institutions have taken, as well as their patterns over time, tell this story of ambivalence. In examining the kinds of LGBTQ institutions that exist in River City, as well as the trajectory of these institutions from the perspective of LGBTQ and ally River Citizens, it becomes clear that pressures to assimilate *and* differentiate persist side-by-side. We can understand these local pressures, the ways institutions have arisen to navigate these everyday pressures, and what the "explosive" and "pooping-out" institutional dynamic suggests about LGBTQ communities in River City and beyond (Ghaziani 2009; Stillwagon and Ghaziani 2019). We might also see the ways that "community" is, in itself, a complicated concept, one not equally beneficial to all LGBTQ folks (Bailey and Shabazz 2014; Eaves 2017; Ferguson 2003; Joseph 2002; Thomsen 2021). Holding the rise and fall of institutions, the visible invisibility of them, and their benefits and drawbacks in tension, simultaneously, is a key theme of this book.

"We've Got Some Gay-Friendly Places": Nonprofits and Bars

If we focus our attention on LGBTQ institutions, especially gay institutions, a familiar narrative about LGBTQ communities emerges: some participants suggest that they are no longer needed because one can be gay and also accepted, if not celebrated, in other areas of social life. Marriage equality is offered as evidence of progress, perhaps the pinnacle of gay and lesbian assimilation into a heteronormative mainstream (DeFilippis, Yarbrough, and Jones 2018; Ocobock 2018). Perhaps there is no need for gay bars if all bars are accessible to LGBTQ people. But what "counts" as an LGBTQ community institution? When I arrived in River City, my first year of research revealed a small, but growing, number of LGBTQ events and institutions. Drag shows were just beginning to be performed again, after a brief absence, at a local fraternal club. Overall, visible gay community in River City was limited largely to specific events like those occurring during Pride Month and drag shows, events hosted by a local nonprofit, and online community spaces hosted on Facebook and, to some extent, informal networking through dating apps like Grindr, Scruff, and, at the time, craigslist.

Ten participants (all LGBTQ) stated that LGBTQ-specific institutions or spaces are no longer needed. For instance, Peter, a white, gay participant who has long been involved in River City LGBTQ community events, lives with his longtime partner in a nearby rural town that is so isolated that he is unable to use streaming services like Netflix due to poor internet availability. He works at a solidly middle-class, professional job in River City; has co-organized the annual Pride event for several years; and is generally known as a go-to LGBTQ community leader, even within his workplace. Peter argued, "I don't think that you necessarily need to have a community center or an advocacy [sic] as much as it once was, because society has progressed a lot, and it's kind of second nature." Peter's knowledge of River City's gay community and its history is extensive, and his comment that an LGBTQ community center is no longer needed reflects a post-gay understanding of LGBTQ community in River City.

Colby, a young, chipper, white, transgender man, is a local college student, and his perspective aligns with Peter's suggestion that LGBTQ institutions—in this case, Pride events—are no longer central to gay identities. Swapping "gay" and "LGBT" in his comments, Colby explained:

> It's like now people can be seen as individuals that are also part of the LGBT community but you don't need to be a part of that LGBT community for people to see you, if that makes sense? So you don't have to go to that Pride picnic for people to be like gay. You can be gay and people can see you as a person now and that's acceptable.

Despite Colby's and Peter's assertions that LGBTQ institutions are no longer central to LGBTQ lives, the appearance, growth, and decline of two LGBTQ nonprofits (River City Collective, followed by River City Pride) indicate some desire for an LGBTQ-focused organization.

These two organizations offer a case study in the challenges of sustaining LGBTQ-specific organizations in River City. River City Collective

(RCC) was active from 2016 to 2019, following the exit of one of the key group leaders from River City. River City Pride (RCP) promptly organized as RCC declined and has most recently hosted a number of 2021 Pride events. Both organizations were founded primarily by Black, Indigenous, and People of Color (BIPOC) leaders who were not "from" River City but saw, and articulated, a need for a particular kind of LGBTQ community and worked to fill the gap with their LGBTQ event-organizing skills. However, both organizations have clashed (sometimes publicly) with long-standing, primarily white, LGBTQ community members, and this context affects the sustainability of these organizations (and whether their leadership decides to stay in River City). In addition, RCC might itself be a post-gay organization like the Pride Alliance, the LGBT student organization that Amin Ghaziani describes (2011), given its explicit inclusion of allies and absence of LGBTQ terminology in its name. And RCP's focus on drag shows and Pride parties as the centerpiece of their work, while popular (especially among non-LGBTQ people), may not serve the needs of a significant proportion of River City's LGBTQ population. It remains unclear whether RCP will be sustained in the long term; my research suggests that strong ties to existing LGBTQ-supportive organizations, cultural shifts among River City's long-standing LGBTQ leadership, and support for an array of programming would be required.

River City has hosted a small handful of gay bars, but, as in larger cities, they have closed. The *disappearance* of visible gay institutions like the gay bar Next Level also suggests a shift toward assimilation in River City. As in other gay communities like Chicago (Ghaziani 2014b; Orne 2017), the closing of gay bars specifically marked a shift in gay community for River City participants. Longtime members of the River City community recalled between one and three bars that opened and closed in rapid succession in the previous 20 years, notably the same period through which, participants suggested, River City was evolving toward LGBTQ inclusivity. Next Level, the most frequently mentioned gay bar, was noted with particular nostalgia among former patrons and bar employees.

Miguel is a Midwestern native, having grown up in small communities throughout the region. When I interviewed him, he had recently returned to River City with his partner of several years and was working to reestablish the gay networks he left behind when he moved away.

Soft-spoken Miguel self-identified as Latino and German, both gay and queer, and he and his partner quickly became known as a young, energetic, power couple in the community, cofounding RCC with a group of friends. Miguel's nostalgia for Next Level, a now-closed gay bar located downtown, was palpable, and he described Next Level as "the hub of [River City]. It was the gay safe place, so like it being around for so long, everybody who moved away would always come back and visit if their family still lived here. You'd always see familiar faces or new people. Like, they would just come. They had a place to go to." In contrast, Miguel lamented that, at the time of the interview, there were no visibly gay bars in River City. He explained that, while some gay-friendly bars existed, "there's no 'safety zone' [sic] or anything like that. There's no rainbow flags in front of anywhere, claiming to be a gay bar, like they were before." Next Level's closing, and the absence of visibly marked gay bars in River City, suggests a transition to post-gay community similar to such transitions in urban gay communities.

While explanations of why gay bars have closed in River City range from internal "politics" (Miguel) to bar raids in the early 1990s (Steve and Greg), the consensus among gay participants was that their gay community was simply too small and unwilling to sustain an exclusively gay bar. As Nate, a white, gay participant and former River City community leader, suggested, "The problem is when we have such small numbers, you have everybody, you only have a very few people to choose from, you know." While the popularity of drag shows challenges this "small numbers" argument, LGBTQ participants listed nongay bars they frequented in River City, suggesting that LGBTQ people did not feel the need to patronize exclusively gay bars.

Others involved in LGBTQ community also noted a decline in LGBTQ institutions. In another example, Shelley, an LGBTQ ally, explained the decision to close the local chapter of Parents and Friends of Lesbians and Gays (PFLAG) in favor of a more broadly focused "Caring Community" group housed within the Center for Multicultural Community (CMC). She asserted that "I think as times have gotten more relaxed, you know, there's been less and less need for the way it has been." She noted that the need for parents, friends, and family to seek support in supporting their LGBTQ kin was in decline, and more *LGBTQ* people were attending the PFLAG group than parents and friends. "Caring Community," at the time of my research, met quarterly, and attendance was slim and mixed between supportive and LGBTQ participants.

Known spaces for LGBTQ community members included two "gay-owned" bars that did not advertise themselves explicitly as gay bars. Participants learned about them through word-of-mouth and assurances that the bar *owners* were gay and lesbian. After I asked Kyle, a newcomer to River City, whether he knew of any gay bars in River City, he responded, "Not that I know of. There are only two that I've been told were gay-friendly. I've been to one; it is owned by a lesbian but it's not a gay bar by any means. Because there's not, there's not one indication anywhere visibly. . . . Just even a little flag, nothing. That I've found." Kyle's comments echo Miguel's in the noted absence of gay symbols, such as rainbow flags, marking gay spaces. Peter explained, "We've got some gay-friendly places in [River City] from a bar atmosphere perspective. [Barney's], which is [a] gay-owned bar, but they don't really focus on just the gay community, has been always receptive. I mean, I've been in there, there's street people in there, nobody's really showed offense. I know some of the local drag queens can go down there and not have any concern." Paul's description of Barney's echoes Peter's: "So you got the whole gay straight alliance happening there. Um, and there's never any judgment ever, you know, it's just nice. It's my new utopia." Barney's function as a gay-friendly, but not explicitly or exclusively gay, bar that welcomes a range of patrons, including presumably poor "street people," suggests a transition to post-gay community in River City and echoes findings about more broadly inclusive gay, or perhaps queer, bars in similar small cities (Mattson 2020).

Barney's is sandwiched between a tanning salon and crisis pregnancy center in one of River City's historic downtown neighborhoods, just across the street from a block that includes an upscale restaurant, bookstore, and coffee shop. Its interior light is best described as golden, and a smattering of couches, tables, and chairs occupies the space between the front door and the bar. Patrons gather to play Cards Against Humanity and trivia in front of the fireplace or to enjoy a pizza procured from one of the upscale restaurants across the street. Callie, a queer woman and Barney's patron who drives a half-hour from her home in a nearby town to spend time there, echoed Peter's inclusive language when she described Barney's as a "queer bar." Callie's distinction between a gay bar and a queer bar summarizes the distinction between gay and gay-friendly spaces in River City and hints at Barney's as a post-gay "queer" space. As she explains,

> I've gone to some of the Pride events [River City] puts on, or like drag shows and things like that, it still feels very um . . . gay white male? [laughs] dominant, so there's that too, which, I was having this conversation with somebody, they were like, well, what's the difference between a gay bar and a queer bar? I was like . . . there's differences! [laughs] There are differences, and I feel, I think it's that kind of a feel right, where it's like where [River City] maybe feels, in any of those events feel very gay, as opposed to them feeling . . . you know, like the difference between a gay bar and a queer bar, where it's like gay white male, not so much anyone else.

When I asked what distinguished a gay bar from a queer bar, Callie explained that a queer bar would include "nongender bathrooms," would have a more "chill" and "come as you are" atmosphere, and would be more welcoming specifically to women. "I think they [the bar owners] didn't want the focus to be just on gender or sexuality, but also on race where it's like just anybody can come and be comfortable." Here, Callie's use of the word "queer" operates as more inclusive and multicultural, echoing a shift toward the use of "queer" as an umbrella term (Casey 2004; Ryan 2016; Warner 1993, 2000; Wortham 2016). However, Callie's description of Barney's as "queer" hints at something more than a post-gay framework and highlights the complexities of LGBTQ spaces. We might think of Barney's as ambivalently queer (Hartless 2018): inclusive and invisible, at least to those not "in the know" about where to find LGBTQ community spaces.

Inclusive (but gay-friendly) bars, or queer bars (Mattson 2020), then, offer opportunities for a range of people to interact, spaces that are not exclusive along lines of sexuality, gender, and race, according to some. Spaces like Barney's, a gay-owned "queer bar," demonstrate inclusion, a key element of post-gay community, and these spaces are defined more by their openness than by their exclusive focus on shared gay (or LGBTQ) identities. This inclusion, according to participants, is meant to encompass specific identities heretofore excluded from white, gay community spaces: women, trans people (symbolically welcomed by the "nongender bathrooms," as Callie suggested), people of color, and straight people. "Queer bars" like Barney's might be considered a quintessential post-gay space, places where all identities are welcome, if minimized.

And, yet, bars like Barney's had not (yet) developed the kind of "questionably queer" (Hartless 2018) credentials earned by other kinds of bars. Participants expressed little ambivalence about the presence of non-LGBTQ people in Barney's specifically. Reflections like Callie's suggest explicit attention to the inclusion of marginalized people (Mattson 2020), rather than an incursion of straight, white, cis patrons. Whether this observation has been demonstrated in Barney's longer-term persistence is now impossible, though; Barney's closed not long after my research in River City concluded.

Also navigating this tension between inclusion and being overwhelmed, nonprofit organizations sought to achieve a balance between signaling their focus on LGBTQ identities while not simultaneously alienating potential ally supporters. As noted briefly above, a small, quickly growing nonprofit aimed to "catalyze and sustain" elements of "the region's diverse LGBTQ+ and ally community" (River City Collective 2016). One of only two River City organizations dedicated solely and explicitly to supporting LGBTQ people, River City Collective's name and mission exhibited the kind of inclusivity and diversity that constitute a post-gay approach to identity (Ghaziani 2015).[2] Again, this approach emphasizes multiculturalism and inclusion of differences while minimizing LGBTQ people's identity specificity and experiences of inequality. Participants also identified the CMC, an organization that houses LGBTQ youth and support groups and offers LGBTQ-specific ally training, as an LGBTQ-friendly organization. The CMC's mission is to "empower . . . all families and community members of [River City] to reach their potential and build unity out of diversity" (Center for Multicultural Community 2016). Aimed as an inclusive statement, the CMC's mission demonstrates both a post-gay and postracial (Bonilla-Silva 2006) approach to difference, as specific identities are not named in the organization's mission or vision. The CMC's efforts to be as inclusive as possible may be the result of relatively small numbers of people who fall under the "multicultural" umbrella. However, an emphasis on unity and "all families and community members" also obliquely references River

City's divisive, exclusive past and, like in a post-gay era, references inclusion rather than persistent inequality.

The line between inclusion and invisibility is quite thin indeed, as "come as you are" may also be interpreted as "come as you are" (as long as you are not too "out"). How such spaces demonstrate a shared value of inclusivity remains an open question (Thomsen 2021). Participants' discussion of spaces like Barney's as inclusive and multicultural, rather than oriented around gay identity, demonstrate the possibility of post-gay spaces in River City. Perhaps gay-specific spaces are no longer needed, in other words. However, I argue that the rise and fall of not only gay but, perhaps, queer institutions offers evidence of institutional (specifically) and community (more broadly) ambivalence. Given the local institutional landscape, local and regional dynamics, and the people engaged in supporting these institutions (or not supporting them), Barney's became possible and legible as a queer institution, for a time. Next Level filled a need in the gay community, for a time.[3] And nonprofits focusing exclusively on the needs of LGBTQ people coalesce around a core of energized people who may then leave or focus on other priorities. Insider/outsider dynamics matter here, too. River City's local context coalesces around individuals who have the capacity to generate and support institutions, both a benefit and a drawback in that creating organizations appears to fill an ongoing community need, but sustaining them remains challenging. The most successful, long-standing institutions engage a broader base of supporters, including allies, reaching across identity lines. This strategy, too, introduces ambivalence on the part of LGBTQ and especially trans community members, as the case of drag shows demonstrates.

"They're at the Drag Show and Having a Blast": Allies in Gay Community

Drag shows, specifically, have become wildly popular in River City in recent years, although they have been hosted in River City since the 1980s, and at least two distinct drag groups regularly hold shows at local venues. Drawing on the explosive popularity of drag culture nationally (Brennan and Gudelunas 2017), which brought drag shows into living rooms beyond large cities, RCP organized an in-person, socially distanced 2020

Pride event that heavily drew on the appeal of drag shows, followed by drag-dominated (but not exclusive) 2021 Pride events. Indeed, drag shows have been central to annual Pride events in River City, where the family-friendly weekend Pride picnic shifts into a traditionally raucous drag show at night. Whether drag shows are examples of LGBTQ community spaces is a question open for academic debate (Rupp and Taylor 2003; Stone 2009), although I spotted a number of LGBTQ community members at the drag shows I attended, both at a casino bar and at the Warehouse, a local bar known for supporting progressive causes. While several participants included drag shows in their lists of LGBTQ events, they also remarked on the overwhelming presence of people they took to be straight at these shows, questioning whether they really "counted" as supporting actual LGBTQ people. Kyle, a white, partnered newcomer to River City who later became an active drag performer in one of River City's two drag groups, noted that he has "been surprised at the people that come to the drag shows here." He went on:

> They're clearly straight couples which, nothing, no judgment. But then it'll be like just, and this is me stereotyping a hundred percent, but the people who normally are the ones yelling, "Hey queer," out of a window, they look like that and then they're at a drag show and having a blast; having a drink and tipping the drag queen. And I really hope that they go home and are just as open about it as they are in that dark room.

My observations at drag shows echo Kyle's description. At one packed drag show held at the Warehouse, I noted a group of white young women whom I understood to be straight closest to the stage, dancing and standing on chairs, waving arms and clapping along with the music (and tipping the drag queens). Just behind them were a few straight men, who, judging by their physical interaction with them, may have been their boyfriends or spouses. The men stood awkwardly and occasionally placed hands and arms around their girlfriends and wives, to signal (both of) their presumed straightness. Just behind the phalanx of straight girls was a layer of gay men, some dancing enthusiastically, some quite young, and some older, standing around and bopping slightly, eyeing each other. My field notes from other drag shows reflected the same kind of spatial orientation: straight women closest to the stage, surrounded by their partners, with a ring of known gay community members toward the edges of the space. This spatial orientation suggests community ambivalence, or specifically, who drag shows are really *for*. Necessarily, the cheering ring of straight women provides support, both audible and financial, for the largely queer performers in a space that simultaneously exoticizes, eroticizes, and celebrates one key expression of gay culture. Examining the contexts surrounding drag shows reveals this example of community ambivalence: national conversations about drag; local desires for liminal, exotic spaces among straight River Citizens; and desires for queer spaces of performance and consumption coalesce to produce wildly popular drag shows.

Participants noted the general inclusion, and centrality, of straight people at drag shows, as well as the acceptance of straight people within River City's drag culture. Some also noted the surprising acceptance of drag culture among straight people in River City. Paul, a straight, white, and active LGBTQ ally, in some ways exemplifies this straight acceptance of drag culture. I shared a meal with Paul and his wife in their middle-class home in a quiet residential neighborhood, and Paul and I sat at their dining-room table for our interview. Bald, with sparkling blue eyes, a contagious smile, and a warm personality, he connected his life's philosophy to the contemporary political moment, explaining, "if you look at Donald Trump, I try to be the opposite." Paul described himself as "gay adjacent," noting that "I should have been born a gay man." In fact, Paul was often identified as gay based on his gender presentation, which he described as more "open and expressive" than typical straight men. Paul grew up on a farm in a nearby town, "population like 70," is a college graduate, and loves science fiction, proudly showing me his enviable room full of science fiction paraphernalia in his basement. Paul's love for his children and his community was also palpable, and he functioned as a local drag mentor for several LGBTQ young people. Paul, at the time of my interview, identified as a straight drag queen, a "comedy queen," and a "bit of a ham" who "like[s] to make people laugh" with his campy, hilarious performances. Paul emphasized his straight friends' acceptance of his drag persona, describing his straight, male neighbors as "totally great guys. You know, they've seen me in drag, they think it's, you know, awesome, they, you know, so it's, it's, you know. I mean, the one actual neighbor, she saw me driving in drag once and was honking at me and waving, you know, so, it's, it's great."

Drag shows may be seen as archetypal markers of visible, gay community (Rupp and Taylor 2003). However, LGBTQ participants' comments in my research suggest that they may also not be, and, in fact, that they might be overtly hostile especially to trans women. While drag shows offer a community space of sexual transgression for straight, cisgender people *and* gay men, they are not *just* for gay people, and most certainly not for trans people, although at least one trans woman plays a prominent role in the local drag scene. They *cannot* be just for LGBTQ people and remain financially viable, given the dynamics of LGBTQ life in small cities (Mattson 2020). In fact, some participants argued that drag performances are too straight to be considered LGBTQ institutions. Fia, a white, trans woman, summed up a critical approach to drag shows as LGBTQ community, noting that she was "surprised by the number of drag shows [in River City], but on the other hand I'm not surprised because drag shows are not really a sign of LGBT community at all." Fia explained that

> it's almost like objectification of the LGBT community. That drag shows are kind of like straight people go to drag shows, it's almost more common, you, you'll, generally you'll find far more straight people at a drag show than you will LGBT people. You'll, you usually find some LGBT people, usually they know the performers, and that's why they're there, um, and, you know, there's, there's that sense of it, it's very voyeuristic. Uh, very exhibitionist . . . a hyperbole expression of femininity, which isn't really femininity. Um, so, it's . . . drag shows are not a marker of LGBT communities.

Drag shows, in other words, demonstrate community ambivalence, containing celebratory and exploitative aspects alongside exclusion and containment of this transgression into a single context. While drag shows in River City offer opportunities to build gay community among the performers (as Steve and Greg suggested), they are also spaces that emphasize straight people's consumption of transgressive gender and sexual performances, performances that have particular implications for trans women like Fia, who live in a national context in which drag queens and transgender women are sometimes conflated. Fia's observations echo previous research on sexual (and gender) transgression. For example, these spaces offer bounded opportunities for subversion, but ones that ultimately re-create the sexual and gender systems they aim to challenge (Bridges 2010; Mitchell 2015; Parker 1991). Drag shows clearly blur the boundaries between largely (but not exclusively) gay performers and largely (but not exclusively) straight audience members, but drag shows in River City are also a straight-inclusive space.

Furthermore, for some of my research participants (especially trans women participants like Fia and Karen), drag shows were spaces of exclusion, places they would not go as members of River City's LGBTQ community. Fia's and Kyle's comments suggest the risks associated with straight inclusion in presumed LGBTQ spaces: a lack of fully inclusive LGBTQ community, and the limitation of sexual and gender transgressions to drag spaces. Drag shows in River City are one example of the kinds of straight inclusion in gay spaces demonstrated in communities shifting toward a post-gay era (Ghaziani 2014b:253–54). Drag shows are one example of contextually determined ambivalent community, a community that is friendly, celebratory, and sexy (Orne 2017) for gay performers, gay community members, and straight allies, but one that leaves trans people, and trans women especially, marginalized.

"Explosive" and "Pooping Out": The Rise and Fall and Rise of LGBTQ Institutions and Events

Participants described a kind of frustratingly cyclical LGBTQ community landscape, highlighting moments of community connection followed by their absence. On the one hand, long-term LGBTQ community members reflected on the feeling of community from a handful of LGBTQ-specific events. Partnered participant Robin, active in local LGBTQ organizations and events, described recent Pride picnics and a local, by-all-accounts well-attended LGBTQ conference as times "where that part of me felt very free." She further described her feeling at the conference: "It was all of the local gay people coming together and not fighting, not being catty. Just enjoying their time together and some connecting and you know I mean generally positive things happening." On the other hand, some LGBTQ community members lamented the senses of loss, of lack of community, and of complacency following some of these events. Robin's reflections about LGBTQ events in River City are telling:

> OK, so what seems to have happened, so this is even in the nine years I've been here. There are people who sort of rise up, take some leadership, and then whatever it is disintegrates. Maybe it's the bar, maybe it's [the conference], maybe it's [Pride events]. You know whatever it is, there's some sort of volunteer leadership that comes up to try to do something good in and or with the gay community that then falls apart. I mean that's sort of the pattern.

LGBTQ events and institutions, in other words, seemed to rise and fall in a noticeable cycle (Ghaziani et al. 2016), rather than follow a clear trajectory from appearance to disappearance, from marginalization to acceptance. We might see this kind of cyclical process as evidence of ambivalence, resolved temporarily in the appearance and disappearance of events and institutions. Karen, an activist and organizer for River City Trans, also described this cyclical community process. She pointedly asserted that people who "come from other walks of life" should decide to stay in River City to create community. Speaking about both the broader River City community and "LGBT community," she explained,

> We don't keep that nucleus healthy, and if it doesn't stay healthy and growing, it doesn't catch on, and it never gains the traction to get so big that you can't knock down, to get to that place where, OK, we are strong. We never get to that place where we're strong. We start things, and we do the best we can with them, [and they] poop out.

While Karen referred to a "nucleus" of LGBTQ people, this idea might also be understood as institutionalized LGBTQ community. In other words, without *long-standing* LGBTQ institutions, and leaders within them, a persistent sense of "strong" LGBTQ community is missing in River City. Research on rural LGBTQ communities, however, explains how and why this process takes place (Gray 2009), but it does not resolve some participants' desire for more persistent community institutions, desires that might be driven, in part, by metronormativity (Halberstam

2005), by desires to be more like imagined LGBTQ community life in larger cities.

Other long-term members of LGBTQ community referenced recent, popular LGBTQ events and their sense of frustration that things had quieted down in recent years. For Peter, who led previous Pride events, this sense of frustration and loss was most keenly felt following the well-attended LGBTQ conference. Shelley, an LGBTQ ally, summarized the ambivalent feeling about LGBTQ events in River City. Speaking specifically about the conference, which she explained was "really sort of like coming out gathering in [River City], in a lot of ways," Shelley described the challenges with the conference and the "explosive" feeling of the conference itself. She explained that "we had issues because it was a very, the community was very bifurcated, at least, bifurcated, but it was not cohesive, as you would expect. . . . And so that one thing isn't enough to pull the whole group together." Despite its challenges, Shelley also noted that the conference "was just the right thing at the right time, it was one of those explosive kinda things that happened and people from different colleges and from different businesses and . . . just people gravitated, and it just came together." The temporary togetherness of the conference seemed to be waning in the first year of my research in River City.

However, the increasing number of planned LGBTQ-themed and -oriented events and organizations suggests that perhaps LGBTQ community was again coalescing in River City. The first indicator that this may be occurring was the incredibly popular drag show in early 2016, described in the introduction to this chapter, the culmination of an increasing frequency of drag shows on the events calendar in River City.[4] In contrast to previous years in which Pride events included a weekend picnic and single drag show, the 2016 series of Pride events were organized by different groups and include at least three picnics, two of which are youth-focused, in addition to RCC's Pride night and at least one Pride-focused drag show. According to RCC's online calendar, five LGBTQ-focused events were scheduled for one summer month alone. These five events do not include ongoing, regularly scheduled LGBTQ support activities, especially organized within the CMC; the LGBTQ+ youth group and adult support groups met each week, although their meeting frequency has declined in early 2017. And RCP's 2021 Pride Week schedule included seven events, including an LGBTQ panel discussion, parade, and ticketed drag events. Whether the most recent LGBTQ events and organizations represent a longer-term institutionalization of LGBTQ community in River City remains an open question. RCC's efforts to institutionalize include registering nonprofit paperwork, fundraising, twice-weekly meetings, and nonprofit board development, all lost when the leaders disbanded the group. While RCP seems to have taken RCC's place, the "pooping-out" risk remains present, although these and other institutionalization efforts suggest that community coherence through this organization could occur.

Follow-up conversations with long-term LGBTQ community members demonstrate some skepticism about the future of organizations like River City Collective and River City Pride, and their hesitation, given the history of LGBTQ community in River City, suggests a sense of ambivalence about the future of the River City LGBTQ community. LGBTQ events continue to aim to be broadly inclusive, balancing the need for engagement from non-LGBTQ people with desires to support LGBTQ community, especially LGBTQ communities of color in River City. For example, the main summer LGBTQ Pride event even in 2020 featured a more racially diverse group of organizers and performers compared to previous years, but the event title lost an explicit connection to Pride and LGBTQ identities, riffing on a popular music event instead. The LGBTQ community in River City seems on the cusp of a simultaneous "coming-out" phase *and* "post-gay" phase, given both the rise of LGBTQ events and fears that community coalescence will decline again, if leaders exit River City. And some leaders have, in fact, left River City, leaving digital traces that hint at new possibilities. RCC's website, for example, redirected to RCP's website, which noted that it is led by "two queer POC with strong social justice ties" and includes an array of local business and nonprofit sponsors. These shifts are taking place within a national conversation about ongoing racial injustice and persistent inequalities, and perhaps more explicitly intersectional approaches to LGBTQ community will emerge in this moment.

Conclusion: Catalyzing Ambivalent Community

It may be easy to forget that national conversations about inequalities were active in small cities well before Donald Trump's election in

2016. Following the shootings in Orlando in mid-June of 2016, I joined a small group of community members gathered to organize a vigil to honor the 49 victims. The evening was warm and steamy, but the downtown square, the location of River City's first Pride march back in the 1980s, was already covered mostly in shade. The large group of about 70 volunteers, recruited in the span of five days, began showing up early, and Mark, ever a public crier, was frequently moved by their physical and emotional labor throughout the evening. We set up the 25 easels, clipping the 49 glossy, professionally produced posters of those killed to sheets of foam board. We discovered the boards kept blowing off the easels, and we improvised, duct-taping, masking-taping, and packing-taping them to the easels. We tested the sound system. We unpacked the candles, setting them up on a table. We put the volunteers to work on these small, mundane tasks, volunteers like the mom with her young-adult child, whose gender identity I could not assume. I watched them, the young person, throughout the evening, wordlessly carrying boxes, posters, and generally being useful without complaining, even though I would have, at their age. A longtime gay community member who has organized many a festival event arrived with 500 bottles of water, plastic tubs, and ice to cover all, and he and his team set them up underneath a tree near the edge of the park.

Mark gathered the volunteers in one place to read them his instructions. There were young folks, older folks, women and men and gender-queer folks, River Citizens and people traveling back to River City, their hometown, from a large, nearby city, a car full of queers whose fashionable gender expression suggested a larger urban home. Participants, overall, expressed their gender in a panoply of styles: a shaved head with a blue mohawk perched atop; shorts and sneakers; nose rings and hair spray; middle-class, middle-aged Midwestern mom clothing; summer dresses and khaki shorts and tee shirts; sunglasses, mirrored and not. Some were shy, quiet, drinking alcohol from water bottles. Attendees began arriving at the vigil early, walking slowly through the volunteers holding the posters of those killed. The mood was both somber and strangely joyful, as people connected, reconnected, newly connected with their neighbors, with people they knew, with people they had not seen for a long time. I spotted nearly every one of my interviewees (those who were in town, at least), and some volunteered, like Sandra, who brought a few boxes of tissues for folks who needed them; Callie, who came with her partner to do some heavy lifting and stand with posters; and Nick, who is in recovery now and hoping to move out of his halfway house soon. The 49 people holding posters stood stone-faced, sad, crying sometimes. Volunteers were largely white, holding the posters and stories of the brown people killed. Some tapped out, after some time at their task, asking the volunteer "floaters" to take their spots for a time, for the evening. They stood for more than an hour in the declining light.

It would be tempting to suggest that the cyclical LGBTQ community events and the disappearance of gay bars and other institutions suggest that institutionalized community is no longer needed. But events like the Orlando vigil, which drew more than 300 community members to a downtown square with little advance notice, require us to consider alternative models of community. The vigil and other community events coexist alongside feelings of disunity, of dispersion, of disconnection. Community is mobilized periodically, strategically; as suggested by the now-defunct RCC's mission statement, "catalyzing" is a good metaphor for the process by which community events occur, as are other chemical processes like "precipitating." The Orlando vigil quickly formed through the actions of a small group of fewer than 10 community members, some practiced leaders, others new to organizing events, and others new to River City (like me).

LGBTQ community ambivalence is highly contextual, as community coalesces and fractures in urban contexts that are different from rural contexts, and regional differences in community matter (Manalansan et al. 2014). For example, Japonica Brown-Saracino's (2011) discussion of ambient community in lesbian-friendly Ithaca suggests that perhaps at least lesbian community members do not feel as strongly about the need for community—one "half" of ambivalence—as those in Midwestern, rural contexts. Perhaps the kind of temporary community that Mary Gray (2009) describes in rural contexts might exist ambivalently alongside post-gay sensibilities in small cities like River City. While this project may be considered a case study (Small 2009) of one community, a similar community landscape is likely in cities and towns with similar demographics: relatively isolated, rural, largely white, and religious cities in the Midwest and, as some participants suggested, in the South (Abelson 2019; Rogers 2018). Brown-Saracino's more recent work (2017) suggests that perhaps, in addition to considering communities as more or less post-gay, understanding communities as more or less strongly ambivalent might yield additional insights into LGBTQ community. In other words, perhaps "friendlier" cities might be seen as less ambivalent, while "hostile" cities demonstrate stronger ambivalence about the need for community (Gould 2001; Smelser 1998). I suspect that River City exists somewhere in the middle of such a continuum, and thick descriptions (Geertz 2002) of seemingly similar community contexts might reveal whether this assertion is true. The benefit of an ambivalent approach to community involves acknowledging the real lives LGBTQ people live, and choose to live, in these spaces, with the emphatic joys and challenges experienced therein.

The relationship between ambivalence and two key dimensions of LGBTQ community requires further examination, specifically, race and gender. First, as I discussed briefly above, white participants' discourse around race suggested an understanding of LGBTQ community as one that is exclusively white, although the emergence of BIPOC-led organizations like RCC and RCP challenge this assumption. White LGBTQ and ally participants often compared LGBTQ community and Black communities, assuming similar, progressive trajectories and neglecting community overlap. Participants of color demonstrated a sense of multiple community memberships (Battle and Ashley 2008; Ferguson 2003; Moore 2010, 2011), some preferring to distance themselves from the largely white LGBTQ community in River City. Transgender and genderqueer participants, most of whom were white, expressed a disconnect with lesbian and gay community that resonates with transgender people's experiences in other communities (Broad 2002; P. Doan 2007; Halberstam 2005), and cisgender participants' comments suggested a conflation between lesbian/gay and LGBTQ community as a whole. Again, a comparison to similar community contexts would be beneficial here, as race and gender dimensions differ across regions.

Comparing identity-based communities in terms of ambivalence might suggest ways for activists to operate strategically to achieve social change. Strongly ambivalent communities might generate different kinds of community events that require, for example, the involvement of allies, coupled with "only" spaces specifically for identity-based community members. Observations in River City's "only" spaces suggest that events specifically for LGBTQ community members sometimes work and sometimes do not, while events focused on allies and featuring ally involvement tend to be successful. Ambivalence may offer activists a way to focus on the "both *and*" of social change: an acknowledgment that multiple dimensions of community mobilization are crucial to support LGBTQ lives.

4

What Do You Mean Your *Gay* Friend?

LGBTQ Friendships

I am sitting with Mark, a white, gay man in his late 20s, at Brews, a dark, downtown coffee shop that doubles as a pub, and we are both nestled into a set of benches surrounding a chrome kitchen table, drinking coffee. Mellow, ambient music wafts into our space as we caffeinate and chat about the challenges of maintaining friendships and finding partnerships and a sense of community in River City. Mark wears comfortable clothes like thin, light-colored hoodies and tee shirts, and he would easily be mistaken for a graduate student in a more urban context. He has a bald, shaved head and a neatly trimmed beard, and as we talk, I think that Mark is the warmest gay man I have ever met. Mark is known among his close friends as an amateur photographer of River City's visually appealing architecture, and his reflections about River City are as descriptive as his ethereal snapshots. While he spent his young adulthood in a nearby Midwestern city, he is originally from an Eastern European country and migrated to the Midwest as a child due to "social unrest back home," as he explains it. His family's experiences in his home country affect his perspectives on community today, and his work and social life revolve around fostering community dialogue and change.

Mark seems to make friendships easily wherever he travels, although he struggles to find the romantic partner he deeply desires. Despite his ability to make friends, his friendship map is relatively small and includes 12 people, five of whom are lesbian or gay, and three of whom he locates close to himself, with the remaining friends spiraling outward from this core group of three. I ask Mark about whether he "gets" anything from his friendships with LGBTQ people, compared to his friendships with non-LGBTQ people, and he hesitates. First, he notes that his response might be different once he is partnered. He then states, "Maybe it's just that I'm not noticing it. All my friends don't, I can talk to them about . . . *well* . . . I guess the thing that is different is that in some cases, maybe the gay friends engage more in the partner conversation, like, actually ask me, like, 'well, who are you looking for, and what are you looking for?' and I have more of an authentic conversation."

Mark's *initial* response, that he can discuss anything with his friends regardless of their sexual identity, resonates with a post-gay analysis: the argument that gay neighborhoods are transitioning toward communities where gayness is deemphasized or invisible (Ghaziani 2014b), or operate, perhaps primarily, as sites of tourism and identity consumption for out-of-town gays (Greene 2014). In contrast with friendships in a coming-out era, where shared identities might determine what could be discussed in a friendship, in post-gay friendships, even straight friends could discuss gay topics like, in Mark's case, "the partner conversation." Yet Mark's quick shift to reconsidering this response, from "not noticing" differences among his friends to having a more "authentic" conversation about romantic relationships with LGBTQ friends resonates with the importance of gay identities in the coming-out era. In other words, Mark's comments about more authentic conversations about partnership with gay friends suggest the ongoing relevance of gay identities in relationships and communities. This seemingly contradictory response characterizes my participants' understanding of their friendships and communities, more generally; participants noted that their friends' (sexual, in this case) identities "don't matter," except when they do. Their responses demonstrate ambivalence about their friendships, indicating mixed, sometimes contradictory observations about the ongoing relevance of LGBTQ identities in their lives in River City.

In this chapter, I approach changing LGBTQ communities and identities through the lens of an underexplored relationship, *friendship*. Research on LGBTQ communities has conflated friendships with community (Nardi 1999; Weston 1991), arguing that LGBTQ friends generate LGBTQ community. However, whether and how these friendships relate to LGBTQ community in a time when the meaning of LGBTQ identities is changing remains underexplored. Are shared-identity friendships still important for LGBTQ people? What might it mean to find that most LGBTQ people in River City have few LGBTQ friends?

In this chapter, I analyze participants' "friendship talk" (Anthony and McCabe 2015) to show how participants' shared-identity friendships mattered, and how they did not. Friendship talk is a type of identity talk that people use in self-identity construction. Individuals' narratives and interpretations of their friendships tell us about how they understand their identities, for example, in terms of gender (Reid and Fine 1992). In what follows, I focus on what participants' friendship talk reveals about participants' *sense of shared identity* and begin to draw connections between shared identities and community. I discuss reasons why participants claimed that shared-identity friendships did *and* did not matter. Two themes emerged on each side of this argument. On the one hand, participants explained that shared identities did not matter in their lives for two reasons: their identity differences are not, or should not, be apparent in their friendships (which I call "minimizing" identity differences), and simply having a shared identity was not enough to generate friendship (which I call "insufficiency"). On the other hand, participants explained that identities still do matter in their friendships, because friendships with those who share their identity offer a sense of affirmation and require less emotional labor to maintain, and these friendships offered connections to shared symbols, interests, and language. This ambivalence about friendships gives us a sense of the complexities in relationships that do (and don't) form LGBTQ community in River City.

I then analyze participants' friendship maps to show which LGBTQ participants were more likely to have shared-identity friendships. In other words, reviewing the social networks that participants diagrammed in their friendship maps reveals a higher proportion of shared-identity friendships for a subset of LGBTQ participants.[1] I conclude by discussing two cases that test the boundaries of a "shared-identity friendship doesn't matter" narrative and reinforce the importance of including community contexts, specifically locally determined norms, in analyses of friendship and in the kinds of ambivalences people experience as LGBTQ community members. River City is a community in which adherence to a range of norms in terms of gender identity, sexual orientation, race, length of residence, age, and partner status is especially meaningful, given its size and Catholic cultural history. LGBTQ River Citizens whose identities challenge these norms are likely to seek within-identity friendships *as well as* a sense of LGBTQ community. These two participants, while similar in some ways, exemplify the challenges of nonnormative identities in a context like River City.

Friendship Talk: Identities Don't Matter, But . . .

Research on LGBTQ friendships suggests that friendships that cross lines of gender identity and sexuality are fairly common, at least in urban communities with high populations of LGBTQ people (Brown-Saracino 2011; Galupo 2007; Galupo et al. 2014; Muraco 2012). In a post-gay (Ghaziani 2014b) or lesbian-friendly (Brown-Saracino 2011, 2017) community, LGBTQ people would form friendships based on shared interests, not around shared identity. Yet recent research has also found that shared identity in terms of sexuality still matters for social networks, at least in the case of lesbians (Logan 2013). Given its low proportion of LGBTQ people, relative to larger cities, we might guess that LGBTQ people in River City would feel isolated and might seek friendships with other LGBTQ people. In other words, the community context of River City might require LGBTQ community members to band together in close friendship or to form chosen families with close friends (Weston 1991).

However, participants demonstrated the same kinds of ambivalence about seeking out LGBTQ-specific friendships that they did about the need for LGBTQ community in River City. Recall Mark's statement above as an example of a typical ambivalent response to LGBTQ friendships. In such an ambivalent response, participants offered conflicting evidence: they stated that shared sexual or gender identities do not matter or should not matter in their friendships, and they also claimed that shared identities do matter.[2] Participants' friendship talk demonstrates a key paradox in LGBTQ identities in River City: a desire to minimize differences and emphasize sameness (with non-LGBTQ people) alongside a desire for identity affirmation and shared culture.

"The People Who Don't Necessarily Care": Minimizing Identity Differences

Some participants' friendship talk resonated with post-gay understandings of identity and relationships. As Amin Ghaziani notes, "Those who consider themselves post-gay profess that their sexual orientation does not form the core of how they define themselves, and they prefer to hang out with their straight friends as much as with those who are gay" (2014b:3). In a post-gay context, we would expect LGBTQ folks to say that the identities of their friends don't matter and, indeed, *their* identities don't matter in their friendships. And, in fact, some participants, like Jack, said exactly that.

Jack is a young, white, asexual trans man who had received what he described as "an external call into ministry" as early as middle school, meaning that others had suggested to him that he become a pastor. He had resisted the call until college, when his connection with a family in Central America during a study-abroad trip made him realize that being a pastor was not all about being "in a pulpit . . . preaching." He realized that, "instead, I can be with people in their times of need, in their joys, in their sorrows. But I can just simply be with people wherever they are and that makes me really, really excited to do ministry." Not a native River Citizen, Jack had moved to River City to attend theological seminary and clearly loved his experiences there, especially its "intentionality of community." Jack's friendship map included 18 friends, 15 of whom were clustered tightly around him and largely interconnected in overlapping friend groups. Jack was close with many of his friends, and of his six closest friends, four are straight, two are pansexual, and none are transgender. I asked Jack why he put some people on his friendship map. He explained:

> I don't know. . . . 'Cause like all of my friends support me. We wouldn't be friends if they didn't because I just don't need that. But these are the people who don't necessarily care I guess that I identify as trans. They just care that I'm their friend. Like so it doesn't matter that to them, like, yeah, I can have really great trans conversations with [these three trans friends] because, well, they understand. Cause we're all FTMs [female-to-male trans folks]. But everybody else just doesn't really care. Like I can talk to them about, "oh, I get to stab myself tomorrow in the morning [with my testosterone injection]." . . . But I can go talk to any one of these people and know that I'm not going to get judged.

For Jack, while friends were supportive and not judgmental, they "don't necessarily care" about his transgender identity. Jack's friendship talk demonstrates one of the benefits of friendships across lines of gender, for transgender people: the feeling of "not [being] judged" (Galupo et al. 2014). However, these benefits come at a price: minimizing one's (marginalized) gender identity. Jack explains twice in the above quote that his friends "don't care" about his gender identity.

This kind of "don't care" language serves a dual purpose. On the one hand, it signals to LGBTQ friends that their identity differences are not the most important aspect of their identities, for non-LGBTQ friends. This language in some ways signals acceptance, that non-LGBTQ friends did not "judge" LGBTQ friends based on their identities. On the other hand, "don't care" language also minimizes LGBTQ friends' identities, potentially for the comfort of their non-LGBTQ friends. Similar patterns have been identified among cross-race friends, where white friends especially minimized the role of race in their relationships with Black friends (Korgen 2002). Minimizing the importance of friends' identities avoids introducing a possible tension in cross-identity friendships but also makes it difficult to discuss identity-specific challenges or inequalities when they arise. When non-LGBTQ friends minimize identity differences by saying they "don't care," then, they demonstrated both acceptance and a possible unwillingness to discuss LGBTQ friends' experiences of marginalization.

Like Jack, Karen had close friends who did not share her gender identity, although her friendship map with 19 named friends showed a clearer distinction between close friends and acquaintances. Karen is a white, transgender lesbian and activist whose close friends have supported her through a number of challenging life transitions. She described Brenda, her best friend and a straight, married, cisgender woman, as her "absolute closest, longtime, most magnificent soul person that I could ever have" and as someone who "brings reality down to the ground." She explained what she appreciated about this close friendship:

> Her acceptance of me is wonderful. I don't think she sees me as male or female. I'm just a person. I'm just, you know, she doesn't have that judgment factor in her about male or female. . . . So you don't, it doesn't matter if you're male or female. And she does masculine, like I said, she rides her own motorcycle, does her own Harley thing and all that stuff, so she realizes that the casing that you're in [is not] who you are inside.

Karen's friendship talk reveals a close, well-loved friend who is also nonjudgmental, even as Karen's gender "doesn't matter." For both Jack and Karen, a friend is someone who does not express judgment *despite* their identity. This kind of "don't care" language resonates with colorblind (Bonilla-Silva 2006), or race-neutral, ideology, although not precisely, as race-neutral ideology is generally asserted by the dominant group and effectively erases inequalities. In Karen's and Jack's cases, this "don't care" ideology suggests a desire to minimize differences from the perspective of a marginalized group, even as it emphasizes the "nonjudgmental" qualities of a dominant-group (cisgender) friend. Researchers have found that some transgender folks reject a framework of identity for understanding their friendships (Galupo et al. 2014:210), and trans folks have historically had fewer ways to find and connect with shared-identity friends, so perhaps it is not surprising that transgender participants in River City were clear about their identities wholly "not mattering." However, it is striking that the participants who were most emphatic about minimizing their friendship differences were trans participants.

Other participants explained that, although shared-identity friendships might have been important in the past, such friendships no longer mattered. They suggested that shared-identity friendships were critical when they were first coming out, but that the need for these friendships had declined in recent years. I asked Leah, a white genderqueer, "queer/lesbian" person in their mid-20s and a native River Citizen, how important it was to have LGBTQ friends, and Leah responded:

> I guess it really wouldn't matter to me. As far as identity, it doesn't matter to me whether like with my friends if I'm straight or not, so they'll listen to my relationship issues either way and vice versa. I guess it's kind of nice because obviously, female-to-female relationship is different than with female-to-male just because there are differences in the way that the mind works and other issues as well. So sometimes it's nice to be able to talk to somebody about those things. But I've talked to [my straight former roommate] about my relationship issues just as much as anybody else, so I haven't really noticed a difference.

Like Mark, Leah had shared-identity friendships that enabled them to discuss romantic relationships, and the complexity of Leah's gender identity comes through in this quote, as Leah refers to "female-to-female" relationships like theirs. Leah then explained that having friends with shared gender and sexual identities was important when they were grow-ing up, but now there is "a pretty even balance for me between whether my friends are straight or LGBTQ. I'm not gonna say, 'You're straight. We're not gonna be friends.'" Here, Leah resists a narrative of exclusion, suggest-ing that being "straight" does not prevent friendship. In the end, for Leah, "relationship issues" are a topic of conversation even with a straight friend, and Leah minimizes the role of shared sexual identity in her friendships today, using sexuality-neutral language (but not gender-neutral language).

Fia's friendship talk also demonstrates a minimizing strategy: her gen-der identity is not a topic of conversation in her friendships. Fia's friend-ship map looks like the spokes on the wheel of a bicycle, her 22 named friends arrayed evenly around her with few connections between them, indicative of what Janice McCabe (2016) calls a "sampler" friendship network. For Fia, a straight, white, transgender woman in her mid-30s, talking about her gender identity was not important in her friendships; she reserved these conversations for an LGBTQ-specific context. She explained, "That's why I went to support group. What I need from the LGBT community I get out of the support group, which is being able to talk to people about being trans, specifically. The rest of my life, I don't really bother talking about that that much. I am 11 years into transi-tion. I don't really need to talk about it that much." Fia still attended an adult LGBTQ support group in River City, compartmentalizing her gender-specific support needs by discussing them only in this group, not with friends.[3] Other participants suggested distinct online networks like LGBTQ-focused Facebook groups as places where they sought identity-related support, engaging in similar compartmentalization processes. Yet Fia's comments share a similarity with Leah's: Fia's note about being "11 years into transition" implicitly suggests that her gender identity may have been discussed in friendships earlier in her transition.

Both Fia's and Leah's friendship talk suggests that shared-identity friendships may have mattered more in the past, but they no longer need to focus on their identities in conversations with their friends today. For Jack and Karen, their gender identities were irrelevant in their friend-ships, beyond a baseline of acceptance, or at least lack of judgment. These examples of friendship talk illustrate the ways participants mini-mized the importance of their identities and the need for shared-identity discussions with their friends.

Not the "Same Raindrops": The Insufficiency of Shared Identity

For some participants, simply sharing an identity was an insufficient cause of a friendship. In other words, simply being LGBTQ did not generate enough commonality to generate or sustain a friendship, a finding echoed by other LGBTQ community and identity research (Easterbrook et al. 2013; Fassinger and Arseneau 2007). For example, when I asked Colby, a young, white trans man and college student, whether there were things he got out of his friendships with other LGBTQ people, he responded:

> Um, no. I don't think there's really any difference. . . . Just because you're LGBT does not mean you have had the same experiences. So it's like, it's not that much different than talking to a cis-straight person that has no experience being LGBT as it is to, you know, sharing your experience with someone else with a different experience that's also LGBT. So, it's like you're under this umbrella together but that doesn't mean the same raindrops have hit ya.

Colby's logic differed from participants in the previous section: identities were not unimportant, but being under the same LGBTQ "umbrella" (Fassinger and Arseneau 2007) was simply not enough to form the basis of a friendship. Colby's comment suggests that the specificity of identities matters and that, to him, the experiences of lesbians and gay men might not differ from those of a "cis-straight person."

Charlie, whom we met in the introduction, was specific about the kinds of lesbians with whom she could not be friends. Charlie is a professional in her early 30s, a woman of color, and a "cisgender woman with gender queer [sic] leanings" who is "primarily attracted to women." At the time of our interview, she was looking explicitly for queer friends in River City. She offered the following interaction with a woman she described as "such a lesbian" as a way to explain the insufficiency of shared-identity friendships:

> It's just, she was very connected to, like, straight culture and, like, heteronormativity. And so she very much, like, wanted to get married and have

kids, and I said somebody was "poly[amorous]," and she said, "Who's Polly?," like as if it was somebody's name. And it's, like, we just had a different lexicon for, like, what, what life was like, basically. Like, she was very much, like, "Everything about me is pretty much straight except for I'm attracted to women." And that's not who I'm used to hanging out with. Like, I'm used to hanging out with people who are, like, "no, I would not wanna be straight, even if you [laughs] had, like, all the money in the world."

While, on the surface, it might seem that Charlie and the woman she describes would share an identity, a common understanding of lesbian and queer identities did not exist, preventing a friendship from developing.

Others explained that simply sharing an identity did not provide an adequate source of connection for a friendship. Grey, a white, nonbinary/genderqueer and queer participant, explained, "I feel like I'm not gonna be friends with somebody just because they're . . . . Like one girl I did peg in high school is gay. Like she's cool and everything, but we just would never click." Similarly, Kit, a white, lesbian- and female-identified college student, offered a mix of answers about whether it is important to have LGBTQ friends: "I don't know if it's important. I think it's important, um, to have friends who identify or who have gone through the same things as you have, in some ways, and part of the same community, as well, but I also think that's not, I mean, you shouldn't place all your importance on that. It should be other people, as well." Like Grey, Charlie, and others, for Kit, "all of your importance" should not be placed on a shared identity in developing a friendship.

Vickie, a white, partnered lesbian, offered the example of a friend she described as "straight . . . well, she's bi but she's married to a man" who is close to her and her partner. Despite being part of the same (LGBTQ) community, Vickie clearly saw that her friend's identity differed from hers, and she contrasted this close friend with other gays and lesbians who were not necessarily close. She explained that her bi friend is "very close to us and she treats me actually better than by far some of the gay and lesbian people. So just because you're gay and lesbian of course doesn't mean by any means you're automatically affirming." For these participants, membership in a shared community was less important than other aspects of friendship: possibilities for affirmation, a sense of "click," shared understandings of identities, or similar perspectives about what those identities mean.

What was important to Vickie and to others was the ability to talk openly about life experiences and elements of identity without fear of reprisal. As Vickie explained about her "straight" friend, she is "affirming. You get the feeling of nonjudgment. You can talk about whatever you want to talk about. Certainly you can talk about your partner and anything to do, if there's a gay pride week going on or anything. It's not like you have to stop and think and censor yourself." Some participants shared a more libertarian approach to friendships: shared identity didn't matter, or shared identity wasn't sufficient to form a friendship, as long as participants could be themselves and not suffer judgment or criticism. And, yet, the insufficiency perspective introduced a paradox in their friendships, highlighted by Leah's and Mark's friendship talk: no matter how accepting, friendships with people who did not share an identity included little space to "authentically" discuss key aspects of LGBTQ participants' lives, like romantic relationships. While participants benefited from cross-identity friendships, there were drawbacks to these friendships, too, like the inability to discuss identity-specific topics (Galupo et al. 2014; Muraco 2012).

"You Get Me": Affirmation and Shared Culture

Even as participants minimized their identities and explained that (some) shared identities were insufficient to form a friendship, they *also* noted that shared-identity friendships were valuable. Some participants were more explicit in their ambivalence about LGBTQ friendships, explaining that perhaps identities should not matter, but they still do. They explained that friendships with those who share identities offer comfort, affirmation, ease (Comerford et al. 2004), and a lessened sense of emotional labor (Hochschild 1979), of needing to work hard to connect with someone with a different identity (Galupo et al. 2014). Sometimes participants' ambivalence came through in the same interview, as was the case for Colby, who later discussed the importance of having transgender friends specifically. I asked him whether there was anything he "got" out of his transgender friends that he didn't get out of his cisgender friends, and he explained:

> Yes, because with my trans friends, it's like trans people know how other trans people feel; therefore we kind of unspokenly go out of the way for each other to make each other feel validated. So, like, when I talk to my trans friends it's always like, "what up bro," "hey man," "how's it going dude," and, like, very like affirming-type things. Or, like, if I'm talking to a trans woman, like, you know, "hey beautiful," like, "I like your blah, blah, blah," give her girl compliments, make her feel very feminine, like always hold the door and be like blah, blah, blah, like super lady things and like super man things. And then, like, they do the same back to me. They're like, "What up bro?" And it's always, like, whereas with a cis-guy, it's, like, "hey." You know, it's not really that extra. It's always like that extra like affirming, validating kind of thing. Like, you get me, like we know who we, we are and we're, like, it just works.

Colby's discussion of shared affirmation and shared gendered language suggests that friendships with trans folks still do offer a source of identity affirmation (Anthony and McCabe 2015). For Colby, this affirmation aligned with stereotypically feminine and masculine gendered behavior—the "super lady things" and "super man things." Shared-identity friendships depended, at least in part, on a shared understanding of transgender identities and gender norms, resulting in a friendship that "just works."

Callie missed the feeling of an affirming friendship after moving to the area and losing her "gay friends." For Callie, a white, queer woman, her sense of "missing" her gay friends was related to a sense of acceptance:

> I remember there being a point when I first moved here that I was, like, wow, I really miss my gay friends. Like, I really miss having those people in my life, and it was, like, well, why is that? What do you mean your *gay* friend? Like you don't mean just your friends, like, why your gay friends? I'm, like, well, it's different, and I still try to pinpoint that of why it's different and what is different about it. . . . I think that, like, there's this level of acceptance, um . . . it's definitely a feeling where it's, like, this, I've found my people.

A sense of finding "my people" is not unique to shared LGBTQ identities (Goins 2011). In sum, Colby's and Callie's comments identify a feeling of shared home, of affirmation; as Colby suggested, "it just works," and, for Callie, "I've found my people."

Some participants described moments where this affirmation occurred. Allyson, a white, bisexual woman who grew up in a nearby small town, offered a specific example of that feeling of validation. Speaking about her closest friend, a bisexual man, she explained that "he's also the friend I get the most validation from probably, too. 'Cause I might be upset or emotional about something and I explain it to [him] and he instantly, it's like, that's totally fair, it's very reasonable that you're upset about this. I'm, like, thank you. Ah, I really needed that . . . you know, he's definitely very . . . he's part of my support system."

Grey also described this sense of "validation," especially living in a small Midwestern town where, as others have found (Comerford et al. 2004), support for LGBTQ people is hard to find. Grey highlighted "comfort" in being around people with a shared identity, explaining that they "feel more comfortable around [their LGBTQ friends]. . . . I really don't care how people identify. It just so happens, I mean, like, sometimes you do need other people in your life who are like you and give you some validation, especially if there aren't, like, a lot of people around here who are like yourself." And despite his comments earlier in the interview that friends "[don't] really care" about his identity, Jack clarified that he loves "being able to talk to those especially who are trans and be, like, oh my gosh, why does this, what is this about. Like, tell me your experience. How did you do this? Like, this is a really hard day because of this, and they understand a whole different level."

Finally, for Teagan, a white, cisgender woman who is "bisexual or something [but] more oriented toward women," people who are "within that spectrum" of LGBTQ identities offer "a little bit of extra understanding. It's not that it's, like, a better friendship or anything like that, but there's just . . . there's a little extra there for sure . . ." That "little extra" is composed of shared understanding, support, affirmation, and, as participants' comments suggest, a sense of "emotional energy" (Collins 2004) generated by a friendship with someone who has a shared identity.

Taking their reflections as a whole, LGBTQ participants demonstrated ambivalence about friendships with other people, even questioning their own approaches and preferences to friendship, as Callie did. What enables this sense of affirmation is its effortlessness, or the lack of identity-based emotional labor needed with these friendships. Participants explicitly identified this *je ne sais quoi* in a number of ways. Colby's description of transgender friends "unspokenly" affirming each other, Allyson's friend who "instantly" understood, and Teagan's "little bit of extra understanding" are good examples. In other words, there *were* ways that shared-identity friendships mattered.

Related to a sense of affirmation, a final theme emerged in LGBTQ participants' discussion of shared-identity friendships: the ongoing importance of shared culture (Eliasoph and Lichterman 2003; Swidler 1986). While shared culture enabled a sense of affirmation, it is distinct in that it refers less to the emotional foundation of a friendship and more to the cultural content of close relationships. In terms of shared culture, participants mentioned cultural objects (Griswold 2013) like insider jokes, symbols, and experiences that they noticed were absent in their relationships with non-LGBTQ people. Lesbian-identified Alimah, for example, explained that

> to be honest, yeah, I think that LGBT people are, like, I think that's one of the reasons that, that should be more of a connection between people who are underprivileged in general, like, you know what I mean? Like, we all have an understanding that we're not gonna be a part of the culture that's, or not gonna be, we're not gonna be perfectly a part of the culture that's the major, the majority, or you know what I, whatever it's called. So it's, like, it's really nice to have that understanding, it's really interesting to see what they see about the world.

Some participants were more explicit about the importance of shared cultural references, humor, and ability to discuss relationship specifics, as Mark mentioned in the opening quote of this chapter. Kyle, a partnered gay man, stated, "I would like more LGBT friends. And I'm realizing that because even the conversations I had on Sunday with [a friend] that I tend to assume people know LGBT things that I don't even realize aren't common knowledge to people who aren't and then I only realize it when I talk to my friends who are straight. Um . . . and the majority of them just don't know." Kyle's comments neatly summarize the value of LGBTQ friendships: the idea that cultural references are "common knowledge" to friends who share identities and require less emotional labor to continually explain.

For Allyson, openness and shared humor distinguished her LGBTQ friends from her non-LGBTQ friends. Reflecting on two sets of her friends, she explained:

> I would say both [of my LGBTQ friends], there's a level of acceptance I get from them that I probably don't get from the [non-LGBTQ] males. And [my female non-LGBTQ friends] I don't think I can be quite as open about that side of me as I might normally be. I don't, you know, hold back or anything too much but it's not the same. I, like, I might make a joke and [my LGBTQ friend is] going to laugh. And I'm going to be, like, totally and they're just going to chuckle and be, like, yeah, that's funny.

When I pressed Allyson to offer a more specific example of something her LGBTQ friends would "totally get," she offered the following reflection on understandings of her romantic life:

> Probably the situation where you're crushing on a friend that doesn't like your gender or sex . . . yeah. . . . It doesn't happen terribly often but it does happen. And I know it's happened to all three of us [LGBTQ friends] and in that situation you're, like, oh yeah. Well, they don't like chicks. Darn it. [laughs] . . . And I almost think both of them are more sympathetic about my relationships period. . . . [My LGBTQ friends] definitely will, they have a lot more insight into relationships.

Like Mark and Leah described, the common cultural knowledge about navigating romantic relationships while being LGBTQ made shared-identity friendships important.

Finally, Robin, a partnered lesbian, reflected on her friendship desires, hoping for friendships with other lesbians with children. She explained the emotional support that similarly identified lesbian couples would hypothetically offer, even as she described difficulties finding similar couples in River City. First, she explained that "lesbians with children are hard to find in [River City]. There are just not that many of us. And so, you know, you hear about them. I'm like Sasquatch." She described a failed experience trying to connect with another lesbian couple with children, one she was excited to build but in which she was ultimately "iced out." While this example demonstrates identity insufficiency, Robin's comments demonstrate the value of shared-identity friendships, made evident through their absence. She was frustrated because "we should be friends with them. If my theory is correct, which it clearly is not, about sharing socioeconomic background and educational level. We should be friends with them." Despite sharing virtually *all* aspects of identity—gender, sexuality, marital and parental status, and class background—the friendship did not coalesce.

This friendship failure, for Robin, demonstrates the hopes she has for shared-identity friendships, particularly around the idea of emotional support. She explained: "Being married, having kids, living in [River City], sharing some maybe pain, sharing some joys. Like, it seems like we should want to hang out with each other because we're rare. We fit these identity categories that nobody else fits. And that nobody else can identify with, you know? Um and so it bums me out that that isn't there."

In brief, shared-identity friendships offered opportunities for both more and less work: more emotional support, and less emotional labor, that is, less need to explain culturally specific symbols and jokes. Participants' ambivalence about shared-identity friendships both challenge and demonstrate the ongoing relevance of LGBTQ identities in River City. Some participants minimized their identities or explained that shared identities were insufficient to generate friendships, while others explained that friends with shared identities were important sources of affirmation and shared knowledge. The future of friendship for LGBTQ participants in River City is murky; most participants expressed a desire for *more* LGBTQ friends, particularly close friends, and regretted that they did not have many close friends who shared their identities. However, analyses of participants' friendship networks demonstrate the ongoing relevance of LGBTQ identities, for some participants more than others. I now turn to this analysis.

Mapping LGBTQ Friendships in River City

Participants' friendship maps offer another layer of evidence about LGBTQ friendships and their relationship to a possibly post-gay River

TABLE 4.1. Average Number of Close Friends by Gender Identity and Sexual Orientation

	Total	Average Number of Friends	Average Number of LGBTQ Friends	Average Number of Non-LGBTQ Friends	Percentage of LGBTQ Friends
Non-LGBTQ	13	17.5	2.5	14.9	14.5%
LGBTQ	41	12.7	4.6	8.2	36.3%
Overall	**54**	**13.9**	**4.1**	**9.9**	**29.3%**

Numbers do not sum precisely due to rounding.

City. I had both LGBTQ and non-LGBTQ ally participants complete an open-ended friendship mapping exercise in which they identified and described their current friends. We might expect that what participants said about their friendships might differ from who they considered close friends, for example, who they seek out in times of distress (Small 2013). Despite some participants' comments that the identities of their friends "wouldn't matter," friendship maps suggest otherwise.[4] First, like ally participants, LGBTQ participants are close friends with largely non-LGBTQ people (see table 4.1); in other words, about two-thirds of LGBTQ participants' friends are non-LGBTQ people. LGBTQ participants do have LGBTQ friends, even close friends, but very few participants had a majority of LGBTQ close friends. In other words, having a shared identity is not enough to generate a close friendship; participants echoed Ghaziani's (2014b) research in noting that sexual orientation, and, to a lesser degree, gender identity was not enough for them to develop a close friendship.[5] However, LGBTQ participants had *fewer* friends overall (12.7 friends, on average, compared to 17.5 friends for non-LGBTQ participants) and a *higher* proportion of LGBTQ friends (on average 36.3%, compared to 14.5% for non-LGBTQ participants).

At first glance, these findings support the idea that River City may be in what Ghaziani calls the closeted or coming-out era. LGBTQ people's overall smaller number of friends suggests challenges making friends, relative to non-LGBTQ people, a possible indicator of a closet era in which LGBTQ people struggle to form relationships that acknowledge their identities. A higher *proportion* of LGBTQ friends among LGBTQ people indicates a possible coming-out era, given a desire for shared-identity friendships in such a community. While this finding is not surprising in River City, it adds a layer to what LGBTQ people and allies *say* about gender and sexuality in their friendships. In other words, as researchers have suggested (Jerolmack and Khan 2014; Lamont and Swidler 2014), what people say about their actions and relationships differs from how they act in situ, and individuals' friendship talk should be analyzed alongside evidence of friendship networks. Based on their friendship maps, LGBTQ participants had a higher proportion of LGBTQ friends than ally participants, suggesting the ongoing relevance of shared identities in LGBTQ friendships.

However, a breakdown by gender and sexuality tells a more complicated story. Table 4.2 compares LGBTQ participants by gender identity, while table 4.3 compares LGBTQ participants by sexual orientation. Note that table 4.3 includes straight-identified, transgender participants, which emphasizes the need to consider sexual orientation and gender as distinct identities when interpreting these data. Analyzing LGBTQ participant data in terms of sexual orientation *and* gender offers a richer understanding of the complexities of LGBTQ community in River City, an approach that would be missed by focusing on sexual orientation alone. First, cisgender women and transgender men have the highest proportion of LGBTQ friends (41.8% and 41.5%, respectively), while transgender women and genderqueer participants had low proportions of LGBTQ friends (27.7% in both cases). Lesbian and queer participants also had higher

TABLE 4.2. Average Number of Close Friends by Gender Identity (LGBTQ Participants Only)

	Total	Number of Friends	Number of LGBTQ Friends	Number of Non-LGBTQ Friends	Percentage of LGBTQ Friends
Cisgender men	13	12.2	3.9	8.3	32.1%
Cisgender women	17	11.8	4.9	7.2	41.8%
Genderqueer/ genderfluid persons	5	9.4	2.6	6.8	27.7%
Transgender men	2	26.5	11.0	15.5	41.5%
Transgender women	4	15.7	4.3	11.3	27.7%
Overall	**41**	**12.7**	**4.6**	**8.2**	**36.3%**

Numbers do not sum precisely due to rounding.

TABLE 4.3. Average Number of Close Friends by Sexual Orientation
(LGBTQ Participants Only)

	Total	Number of Friends	Number of LGBTQ Friends	Number of Non-LGBTQ Friends	Percentage of LGBTQ Friends
Bisexual, pansexual, asexual	6	13.8	4.7	9.2	33.7%
Gay	14	13.7	4.8	8.8	35.4%
Lesbian	10	10.2	4.5	6.3	44.1%
Queer	9	9.5	3.4	6.1	35.5%
Straight	2	28.5	8.5	20.0	29.8%
Overall	**41**	**12.7**	**4.6**	**8.2**	**36.3%**

Numbers do not sum precisely due to rounding.

proportions of LGBTQ friends, while straight and bisexual, pansexual, and asexual participants had lower proportions of LGBTQ friends. These averages should be treated with extreme caution, given the low numbers of participants in each category (only two trans men and only two straight, transgender participants, for example) and the fact that this is not a random, representative sample. Notably, cisgender men and gay men have *middling* proportions of LGBTQ friends (32.1% and 35.4%, respectively), as well as middling numbers of friends, compared to other LGBTQ community members. These findings do not offer clear evidence that River City is post-gay, but they also do not suggest that gay men are especially closeted or out, in terms of their friendship numbers and proportions. These findings could also be the result of small numbers of gay men, and LGBTQ people more generally, in River City, although it is difficult to know without data comparing River City to similar, and similarly sized, cities. In sum, cis lesbians, cis queer women, and trans men had the largest proportions of LGBTQ friends, followed by cis gay men; trans women and genderqueer people had the lowest proportion of LGBTQ friends.

Two findings emerge from my analysis when we focus on the range of LGBTQ identities present in River City. First, shared-identity friendships are more common among lesbians and queer women. Second, those whose gender and sexual identities challenge normative boundaries have lower proportions of LGBTQ friends, a finding that must be interpreted given the particular community context of River City. First, contra what research about rural contexts and lesbian identities and communities suggests (Brown-Saracino 2011; Kazyak 2012), cisgender lesbians, queer people, and trans men have the highest proportion of LGBTQ friends. River City, in other words, is certainly not post-lesbian; in other words, shared-identity friendships still seem to matter for the cis lesbians, queer women, and trans men in my study. Given that five of the nine queer-identified participants also identified as women, lesbians and queer women more generally in River City likely have higher proportions of LGBTQ friends than gay and queer men. In this small sample of LGBTQ River Citizens, shared identities matter in lesbian and queer participants' friendships, despite research suggesting some lesbian integration into the straight, cisgender mainstream (Brown-Saracino 2011, 2015). Post-gay (or post-lesbian) frameworks may not be relevant for lesbian and queer women, trans men, or community contexts beyond the urban gayborhood.

Second, groups with the lowest proportions of LGBTQ friends include genderqueer participants, transgender women (both straight and lesbian), and bisexual, pansexual, and asexual participants. However, transgender men and queer participants have high proportions of LGBTQ friends. Keeping in mind the low numbers suggested by these tables, it is difficult to know what to make about this array of identities. While the numbers of these participants are relatively small, this finding raises questions about shared-identity friendships and fit with community gender and sexuality norms in River City. We might think that, for example, transgender participants as a whole might have more shared-identity friends than cisgender participants. However, comparing gender and sexuality for transgender participants suggests that these identities might matter in different ways, in the context of River City. However, this finding may have more to do with the age of participants than gender identity specifically, as the trans women I interviewed were generally older and transitioned later in life, while the trans men were younger and came out as trans at a much younger age. Friendship networks for older trans participants tended to include non-LGBTQ friends known prior to transition, while younger trans participants' friendship networks included friends they had known during and after transitioning. It is also possible that the coming-out process for trans participants affected friendship networks differently for older compared to younger trans folks, and younger trans participants were able to find and make trans friends online more easily.

While average numbers of friendships do not necessarily signal community integration or coherence, initial patterns in proportions of LGBTQ friends suggest that gender and sexuality *normativity* is a dimension along which LGBTQ community change should be assessed. Researchers have examined how, for example, heterosexual (Rich 1993) and gender normativities are enacted in urban public spaces (P. Doan 2007, 2010), resulting in exclusion of nonnormative or queer people (Ingram, Bouthillette, and Retter 1997; Warner 1993). River City's local gender and sexual norms, in some ways typical of the Midwest (Kazyak 2012), meant that some LGBTQ participants struggled to fit in to restrictive community norms. In what follows, I offer two cases from my interview data to demonstrate the need to further explore both post-gay and queer dimensions of LGBTQ community.

The Loneliest among Us: Friendship, Normativity, and Legibility

Teagan and Kai are young, low-income LGBTQ community members who have lived in River City for more than 20 years. Teagan is a white, cisgender woman in her mid-20s with long hair and Ray-Ban glasses, which she explains are stereotypically lesbian. While she is not partnered, she is dating a genderqueer person who is not a River Citizen and who lives in a distant state, and she is well connected to LGBTQ concepts and ideas through her tumblr friends. Teagan is active in what might best be described as online geek and gaming communities, and her friendships involve connections to those communities. Kai is in their early 30s, is also white, single, identifies as a lesbian, sports a short haircut, and locates themself under the genderqueer umbrella.[6] Kai is active in the local recovery communities, and their friendship networks extend into recovery-specific spaces. Both Teagan's and Kai's close friendship circles include LGBTQ people; Teagan's large friend group of at least 20 people includes couples and individuals of a range of gender identities and sexual orientations, while Kai's slightly smaller close-friend group of 16 includes a mix of lesbian and straight friends. However, Kai's and Teagan's experiences of community differed radically in ways that are prototypical of my participants and indicate a next step for research about friendship, identity, and normativities: Teagan seemed comfortable feeling disconnected from LGBTQ community in River City, while Kai described a sense of loneliness and longing for LGBTQ community. Fitting with normative frameworks of gender, sexuality, partnership, and class are, I suspect, key to the differences between them, and these themes were echoed by other participants.

More generally, among my interviewees, those who expressed the greatest sense of loneliness were those who challenged gender *and* relationship norms, especially if they were uninterested in "passing" as cisgender or straight *and* were single. For example, three LGBTQ participants (one genderqueer and lesbian-identified, one genderqueer and queer, and one straight-identified, trans woman) cried during my interviews when discussing what they felt was a lack of friendship and community. In each case, participants expressed their gender identities in complex ways that did not align with local gender norms. However, other participants' nonnormative gender identity or expression did not automatically lead to a sense of loneliness.

The difference for these three participants is that they were *single* and struggled to find dating partners who would acknowledge and recognize their sexual and gender identities. In other words, partnership offered a protective effect against loneliness for nonnormative participants as a whole, and queer, genderqueer, and trans participants who were single were not able to enjoy this protection. While all participants described LGBTQ community in River City as disconnected and temporary, at best, single, nonnormative participants seemed to feel this disconnect most acutely, *despite* the presence of generally supportive friends. The lack of dating prospects, for these three participants, contributed to their sense of loneliness. For Charlie, a lack of partnership *and* a sense of connection with queer friends was sorely lacking in River City:

I just feel like I don't get my needs met in the same way. Um, because I don't have queer friends. . . . I don't have queer friends here, basically, at all. Um, and I don't know, that could be because of my age and because lots of people are partnered up and I'm not, and so it feels like there's not really hanging out that happens . . . like, I just don't have the variety, I guess, is what it feels like. And so I feel really lonely sometimes amongst the friends that I have now. And I realize there are times when I just don't need to hang out with them. Like, there are times when I'm lonely, and so I think of, like, I should go hang out with them, and hang out with them and I'm, like, they don't, no, this is not hitting the spot. Um, and it's because I don't have, like, other sets of friends to, like, offset that feeling. So yeah, these are reflections I've had since being here.

For Charlie and Kai, this sense of loneliness contributes to a desire to leave River City; indeed, they have each resolved their ambivalence about friendship in River City, with one moving away and the other committing to an at-times painful (and also joyful) single life.

Interestingly, gay men I interviewed had few complaints about the lack of LGBTQ community in River City, regardless of their relationship status, and their middling proportion of LGBTQ friends reflects this approach to what might be described as optional LGBTQ community. These preliminary observations suggest that there are limits to understanding a particular LGBTQ community as post-gay, or as following a post-gay trajectory. The context of River City may well reward more normative gender identities and sexual orientations, white racial identity, and normative family formations, leaving those whose identities cannot follow a locally legible trajectory involving partnership, family, and identity lacking friendship, community, and a sense of belonging. While evidence of LGBTQ community exists in River City, as discussed in the introduction and chapter 3, this community may also be segmented along lines of gender and community-based normativities. In other words, LGBTQ community is, and has always been (Armstrong 2002; Ghaziani, Taylor, and Stone 2016), fractured by gender, race, and class. I add that local norms also divide LGBTQ community insiders from those who are more on the community's periphery.

Conclusion: Friendship Ambivalence and LGBTQ Futures

Friendship talk and friendship mapping indicate that the story of LGBTQ community in River City is not clearly post-gay, definitely not post-lesbian, and, still, not entirely queer-friendly. These friendship findings illustrate a dimension of ambivalence in relationships, contextually determined like individual and institutional ambivalence. Focusing on friendship reveals aspects of LGBTQ identities and communities that remain invisible with an exclusive emphasis on gay institutions. In my research in River City, participants explained that shared identities did *and* did not matter in their relationships with other LGBTQ people. Participants' "friendship talk" (Anthony and McCabe 2015) suggests that some participants minimized the importance of *their own* sexual and gender identities in discussing their friendships, while others saw shared identities as insufficient to generate a friendship. Other participants explained that friendships with LGBTQ people offered a sense of affirmation and shared cultural understanding, requiring less emotional labor than friendship with non-LGBTQ people.

In contrast to participants' friendship talk, friendship mapping told a different story for a notable, and surprising, group of participants: cisgender lesbian women.[7] These findings suggest that the presence of post-gay discourses among LGBTQ community members may not align with friendship patterns. A post-gay narrative of progress hides the complex reality that, in the context of River City, those with the highest proportion of LGBTQ friends (lesbian and queer cisgender women) are also those seemingly most likely to be integrated into the straight community (Brown-Saracino 2011; Kazyak 2012). Finally, findings from my research support LGBTQ friendship research that identifies the limits of friendship as a progressive foundation for LGBTQ communities (Muraco 2012). That is, gendered and sexual *normativities* that emphasize conformity, traditional gender expression, and monogamous, heteronormative families persist even in friendships, indicated by a lower proportion of shared-identity friendships and a sense of loneliness experienced by LGBTQ community members who do not align with heteronormative community norms around gender, race, and community insider status. In other words, focusing on communities through the lens of friendships in River City highlights the role that normativities play in ambivalent community, and those normativities are determined, in part, by community contexts (Bell and Valentine 1995; C. Johnson 2013; Seidman 1996; Warner 1993).

While it would be easy to dismiss friendship talk as what people say, not what they do, understanding the meaning-making process of friendship (Anthony and McCabe 2015; Duck 1994) alongside friendship-mapping data suggests that shared identities matter for LGBTQ participants' friendships. LGBTQ friendships "matter," specifically, in ways that differ along lines of gender and sexuality. Furthermore, I have shared examples of friendship talk that demonstrate an ambivalent approach to identity:

the "identity doesn't matter, but . . ." idea. Some participants focused on minimizing identity differences and describing identity insufficiency for friendship, while others described the benefits of shared-identity friend-ships: affirmation and shared symbols. Ultimately, there are real conse-quences for LGBTQ people in River City: friendship thinking and talk informs how people approach friendships, community, and decisions about futures.

Importantly, friendships offer a lens through which to explore LGBTQ communities, even in places where communities remain difficult to find. The range and organization of LGBTQ friendship suggest that communities may not follow a linear trajectory through gayness. For ex-ample, my friendship data demonstrate that, while some say that shared identity is no longer important in selecting friends, *recognition* of identity is critical to that friendship persisting, as Colby suggested. Similar to Elizabeth Armstrong's idea of "gay plus one" (2002:22), a concept that refers to the development of organizations that are both gay and "some-thing else" (like churches or sports teams), these friendships are not cen-trally organized around LGBTQ identities, but those identities must still be acknowledged and, at a minimum, "not judged." These friendships highlight the complexities of LGBTQ community raised in the introduc-tion: the idea that recognition and validation of LGBTQ identities remain important in LGBTQ communities even as its members' friendships might look quite different. Exploring what friends *do* together is part of the work of friendships, as allies support LGBTQ acquaintances and see the importance of supporting friends and, in some cases, showing up for LGBTQ events, a theme I explore in my next chapter.

An exclusive focus on urban gay enclaves and gay relationships, while an important start to the discussion, limits our ability to analyze and fully understand the complexities of LGBTQ communities and re-lationships. Furthermore, researching friendship dynamics in places with *queer* institutions, networks, symbols, and geographies, compared to River City, is a compelling proposition and raises questions about what such institutions, relationships, symbols, and spaces might be. Ul-timately, friendship research has the potential to offer critical insights into processes of assimilation, community shifts, and social change, and integrating an analysis of friendships into LGBTQ community research offers a queer corrective to post-gay theories of community change.

5

Straight Woman in a Gay Man's World

Allyship and Diversity Resources

Angela and Brenda, middle-class, straight, white, cisgender women in their 40s and 50s, are both close friends with LGBTQ people in River City. Both are River City natives, although Angela had moved to several different US states, especially as a young adult, while Brenda explains that "I've grown up here, been here my whole life, probably die here, my whole life. [laughs] So, born and raised, um, just a [River Citizen]." Brenda sees herself as a long-term River City community member, while Angela left when she was "almost 21, kinda sowing some wild oats, just, I just needed an adventure." Both live in River City and value their close connections with nearby family, although their friendship maps differed in one key way: Brenda's included primarily family, while Angela's map included nonfamily friends exclusively. Brenda's friendship map reflects her social life in River City, one that revolves around shared family activities with peripheral connections to friends. Angela's demonstrates her lively, friend-based social life and documents her travels around the country.

Brenda is best friends and was a onetime business partner with Karen, a transgender woman, activist, and public speaker. Angela's close friendships with two gay men began in her young adulthood and have continued despite her migration to cities in the West and Southwest. On the surface, neither of them seem likely candidates for LGBTQ political activism, and, yet, both offer support for their friends as well as LGBTQ events and institutions in River City. They might both be considered active allies, people who are not LGBTQ but who support LGBTQ people and communities through their actions, in contrast to more passive allies, who might post messages of support on social media but who fail to show up for their LGBTQ friends at community events and on election days. Angela works for a nonprofit multicultural organization, the Center for Multicultural Community (CMC), and has played a leadership role in supporting LGBTQ groups and events. For example, she helps manage and advertise LGBTQ youth and adult support groups housed at the CMC, and she spearheaded an initiative to create transgender-inclusive bathroom signage at the CMC. Brenda works at a convenience store and occasionally accompanies Karen to local LGBTQ events like a downtown walk to honor Transgender Day of Remembrance.

It might seem that Angela is the more politically engaged, active ally, albeit through her work. But Brenda's comments about supporting a young visibly gay man of color in her workplace should give us pause in considering the role of allies in supporting LGBTQ community. In response to a question about whether her friendship with Karen caused her to talk with others about LGBTQ issues, she offered the following story:

> Once in a while maybe, yeah, if something would come up. . . . Different people that I meet, you know, for instance there was a young Black, uh, male that came in the store this morning, and you could tell all over that he was gay, you know? [C: How could you tell?] I just had to think of *The Birdcage* [film] when I saw the one, you know he is, but very feminine, he was very, very feminine [chuckles], and even the voice was very feminine, and because he was still male appearance, and I don't know, maybe he could be, um, transgender, too. Maybe he wants to change, I don't know because I don't know him, but I found myself being very pleasant to him and probably a little extra special care to him, you know, conversation or whatever, strike up a conversation with him and that, and, oh, are you having a good day? Or you know, where do you work at? Or where are you headed out so early this morning, or you know? Which normally I'll just kinda wait on somebody, oh, hope you have a good day, thanks, good-bye!

In urban contexts like Chicago (Ghaziani 2014b) or San Francisco (Muraco 2012), such an interaction might not be noteworthy. In River City, where being *Birdcage* queer is noteworthy and relatively rare, such support is seen as uncommon. Recall Steve's comment about being able to "pass" as not "flamboyantly, rah-rah-shish-koom-bah gay," which was confirmed by my community observations where, even in the gayest of spaces like gay-owned bars and drag shows, masculine gender expression was a norm (Silva 2021). Brenda's extra effort to engage this anonymous, presumed member of the LGBTQ community highlights the complexity of LGBTQ community support and allyship in contexts outside urban centers. In other words, does Brenda's emotion work (Hochschild 1979; Hochschild and Machung 2003) in support of this young man "count" as support for the LGBTQ community?

In Angela's interview, she described her pleasure in participating in gay and lesbian communities, particularly when she left River City for the larger, gay- and lesbian-friendly cities of the Midwest and Southwest. Angela's involvement in gay communities has clearly contributed enjoyment and fun to her life, as she visited gay bars in Chicago's Boystown and lesbian communities in the Southwest. It also contributed to her personal development, and after returning to the River City area, she became involved in a community organization that supports LGBTQ people, the CMC. While Angela's active support for LGBTQ community in River City is clear, and frequent, she also still benefits from her engagement with these communities. Her work as an ally might be considered alongside the benefits she gleans from connections with this community. How might we weigh evidence of allyship against a sense of what allies "get" out of their connections to LGBTQ community (Bridges 2014)?

Brenda's and Angela's allyships raise the two key themes I address in this chapter, where I consider the role of self-identified non-LGBTQ allies in River City's LGBTQ community. I address how allies *benefit* from their engagement with LGBTQ people and how they *contribute* to supporting LGBTQ people. These benefits and contributions are not unique to River City (Bridges 2014), as they appear in other small cities specifically (Mattson 2020), and LGBTQ people are distinctly ambivalent about the role of allies in their small-city community spaces (Hartless 2018). This two-sided allyship coin arose in my research in River City's LGBTQ community in two ways: within friendships and within community institutions. Both are equally important. A focus exclusively on community institutions would miss Brenda's everyday contributions to LGBTQ community, while a focus solely on friendship would ignore Angela's important work within community institutions.

Implicit in the literature about non-LGBTQ involvement and activism in LGBTQ communities (what I am calling "allyship" in this chapter) is a question about what constitutes allyship and which non-LGBTQ people can claim an ally identity, according to LGBTQ people. For the purposes of this chapter, "allies are movement adherents who are not direct beneficiaries of the movements they support and do not have expectations of such benefits" (Myers 2008:168). Even this seemingly simple definition is complicated (Dean 2014; Hartless 2018), as I am arguing here that allies do indeed benefit from their participation, if not activism, within LGBTQ communities.

Sociological research offers conflicting evidence about the role of allies in LGBTQ communities. On the one hand, allies offer concrete, often material support for LGBTQ communities, contributing time, money, transportation, education, and their privileged voices and bodies in heteronormative spaces (Broad et al. 2008; Ghaziani 2011; Myers 2008). On the other hand, allies consume LGBTQ community resources and reinforce heteronormative and gender norms (Bridges 2014; Hartless 2018; Mathers, Sumerau, and Ueno 2018; Muraco 2012). Furthermore, allies play particular roles in different *types* of communities. In urban gay communities, for example, allies engage in what Amin Ghaziani calls "performative progressiveness" (2014b:255; see also Brodyn and Ghaziani 2021), an orientation to gay communities marked more by consumption and celebration of these spaces, rather than knowledge and active support for LGBTQ rights (through volunteering, marching, or writing a local legislator, for example). In rural communities, allies play a central role in LGBTQ community institutions (Burgess and Baunach 2014; Gray 2009; Mattson 2020), even as their participation entails some risk to their community standing. And in a variety of community contexts, allies support their individual LGBTQ friends, offering emotion work and direct and indirect material support to LGBTQ community members who are themselves engaged in a variety of activist labor. Overall, allies both support and benefit from connections with LGBTQ people and communities.

I use the concept of "diversity resources" to consider the ambivalent relationship between allies and LGBTQ community in River City. The concept of diversity resources builds on the concept of "gay capital" (Morris 2018), which describes a "form of social privilege" (2018:1199) that gay men use to develop strong social networks, specifically with other gay men. Gay capital, in other words, is

> an umbrella term which describes the unique forms of cultural, social, and symbolic capital available to young gay men in gay-friendly, post-gay social fields. In other words, cultural gay capital describes insider

knowledge about gay cultures, social gay capital describes belonging to social groups which are exclusively or predominantly gay, and symbolic gay capital describes having one's gay identity recognized and legitimized as a form of social prestige by others. (Morris 2018:1199)

The concept of "diversity resources" expands on "gay capital" in four ways. First, while the "others" Max Morris explores include gay men, I consider how such resources can be exchanged by allies who are not part of gay or LGBTQ communities (Bridges 2014). Second, I analyze the exchange of resources in River City, an ambivalent community context that is not clearly a "gay-friendly, post-gay social field." Third, I expand the understanding of "capital" beyond cultural, social, and symbolic dimensions. In addition to community-based knowledge as cultural capital (Bourdieu 1986; Green 2013; Greene 2014; hooks 2000; Orne 2017), diversity resources include material contributions to community as well as emotion work (Hochschild 1979), forms of labor that allies draw from and contribute to LGBTQ communities. Finally, the concept of diversity resources may well apply to other marginalized groups, and I suggest possible, and problematic, diversity "exchanges" and equivalencies below. Sara Ahmed's (2012) discussion of "diversity work" as a kind of labor that ultimately inhibits social justice is central to this concept, as the "work" in which allies engage holds the potential to prevent social change.

I argue that the concept of diversity resources grounded in the context of an ambivalent community helps us think through, if not fully resolve, the tensions between individual and organizational support for LGBTQ communities (L. Doan et al. 2014) and who "counts" as an ally. However, the net balance of diversity resources, or whether and how ambivalence is resolved, remains an open question, and researchers offer conflicting results. Do allies ultimately deplete or generate LGBTQ community? What quantity of diversity resources is required for allies to offset the resources they draw from LGBTQ communities? To address this question, I first describe friendships between LGBTQ people and non-LGBTQ allies, identifying the ways that allies see their LGBTQ friends as diversity resources *and* offer material, emotional support as diversity resources. I then identify the ways allies constitute LGBTQ community, as both community consumers of diversity resources and as pillars embedded in LGBTQ institutions, offering institutional diversity resources of their own. I conclude by offering comments about the continuum of politicization (Muraco 2012) allies represent and the importance of considering community context in interpreting allies' ambivalent relationship with LGBTQ communities.

Allies in Friendship

In this section, I discuss the ways allies and their LGBTQ friends exchanged diversity resources. Allies drew on their LGBTQ friends' identity-based diversity resources and offered their own resources to support their "diverse" friends. In what follows, I identify the ways ally friends drew on the identities and experiences of their LGBTQ friends to signal their own inclusivity, and in the next section I describe the material and emotional resources that allies offered to their LGBTQ friends.

Seeing LGBTQ Friends as Diversity Resources

LGBTQ people operated as diversity resources for their ally friends in three ways: as indicators of River City's progress, as an aspect of personal self-development, and as a demonstration of "coolness" or cultural distinction (Bourdieu 1986; Green 2013; Orne 2017; Richards 2020). Allies' diversity talk—defined as a discourse that "simultaneously acknowledges racial (and other) differences while downplaying and disavowing related social problems" (Bell and Hartmann 2007:905)—was offered as evidence of their progressiveness (Ghaziani 2014b), a newly valuable reputational enhancement in River City (Fine 2001).[1] In other words, in discussing their friendships with LGBTQ people, allies demonstrated their broadly inclusive progressiveness both at the community level and at the level of the self, where diversity and multiculturalism indicate self-development.

Ally participants described their LGBTQ friends' experiences as an indicator of a progress narrative for River City, a sign that the community has come a long way. Sharing the recent wedding of a gay friend, Angela juxtaposed the ongoing "hardness" of growing up gay in the River City area with the "cool" ability to get married in a small town in the River City metro area:

> He just got married last weekend in [his hometown] to his partner. So these are two guys that grew up gay in [this town], which back then was

harder, you know, much harder. I mean, it's always hard I'm sure, I mean, in small communities maybe, maybe . . . I mean, so it's just hard to, to like, you get to marry your partner now in your hometown, you have two children together, and you know, just cool, you know.

Angela's discussion of her gay friend's ability to marry his partner illustrates, for her, River City's progress in recent decades. Marriage was used by LGBTQ participants to demonstrate River City's progress, as well, indicating the symbolic value of marriage as a marker of social change (Ocobock 2018).

Gay friends' weddings, a long-standing possibility in River City predating *Obergefell v. Hodges* by more than six years, also marked River City's progress for Shelley, a straight, white woman in her 50s and a community leader who had been officiating weddings for same-sex couples since they first became legal in River City.[2] Shelley's journey as an ally began relatively early in her life, when she first began questioning the strict, conservative religion in which she was raised. She explained that she had originally not questioned the frameworks of her childhood, "buying it, hook line and sinker . . . but I think it was, whenever I threw open the door to the religion and all that, then I decided to really reassess the whole thing, you know. Some of these things weren't true, then what else wasn't? And so that's why, that's when I started, I guess, questioning." Her active support of LGBTQ people evolved through "just knowing more and more people" and showing curiosity about their lives, and her allyship predated her daughter coming out as a lesbian.

She described the marriage of a gay man and recent transplant to River City as a kind of bookend to her process of understanding and supporting LGBTQ people. He had moved to River City, was looking for community connections, and volunteered to speak at the local LGBTQ youth group. Shelley explained:

In fact he was my first same-sex wedding, later, but I was leading this youth group that we could talk about everything. . . . So I asked him and his partner [to] come in, and told them they could tell their parents if they want to. I don't think they did. [chuckles] But for two, two different nights they came. And [they] answered every question these kids wanted to know. And, um, I think that was a, that was a big, you know, just listening to him, too, really solidified it. I guess I was already there but it really solidified it. I can, now that as I remember that, and then I, and then I married them on their thirtieth anniversary of being together.

In Shelley's case, this "first same-sex wedding" signaled both the evolution of her allyship and the move toward gay acceptance in River City.

For some participants, welcoming LGBTQ friends was part of a conscious strategy to incorporate LGBTQ people into the broader River City community, or at least, as in Wendy's case, to make them feel "welcome" and "connected." Wendy and her husband, Drew, met when they were students at a small liberal arts college, and they have lived in River City, raised their children, and worked in colleges and universities in the area for more than two decades. Both are invested in supporting LGBTQ people in River City, and their recent support is focused on a lesbian couple with small children. Answering a broad question about LGBTQ friendships and discussing her and her husband's closeness to this couple, she explained that

> my thought is . . . I wonder if part of the reason we're so close to them is we really wanted them to feel welcome and connected back to the community, so I think we put more time and energy into making that relationship happen when they came when [one member of the couple] came back 12 years ago. And, of course, we loved [her partner], so it's, like, but then it was, like, we just like you so we're friends.

Processes of creating both friendships and community were intertwined for allies like Wendy, suggesting the importance of understanding friendship in community contexts (Adams and Allan 1999). In an urban context, the need to attract and welcome LGBTQ people might not be seen as important, necessary, or urgent, at least not in the same ways. Allies' LGBTQ friendships operated as diversity resources in their friendship talk (Anthony and McCabe 2015), marking River City's progress through marriage and the conscious emotion work of allies to attract and support LGBTQ people.

Allies also used friendship talk about LGBTQ friends to share a *personal* narrative of progress or acceptance, demonstrating their "moral careers" as active allies advocating on behalf of LGBTQ people (Becker 1963; Johnson and Best 2012). Without knowing her transgender, lesbian friend Karen, ally Brenda admitted that she would not have questioned others' negative attitudes toward LGBTQ people. She reflected on the source of those attitudes in her discussion of her friendship with Karen: "In my mind, going from when I was young, you know, everybody saying, oh, yeah, there's a lesbian, you know, or, but now knowing what they actually are. . . . My whole relationship with [Karen] has made me all aware of, of that, I don't think I would be like that if I hadn't met her." Brenda's "moral career" (Johnson and Best 2012) supporting LGBTQ people in River City would not have existed without her close friendship with Karen, and her personal story of self-development and growing acceptance depended on this friendship.

Brenda also benefited personally from her relationship with Karen, like she would in any other friendship, and something about her friendship with Karen and Karen's friends helped her to understand her own life experiences and changed how *others* viewed her, as Brenda suggested laughingly, as a "bitch, probably." She described meeting other transgender people through her friend Karen, explaining that "they're just so easy to talk to, so more friendly, so not judgmental, you know." Connections with trans people, in other words, put Brenda at ease in a way that interactions with cisgender people did not.

While Brenda met Karen through work, others met LGBTQ friends through institutions like colleges and leisure organizations. For Drew and Wendy, gay and lesbian friends were part of a moral career developed through a process of learning in college that emphasized the benefits of exposure to differences, diversity, and multiculturalism (Anthony and McCabe 2015). Drew explained:

So, at [my small liberal arts college], I met a number of friends and so this expansion of the mind, from small town to I know there's more out there, OK, I've read a lot, to meeting people who are visibly different, who are sharing different things, who have a different perspective on politics and everything else, um, and I was involved in choir for four years so I had lots of gay and lesbian friends.

Wendy, also involved in the choir at the same college, reflected that the closeness with gay choir members and the historical and political context of the 1980s led her to change her perspective on LGBTQ people and become more accepting. Her choir was

a close group of like 70 people. And, well, each year it changed, the membership changed a little bit. It was really in that group of friends it was, like, oh, you're gay. And then there was, like, suddenly, like I guess that doesn't matter because we're friends and that's whatever, that's fine, ya know. So I think it was really through those friendships that I realized and let's see, oh OK, so that was happening, I know people and they're gay and they're cool and they're my friends and I love them and I would do anything for them. . . . But also what was emerging at that time was homosexuality is not a choice: this is the way people are born so that was happening kind of at the same time. So it was, like, not only are these people, like, good and they're my friends and ya know this, but there's nothing wrong with it. Religion has put this label on it, has interpreted it in these ways historically but we know now the science behind it and this is the reality. So it was those two things coming together kind of in that decade in the 80s, that was what changed it for me.

While, for Wendy and Drew, friendships with LGBTQ people marked specific shifts in acceptance and awareness, for Shelley, friendships with LGBTQ people demonstrated a more spiritual process of self-development marked by realizations of *similarity*. She described her LGBTQ friendships as

just the eye-opening ones, the ones that help you understand how similar we all are. It doesn't make any difference, but it is lovely in a way that you get a chance to understand how some of the different things that people have to deal with because of that, that you just don't think about. . . . Like, one couple in particular I'm thinking of, they're, I just love 'em to death, and I love, I just enjoy watching them. I enjoy watching them with their children and reminding myself over and over, it's all the same, it's all the same.

Reflecting specifically on her learning about her daughter's transgender friend, she emphasized this theme of learning and realizing connection and sameness in difference:

> When you start getting down deeper into the alphabet, that I'm still, well, and, you know, wrapping my head around, you know, the trans, but then the, all the different levels within, all that stuff, I just find it fascinating, it's just lovely if you can just get past the idea that there's normal, and just go to, wow, we're all people and then there's all these different gradients of us.

For Brenda, Wendy, and Drew, the diversity resources accessed via their LGBTQ friendships helped them recognize the value of difference, while, for Shelley, these relationships demonstrated a fundamental human sameness. For each of these participants, friendships with LGBTQ people connected with a narrative of self-development, whether realized through intimate knowledge of a friend, in the context of college and exposure to diversity discourses, or as part of an ongoing spiritual process. These narratives of self-development aligned with claims of "moral worth" (Ueno and Gentile 2015b), the idea that friendships with LGBTQ people play a role in personal enlightenment. LGBTQ friendships offered diversity resources to help allies move forward in a process of self-development, demonstrating their "moral worth" and "moral careers" as supporters of LGBTQ people.

In sharing these friendship stories, ally participants also drew on their LGBTQ friends' identities and experiences as a source of "coolness" and fun. Friends' "difference" operated as a source of cultural capital (Bourdieu 1986) for ally participants, as well as a source of pleasure. Paul, for example, described his LGBTQ friends as simply more fun than his non-LGBTQ friends. Speaking about his friends from the LGBTQ youth group, he explained that "my LGBT friends [who are also leaders in the youth group], you know, when we're out at [a restaurant] having a mentor meeting, I mean, oh my gosh, the laughter and, you know, the stories and it's just, you just leave there on such a high. Um, and that's what I love." Some ally participants' comments about their LGBTQ friends suggest that these friends specifically are offered as evidence of *allies'* hipness, coolness, or taste. Angela explained her attraction to her first gay friends:

> I think in the very beginning, I mean [my two gay friends] were just so interesting and just different. You know, they were just different from any of my [River City] friends, I didn't have any openly gay friends and just different and fun and funny, you know. Like, and so, I'm, like, OK, this is cool, these people are cool and I didn't care about their sexuality, you know? I mean, I didn't care what they did in their bedroom or who they loved, I'm, like, that's fine with me, you know? Um, you know, I guess I, if I had to say, just really interesting people. [laughs] You know? Just different and interesting from, definitely from growing up in [River City], you know? Was just attracted to that. Diversity. I was attracted to that diversity.

Angela's comments make LGBTQ identities as diversity resources explicit, and allies' comments about their LGBTQ friends being more "interesting" than non-LGBTQ friends demonstrate the unique diversity resources that LGBTQ people offer as friends to allies. White, cisgender community leader Nadine explained, "I feel like in general . . . I don't know, LGBTQ people tend to be interesting and smart." Allies suggested that what made LGBTQ people "interesting" was their subordinate status and assumed struggle. For example, Nadine also explained that

> I mean, maybe another thing that's I think my LGBT friends like, just by virtue of being LGBTQ, they have to . . . they have to have done some self-reflection so not all, but I'd say generally LGBTQ people tend to maybe [have] more self-reflection about their identity and their place in the world, and that's something I can connect with, you know. I think it forces a certain amount of soul searching for lack of a better term. Um, which just makes you a more interesting person, a deeper person and that's attractive to me, yeah.

LGBTQ peoples' experiences of marginalization make them more "interesting" to Nadine.

Similarly, for Wendy, what makes LGBTQ friendships valuable is the way struggles shape LGBTQ people's lives and make them more "comfortable with who they are." She stated:

> I think there's some excitement in having friends who are a same-sex couple because none of our other friends are, so, I mean, I think it's interesting, I think they're just really great people. I think that's true of a lot of people in the LGBTQ community. . . . I think part of that is what people have to go through. I think they tend to be, I think they tend to know who they are once they're out, maybe they tend to know who they are and they're very comfortable with who they are a lot of time, I guess sometimes they can't be out with some populations. And I wonder if that also is kind of, like, ya know, they're just really good people.

Nadine's and Wendy's comments highlight the ways allies conceptualize their friends' struggles as diversity resources, ones that generate for allies a sense of fascination and connection. In brief, ally participants saw LGBTQ friends as diversity resources, as sources of fun and interest, resources honed in the face of shared struggle. Much like the straight friends in Anna Muraco's "intersectional friendships" (2012), allies benefited from the resources available in their friendships with LGBTQ people. In their friendship talk, ally participants demonstrated their community progressiveness, their personal development, and their cultural distinction through their LGBTQ friends.

Offering Material and Emotional Support

While ally participants' friendship talk demonstrated an understanding of friendships with LGBTQ people as diversity resources, this flow of resources might be viewed ambivalently. In other words, allies also offered their own resources in support of their LGBTQ friends. Specifically, allies offered education to their non-LGBTQ family and friends as well as emotional labor and material support directly to their LGBTQ friends. First, allies educated those around them about their LGBTQ friends' identities and the experiences of LGBTQ people, as they understood them. This education work could take place in both formal and informal settings.

For example, Drew, a college professor, taught about same-sex families, asked his close LGBTQ friends to speak in his classes about their experiences, and offered a safe space, marked by a "safe zone" pink triangle, to LGBTQ students. He provided educational and emotional support to these students specifically, noting that students seem willing to come out to him because

> I think [it] is a combination of [my] discipline and then some of it is, um, I appear to be the kind of person, well, not just appear, I, so there's that and then there's, I have a triangle on the door and that kind of stuff that students are comfortable coming out to me. It seems because they do that more with me than a lot of my colleagues.

Other allies work to educate those around them in more informal settings. Brenda's friendship with Karen included ongoing education work among even the closest of Brenda's family members. Brenda explains that

> to [Karen's] face, they treat her fine and everything but there are some that will talk about it behind her back. I know my kids have had problems with it. My sons mostly because they think of it as, OK, is she gay or what? You know? They always thought it was gay, and I'm like, gay and transgendered are not the same thing, you know, try to explain that to 'em and, uh, [they] don't want any part of it, you know, whatever. But I'm, like, hey, it's my friend and I expect you to respect her, you know? And they do. So, and you know, the more they get to know her, then I think they're more comfortable with it, too.

What is striking is that this education work is being undertaken across class backgrounds: Drew, a married college professor with his own children in college, is part of the River City upper middle class. Brenda's background is working class, and she did not attend college. Allies themselves become "diversity resources" for the larger River City community based in part on their friendships with LGBTQ people, and these resources, at least in theory, help the River City community become more welcoming and accepting for LGBTQ people, one relationship at a time (Barth, Overby, and Huffmon 2009; Tompkins 2011).

In addition to these education services, allies offered resources in the form of emotion work (Hochschild 1979) and material support to their LGBTQ friends. Brenda, for example, offered her "shoulder" to her friend Karen. After meeting Karen in the same workplace, Brenda explained:

> We never talked or were really that close to her, she just worked in the same store I did. Um, and then she went through her divorce and then came over to my department where, that's where I really got to know her. More she, was lonely, I would say, with the divorce going on and stuff like that, and, I don't know, just needed somebody to talk to. I was the shoulder to talk on, and, and more and more confided more and more in me.

Brenda supported her friend Karen through a difficult time; similarly, Elina, whose close friends include Mark, a gay man and former coworker, also offers a listening ear to her closeted gay cousin. She explained:

> He doesn't have a lot of friends, and I also feel that I'm the only person that he shared such a big, like, fact about his life that I feel more of his friend than a family member, given the context of our family. I mean we're very open, but apparently not, right, because he's not sharing it with anyone. It's only one way. I don't share a whole lot about myself with him. It's mostly me listening. Um, but, yeah. So it's actually a pretty much a one-way thing because we don't hang out when I need to, but it's mostly when we go out on family trips, him and I talk and it's mostly him coming to me and then talking. Now that I know, I reach out to him.

While this work would be typical of any close friendship (Fischer 1982b), for ally participants' LGBTQ friends, this support enabled their coming-out processes and, in some cases, their very survival, especially for friends who considered or attempted suicide. This kind of support and recognition also manifested in the intersectional, cross-gender, and cross-sexuality friendships Muraco (2012) described. What distinguishes this emotion work from general friendship support in times of crisis is its LGBTQ specificity, that is, the way it enables LGBTQ friends to live, and live proudly.

Material support included direct services from childcare (Drew, Wendy) to time spent shopping (Brenda, Drew) to shared volunteer work (Paul, Lindsay, Shelley, Sandra). For example, in addition to supporting her friend Karen by offering emotional support, Brenda explained that "as I learned more about her, we went shopping, you know, tried makeup or clothes or whatever, and, um, we go out to lunch a lot, we still keep in touch that way. I worked with her a lot, um, we opened the shop together at that point for a couple years." Brenda's investment in her friendship with Karen also included a substantial financial commitment to a shared business. Drew's support for his lesbian friends included an educational role for his friend Keri. He explained that "in some ways I see myself mentoring [her] when we're doing a project 'cause she wants to learn. Tell me how to do that, you know, can I, you know, and I'll say, well, here, you make the next cut. See how I do this, OK, here now you, you try it. And she, she's eager and happy to do that, you know." In fact, Drew explained that they were "going to pick up materials for a swing set tonight." Material, emotional, and educational support offered by allies are examples of diversity resources that help LGBTQ people manage day-to-day life.

However, it is important to examine whether the diversity resources offered by allies to their LGBTQ friends and the resources offered by LGBTQ people in friendships with allies should be seen as equivalent (Korgen 2002; Muraco 2012). In either case, resources are offered *because* one friend is marginalized. In her study of Black-white friendship pairs, Kathleen Korgen describes the unidirectional flow of insider knowledge between Black and white close friends (2002:41), yet acknowledgment and explicit discussion of race and inequality were largely absent. Focusing on the status inequality between GLB and straight friends, Koji Ueno and Haley Gentile's (2015a) research demonstrates the ways friends manage their status inequality, and, not surprisingly, the burden to maintain a sense of equality (even when it is not realized) falls on GLB friends, who rationalize their straight friends' discriminatory behaviors. This rationalization occurred within friendships LGBTQ participants discussed. In one example, transgender participant Colby described an "uber-Catholic" friend who may not be aware of his gender identity and who is not currently "necessarily accepting of the LGBT community." He explained that his friend "was home schooled for seventeen years . . . went to, like, one year of public high school." Colby, in this case, rationalizes his friend's discriminatory perspectives by describing her presumably isolated background.

Inequality was evident in other River City friendships, as well, even as allies were aware of this inequality. Some allies worked to provide support to LGBTQ community members and institutions as a way to work more actively toward challenging this inequality (Muraco 2012). Sandra's shift in techniques of support is one example of the way such activism changed in an ally's lifetime. Sandra, a white, cisgender, middle-class woman and not an obvious LGBTQ activist, described her career as a former pharmacist, especially in the early 1990s. She located this experience in the context of the growing AIDS epidemic, highlighting the role small cities like River City played as the epidemic began to unfold. She described her experience providing medication for gay men when other pharmacists did so reluctantly, explaining that she had developed a reputation through word of mouth as a nonjudgmental supporter of HIV+ gay River Citizens who, in her words, were "coming home to die," only to be rejected by parents and friends. After she changed careers and met Karen, her LGBTQ community support expanded to advocacy for transgender-protective legislation at the state capitol, where she traveled to offer testimony and support on such legislation. While some participants, like Sandra, took a more active and activist role in supporting LGBTQ community members, this level of activism was rare among ally participants in this study, even as allies supported individual LGBTQ friends and participated in River City–based events. Diversity resources in LGBTQ friendships sometimes extended to LGBTQ community, although allies also drew resources from LGBTQ community, a tension I explore in the next section.

Allies and LGBTQ Community

Allies have long supported LGBTQ community formation, for example, by offering labor and resources to LGBTQ advocacy groups and participating in LGBTQ community institutions like gay bars (Casey 2004; Faderman 2015; Ghaziani 2014b; Hartless 2018). However, the role of allies in LGBTQ communities has also been ambivalent, as allies and LGBTQ community members grapple with managing experiences of privilege and marginalization (Hartless 2018) and the role they play in ally-LGBTQ community engagement. Allies must work to continually assert their membership in LGBTQ social movements (Myers 2008), for example, by showing up at LGBTQ community events, even as they risk being seen as community intruders. In some ways, the very presence of allies in LGBTQ community spaces like bars reduces LGBTQ people's sense of safety and community (Casey 2004; Hartless 2018). And, yet, LGBTQ social movements and community spaces have required allies' involvement to be successful (Fingerhut 2011; Mattson 2020). In a recent example, Mathers and coauthors (2018) demonstrate the trade-off between ally inclusion and access to power within a southeastern LGBTQ advocacy group. They note that this advocacy group became "heterosexualized" when straight ally participants became increasingly involved in the group. Similarly, when allies advocate for LGBTQ people in other community institutions, this trade-off has ambivalent effects, reproducing normativities even as allies contribute resources (Bridges 2010, 2014; McQueeney 2009). In other words, allies often unintentionally reproduce the gender and sexuality norms they seek to undo. Ally involvement in LGBTQ community both allows community institutions to persist and reinforces normativities along the way.

River City's local culture affected ally engagement with LGBTQ community, as LGBTQ community spaces necessarily included, sometimes actively, allies. LGBTQ-supportive programming at the CMC, for example, features the following statement: "The [CMC] is committed to being a welcoming place for members of the LGBTQ+ community (lesbian, gay, bisexual, transgender, queer, +) and its allies."[3] Historically, allies played a significant role in the creation of LGBTQ institutions like Parents and Friends of Lesbians and Gays (PFLAG) and LGBTQ support groups. River City's dispersed, "cliquey" LGBTQ community meant that LGBTQ community organizations could not survive without the support of allies. LGBTQ community institutions were more temporary (Gray 2009) than institutionalized and were more ally-inclusive than explicitly and exclusively LGBTQ. For example, allies most frequently referenced the annual family-friendly Pride picnics (notably, not parades) and drag shows (notably, not family-friendly) as sources of community. Community organizations included the now largely defunct PFLAG and the LGBTQ youth group, housed at the CMC, a space self-consciously designed to be welcoming to allies across a spectrum of identities.

Traditional gay institutions like gay bars existed in River City, a gay-owned "queer bar" is also cited as a local LGBTQ-friendly institution, and there are signs that a new gay bar has opened in town, sponsored in part by the owner of a former gay bar. The rapid rise of yet another LGBTQ-oriented nonprofit focused on social events (River City Pride) has surprised community members and allies alike, but its future is far from secure. And some allies described Facebook groups as evidence of LGBTQ community, although their engagement in these spaces primarily involved sharing event announcements and local resources. Despite suggestions from both LGBTQ and ally participants that LGBTQ social life is moving online, River City LGBTQ Facebook groups serve largely as bulletin boards, sources of local events rather than spaces of interaction.

Given the centrality of churches in the River City community more generally, some allies also identified more LGBTQ-friendly churches as elements of LGBTQ community. However, neither the Metropolitan Community Church, a church founded explicitly for LGBTQ people, nor Dignity, an LGBTQ Catholic organization, exist in River City, and no allies demonstrated an awareness that such organizations existed. The absence of such LGBTQ-exclusive religious organizations illustrates the broader focus on inclusion, rather than differentiation in River City. Similarly, no LGBTQ-exclusive organizations to date have survived without institutional support from larger community organizations. Long-standing LGBTQ events and organizations became enfolded in other organizations, like the LGBTQ youth group and former PFLAG group. Allies' roles in these institutions are declining, as some participants admitted they had taken a step back from their leadership in recent years, as LGBTQ people have taken a more active role in building community organizations and, perhaps, the need for such organizations has simultaneously declined in allies' eyes. And, yet, allies still participated in social LGBTQ events, even as their involvement in LGBTQ-supporting organizations has waned in recent years.

Consuming LGBTQ Community Resources

Unlike in larger cities (Ghaziani 2014b; Orne 2017), few allies identified River City–based LGBTQ community institutions as sources of recreation and consumption, as "diversity resources" for their enjoyment. The presence of straight allies in gay spaces affects the safety, comfort, and ownership LGBTQ people feel in such spaces (Casey 2004; Ghaziani 2011; Greene 2014). Drag shows, in particular, offered opportunities for allies to consume a particularly flamboyant, subversive expression of gay culture (if not gay space) and to be entertained by the gender play these drag shows displayed (Parker 1991; Rupp and Taylor 2003). Aside from drag shows, the relative lack of LGBTQ community institutions meant that there were few places like gay bars for allies to intrude upon, few spaces in which to benefit from gay culture (Green 2013; Orne 2017).

Still, some ally participants noted LGBTQ spaces and events where they would go to have fun. Elina and Paul explained that they enjoyed attending LGBTQ events and institutions. Elina, for example, explained that she does "attend [LGBTQ events] when I can just because I like events. I like new things. . . . There's always something new that I find, new information. New people I meet. So, for that reason, I like it." LGBTQ events, like LGBTQ friends, offer the diversity resources of "newness." For Paul, the local gay-owned bar Barney's offered an opportunity for comfort. In describing the kinds of activities he enjoys with gay friends, he explained:

> We do go to bars. We'll, um, there's one bar in particular downtown that I tend to go with more of my gay LGBT friends, just because that's, you know, and I feel very comfortable. It's not a gay bar. It's just a, you know. . . . Um, I love it down there. And actually I love going there just because their music is toned down, that they usually play the 80s, love it. I'm at the age anymore where I can't and I can't go to a really loud, it actually hurts my ears.

Paul's experience of Barney's was one of comfort, relative to other, louder bars in the area. Angela and Drew remarked on connections with LGBTQ institutions in contexts outside of River City, participating in "vicarious" LGBTQ community much like the gay community members in Theo Greene's research (2014). Drew, for example, would visit a gay bar with a colleague from his college while attending conferences. He recalled, "I would go with her to those kinds of things, too. She's, like, if she and I were ever at a conference, no matter the city, she was going to find a gay bar so I would go with her." For Angela, perhaps the most out consumer of gay culture, living in Boystown in Chicago was a key part of her life experience. She recalled:

> Like, I remember, in Chicago, too, and we were in the thick of it, like myself, [my friends], some of these friends, [local] friends that lived in Chicago, um, and always in Boystown and you know, one time, I said I was going to, I was, like, I'm gonna write a book, it's going to be called "Straight Woman in a Gay Man's World." So we'll bring it up every now and then, like remember that book I was going to write? Like, 'cause I'm, like, that's going in this chapter, like, you know, "Straight Woman in a Gay Man's World," 'cause I was just, lived in it and was around it quite a bit, you know?

She frequently attended gay events in Chicago, like Pride and the Halsted Street Fair, events that featured a "lot of good memories with a lot of friends in that area." Allies like Angela were more likely to consume LGBTQ community resources through local institutions in other, larger cities, generally because such institutions did not exist to the same extent in River City.

More generally, allies seemed to see their *friendships* as diversity resources more frequently than local LGBTQ institutions. Nadine, for example, was critical of the framing of LGBTQ community participation, swapping out gay friendship for these institutions. After I asked whether participating in LGBTQ community was important to her, she offered the following: "I mean, I wouldn't say that it was a priority. It's not like when I moved to [River City] that I like wrote on my 'to-do' list like 'Hmm, well, I need to get my [state] driver's license, and my [state] license plates and unpack my stuff and make some gay friends.'"

I discuss the connection between friendships and community in the next chapter, but, generally speaking, allies were stepping away from LGBTQ community organizations and institutions at the time I interviewed them, even as they continued friendships with LGBTQ people in River City. Whether and how allies engage with new LGBTQ-led organizations like River City Pride and a new gay bar remains an open question, one that is likely affected by the overarching political context in River City and, importantly, the United States, as a whole. Initial observations suggest that there is some recognition that these organizations are not "for" allies. Simultaneously, the growth of drag shows as a venue for LGBTQ community consumption went strangely unremarked in allies' interviews, with one notable exception: Paul, a drag queen himself. However, the absence of drag shows as a site of community consumption speaks more to the type of ally recruited for participation in my research than to any absence of non-LGBTQ people at drag shows. Indeed, future research might target the kinds of non-LGBTQ people who specifically attend drag shows to temporarily benefit from a kind of "gay habitus" (Green 2013; Orne 2017) without traveling to gay neighborhoods in larger cities. Ally participants in this study were generally not interested in attending drag shows, although they were aware of them, and those who were involved in River City drag shows tended to be involved as performers and MCs, suggesting a leadership role in LGBTQ community.

Allies as Pillars of LGBTQ Community Institutions

Indeed, allies *were* involved in the few LGBTQ community institutions that exist in River City. Even people unlikely to be involved in community institutions more broadly, like Brenda, who explained that participating in a community was "somewhat, but not a lot" important, attended LGBTQ events. When I asked whether Brenda engaged in any activities due to her friendship with Karen, she responded: "Probably, yeah. Because I do support the LGB if there's a walk or stuff like that, I will go on it. No, probably none of my other friends would. Um, so, yeah, there are things that way that I do." Brenda overcame her "shyness" to participate in LGB-focused events with Karen, a big deal for someone who is "not real comfortable with the other people, people I don't know." Angela, whose job required engagement with a variety of River City communities, offered a long list of ways she supports LGBTQ community organizations and groups, including attending local Pride picnics and drag shows and supporting the CMC-based youth group and adult support group. Angela's advocacy within the CMC has generated material resources in the form of funding to support LGBTQ community events like workshops. As she explained:

> Well, I think, I mean, because I have this position where I'm like, OK, I can help, the resources, like I have the resources where I'm like, OK, and then you know proud that within the budget I've been able to, like, OK, it's not much, but I'm like we need to add this to the budget so that we could possibly do more things with this group, and luckily committees and boards have agreed. But it was me pushing for that so I've got, so I have funds in little pockets to help with that, and that's important, that a little piece of it, right? Like, hey, there's some backing here, you know?

While Angela's offerings to LGBTQ community include material resources through her organization, other allies are actively involved in LGBTQ organizations in River City. Paul, for example, both volunteers in the LGBTQ youth support group and is an active participant in one of two local drag queen groups. Elina spearheaded an LGBTQ community workshop that, while yielding a small turnout, kickstarted initial conversations and reactivated a dormant LGBTQ Facebook group. Elspeth, a temporary River City community member and young ally, cofacilitated a communitywide Safe Zone training in which local leaders, family, and friends of LGBTQ River Citizens learned about LGBTQ terminology and techniques for support. And Shelley founded a local PFLAG group that recently disbanded, although similar supportive conversations were scheduled quarterly through the CMC. In brief, it is difficult to imagine LGBTQ community institutions in River City without the central role of allies.

And, yet, allies also noted the ways they have been absent as a diversity resource in River City, even as they acknowledged ambivalence about being an ally. Drew, for example, noted that he was not involved with LGBTQ institutions in River City, despite offering support to individual students and friends. I asked him whether he wished he was involved more in LGBTQ community, and he responded:

> A lot of times I do, um, it, yeah. This is, I want to be useful. I want to be able to make a difference and I can see I care about lots of different populations, right, so it's this, kind of this big, [gasp] so, how might I contribute,

you know. And in some ways it's, were I invited, I probably would. Just like, were I invited to do something with the NAACP, I probably would, you know, like, that kind of feeling. Um, but at the same time, it's not, like, I don't want to say, hey pick me, cause you know, that, something seems self-serving about that or something like, I want to do something for you! And that doesn't feel right. Pick me, I'm a good guy! I'm not, like, you know, and I'll, I want to be part of your group because this is the group that I think is cool anyway, you know, or something like that, right?

This conflict between wanting to support LGBTQ community and not wanting recognition for this support is navigated in complicated ways by other allies who admitted they had been less involved in LGBTQ community events in recent years. Many of the allies I interviewed explained that they had once been involved in LGBTQ organizations but were no longer involved or connected. And those who were involved were also critical of the kinds of events LGBTQ organizations were creating. Elina, for example, described a tension within River City LGBTQ community events:

I think a lot of people don't go to these things because they don't feel informed or they don't know about it or that they don't really see value in it. Like I'm not a member of LGBT community, but even as a strong ally, I wouldn't want to go to this if all it's doing is just showing me a play. I mean, yeah, I loved that discussion. That was great. What is going to come out of it, you know? There are issues people are facing. People are like gay couples are not being looked at or stared down when they apply for housing or when they're going to rent apartments. There are those things, and who do they go talk to? It's not necessarily, being stared at is not a civil rights violation.

Elina's concern is shared by LGBTQ community members: LGBTQ community events are focused on entertainment and social support and not on identifying and solving the widespread "issues" LGBTQ people face in River City, like civil rights violations. Elina's comments raise questions about what constitutes LGBTQ community and what "diversity resources" might mean if those resources are dedicated to social activities and not social change (Muraco 2012). Examining the complexities of allies both seeking and serving as diversity resources reveals broader tensions within LGBTQ communities, tensions that are playing out within the organizations and events engaging LGBTQ people in River City.

Conclusion: Allies, Diversity Resources, and Activism

Diversity resources demonstrate the ambivalence of LGBTQ community allyship in River City, as allies both offer and appropriate diversity resources from these communities. I have discussed the ways that River City allies draw diversity resources from their LGBTQ friendships and, to a lesser degree, community, as well as the ways in which allies contribute their own diversity resources to support their friends and LGBTQ community. In other words, allies' role in River City's LGBTQ community is a strongly ambivalent one, as they both support and benefit from community (institutions and friendships). However, whether this exchange of diversity resources generates social change remains an open question and is, I suggest, context-dependent. In Muraco's research on friendships between gay men and straight women and between lesbians and straight men, she asserts that allies demonstrate a "continuum of straight politicization" in their support for LGBTQ social change, ranging from "shifting attitudes to inspiring activism" (2012:124). However, she concludes that these friendships do not substantially contribute to social change, explaining that these friendships demonstrate "a limited ability to create social change at the societal level, despite the actions of many straight individuals motivated by gay male and lesbian friends. In addition, while these intersectional friendships reportedly provided both a greater appreciation for difference and a context in which heterosexism was challenged, discriminatory attitudes coexisted with movement toward social progress" (2012:144).

While the allies who participated in my research demonstrated some similar motivations, appreciation for difference, and discriminatory attitudes (L. Doan et al. 2014), I want to highlight that the community context matters here. Muraco's research was conducted in the San Francisco Bay area, a haven for gay community and visibility quite unlike the similarly hilly downtown streets of River City. In River City, given what LGBTQ participants described as a dis-unified LGBTQ community, as well as the impact individual LGBTQ people have had on their community acceptance, I argue that support for an individual friend might well move the community toward social change.

Karen and her friends Brenda and Sandra are good examples. Karen's work speaking as an individual transgender woman in a variety of community contexts has generated discussion and influenced social change at the state level. This work has been supported through her close friendships with both of these cisgender women, one of whom has primarily offered her "shoulder" and the other who has accompanied her during legislative testimony. While Muraco describes these friendships as "political" simply because marginalized identities are politicized (2012:143), I add that we might also consider the extent to which such friendships can generate social change. Brenda's definition of community as "politics" perhaps inadvertently reinforces this point. She explained that

> community, I think, means the whole thing, the outreach, um, the, I guess, the politics of it all is what it means to me, community. Politics. [C: What do you mean, like?] [sighs] Uh, like, you know, the fundraising, the building, the streets, the expanding, the, all of that, you know, getting the licensing, it's all politics and I don't like the politics. I just wanna do it, you know, and do it or don't.

While Brenda's aversion to "politics" as she sees it means that she does not feel involved in community, her support of Karen, in some ways, enables Karen's activism.

And, yet, there is reason for caution in claiming that individual friendship support "counts" as activism, for two reasons. First, despite cross-identity friendships' inherent politicization, shared emotional labor is a characteristic of close friendships more generally, and it is important to distinguish general friendship support from an exchange of diversity resources that specifically supports marginalized friends. What might the lower end of the "continuum of politicization" look like, in other words? When is an exchange of resources enabling LGBTQ survival, and when is that support part of a general process of exchange in friendship (Blatterer 2015; Rawlins 2008)?

Second, consider the other "side" of diversity resources. Drawing these resources from LGBTQ friends and deploying them in the broader community might also be considered a political act, but how that process harms LGBTQ friends (for example, by "outing" them) should be explored. Using the experiences of friends as resources to educate others might change River City's perception of LGBTQ community, but it is a complicated political act with implications for those who "own" these resources: LGBTQ people themselves. Furthermore, allies are not merely passive consumers of LGBTQ culture and community resources; allies actively constitute community and are self-reflective about their role in this process. There is also a political element to using LGBTQ events, institutions, and people as a marker of "fun," the political benefits of which are dubious (Casey 2004; Ghaziani 2014b; Greene 2014).

It is also worth considering how allies differentially value diversity resources, demonstrating acceptance for (primarily white) LGBTQ people while devaluing contributions of Black, Indigenous, and People of Color (BIPOC) and especially Black people in River City (Richards 2020). For example, more than one ally I interviewed used explicitly or implicitly racist terminology, and perhaps being able to lay claim to an LGBTQ friend demonstrates growing acceptance of white LGBTQ people while allowing, enabling, and supporting racist attitudes and behavior. Brenda, for example, reflected on River City's changes late in our interview, lamenting that

> I see our economy, our country getting worse. I fear for my grandchildren when they grow up. You know, what kind of a place it's gonna be. I mean, even look at [River City] now how, since they, I shouldn't say this because that's judgmental, too, but, you know, when the mayor decided to bring in the race people from Chicago and New York from the ghettoes, all that, um, gang people, when they brought 'em here, look at how we've become. We've never locked our doors before. You know, and now you have to lock your doors. You're afraid to walk the streets.

Terms like "people from Chicago" and "gangs" were frequently used as coded language for Black people in River City, language that has been used for decades both in River City and nationally (Bonilla-Silva 2006). This kind of racist rhetoric is still common in River City among allies *and* LGBTQ participants, even in visible, online spaces like Facebook groups, where participants are identifiable by name. Brenda continued this thread of conversation by sharing a story about a negative experience with a Black man at her workplace, which she used to make stereotypic inferences about Black people in River City. This story contrasts with her earlier story about the *Birdcage* young man with whom she sought a connection.

It is important to clarify that Brenda was not seeking credit for supporting a "diverse" (transgender, in this case) friend. However, if we view diversity resources as differentially valuable, we might consider how and why friendships with white LGBTQ people, or LGBTQ identities themselves, operate as a public symbol of diversity bona fides (Ahmed 2012). In other words, in a largely homogenous (read: white, Catholic, straight, and cisgender) community, those with white LGBTQ friends may be able to claim acceptance and inclusivity while reinforcing harmful racist stereotypes and, importantly, voting for policies that continue to reinforce inequalities. How might diversity resources be examined intersectionally, as a medium of exchange, in a context where marginalized identities are differentially valued?

Given the limitations of this small sample, a number of questions remain to be explored. First, this sample likely included more activist-oriented allies than a more representative sample of LGBTQ friends and family. Brenda is one example of an ally who generally avoided community engagement, while most other allies were more visibly active and, it's worth noting, middle class. Considering allyship and activism across class contexts might flesh out a broader definition of activism and challenge models of activism enabled by greater resources. How LGBTQ people act as allies to their LGBTQ friends is another dimension that should be explored in future research. For example, some research demonstrates that gay and lesbian allies of transgender friends exhibit the same kinds of diversity resource exchanges discussed above (Stone 2009), and whether and how allyship operates across gender should also be explored (between lesbians and gay men, for example, or trans women and trans men).[4] In recent years, sociologists have analyzed the allyship of cisgender people in romantic partnerships with transgender people, offering insights into new community, activist, and relationship identities (Pfeffer 2016; Tompkins 2011, 2013).

Another key consideration of allies and activism in River City specifically is whether allies and LGBTQ friends are longtime River Citizens or newcomers to the area. Their friendship support likely differs depending on their insider/outsider status as a community outsider, at least initially, a "stranger" (Simmel 1917) in River City. Finally, there is some hint that ally support of LGBTQ friends may have turned a corner following the 2016 election of Donald Trump as US president. Some progressive LGBTQ people jettisoned Trump-voting friends, while, for others, discussions of differences have been further "disarmed" (Korgen 2002) or actively avoided. How allies will engage in activism in support of their marginalized friends, and what moves allies across a continuum of activism, will need to be explored in the coming years, especially given changing and perhaps decreasing support for the diversity resources that allies ambivalently contribute and pull from LGBTQ communities.

6

"There's Varying Degrees of Friendship in Here"

Creating Ambivalent Community

I first met Teagan at a local college, where we chatted following a screening of a documentary about transgender identities. In our interview, 25-year-old Teagan described herself as "funny," a personality quirk she demonstrated frequently throughout the interview by gently mocking both herself and her mode of interaction with me, describing her coughs and hand gestures into my recording device. When I asked her which parts of her identity were most important to her, she explained that "being a queer woman pretty much sums it up," and she described these two elements of her identity (sexuality and gender) as being central to how she saw herself. Teagan suspected that she might leave River City, but she planned to return and expected that she would "probably end up settling here." When I asked Teagan what might keep her in River City, she described her family first and her friends second. She explained:

> Family is a big factor for me. Um, it's just always been nice to be close to . . . my sister lives in town here, with her husband, and I know they're gonna start a family soon and I'd like to have a pretty big role in [their] lives. You know, my parents are here, my grandparents, the three that are still here are here. Um, and that's, that's been a big draw. A lot of my friends have sort of scattered, like, since high school, which, you know, happens, it's typical, but I have a good group of friends here, I just have a lot of roots put down and I think that's important. . . . Hometown is important to me, and that kind of thing.

Teagan's "good group of friends," according to her friendship map, included 21 named friends (one of whom was a family member) and a more distant group of "tumblr friends," friends with whom she connected using the microblogging, social networking site tumblr.[1] As with other participants, I asked Teagan whether her friendships made her feel more connected to community, LGBTQ or otherwise, and she responded:

> No, I don't think so. I think most, I mean most of my friendships are kind of interconnected and are their own community but in terms of connecting with a wider community: not really. Um, I think it is a little community that we've sort of built and you know there's varying degrees of friendship in here . . . but as far as connecting with a wider community, not really. Um, yeah. It is what it is.

While Teagan was close with her friends and family members, relationships that she perceived as constituting its own "little community," she did not feel that this group connected her with a broader sense of community. Yet her little community included shared "roots," interests, and activities, like her "crochet friend," for example.

We might interpret Teagan's reflection as evidence of what Japonica Brown-Saracino (2011) calls "ambient community," a sense of community dependent on shared tastes and activities, rather than shared identities. However, it is striking to encounter ambient community in River City, a geographic context that, as I described in chapter 1, is quite unlike the well-known lesbian enclave Brown-Saracino describes: Ithaca, New York, in this case. Given that Brown-Saracino's research was conducted nearly a decade prior to this interview, perhaps River City's LGBTQ population has experienced the same kind of assimilative cultural shift that has allowed them to experience a sense of belongingness predicated on interests, rather than identities.

As noted in chapter 1, River City is not known regionally as an especially LGBTQ-welcoming community. A number of participants, LGBTQ and ally, explained that their friendships *did* connect them to a sense of LGBTQ community; in fact, very few participants claimed no sense of community, even as they found LGBTQ community disjointed and disconnected.[2] Teagan's comments, however, raise questions about whether and how friendships constitute LGBTQ community, as well as the meaning of community for both LGBTQ and ally participants. In this chapter, the relationship between friendship and community is a strongly ambivalent one.

Sociologists have long analyzed the reciprocal relationship between friendship and community, focusing on the ways friendships create community and, conversely, the ways community creates friendships. In the latter case, researchers have demonstrated how community contexts like cities (Fischer 1982a), neighborhoods (Bell and Boat 1957), and work and family (Adams and Allan 1999) influence friendship possibilities. Scholars of LGBTQ communities have also argued that community contexts have enabled friendships between LGBTQ people; historians and ethnographers have shared rich data describing LGBTQ community formation and the friendships that resulted from these new networks. Urban communities in New York and San Francisco (Armstrong 2002; Chauncey 1995; D'Emilio 1998; Esterberg 1997; Faderman 1991) have drawn the most focus, with some notable exceptions that describe midsized cities like Buffalo, New York (Kennedy and Davis 1993), and temporary, mobile communities like festivals (Rothblum and Sablove 2005).

As I discussed in chapter 4, some researchers have considered how shared-identity friendships generate communities, for example, among lesbians (Jo 1996) and gay men (Nardi 1999). Recent research on the decline of lesbian and gay institutions (Brown-Saracino 2011; Ghaziani 2014b; Greene 2014) has referred, often obliquely, to a vague sense of "friendship" as a cause of community, and a potential loss, if LGBTQ community institutions disappear. In some ways, the concept of "community" has been used too narrowly to refer largely to LGBTQ institutions in large cities, while the concept of "friendship" has been used too broadly to refer to a host of personal relationships, from acquaintances to lifelong partners. How friendships constitute LGBTQ communities has remained obscure, even as friendships are described as central to LGBTQ community formation, maintenance, and dissolution. In other words, for LGBTQ people, just because one has LGBTQ friends does not mean these friendships generate a sense of community. Conversely, just because one has a sense of community does not mean this community generates LGBTQ friendships.

In this chapter, I extend Brown-Saracino's (2011) call to examine the role of affective ties in LGBTQ community, a challenge, given that River City features few LGBTQ institutions (which makes it different from the settings that Brown-Saracino and other scholars mentioned above have studied). I analyze the relationship between friendship and community specifically, given previous literatures that presume a causal, if unspecified, connection between LGBTQ friendships and senses of community. I consider LGBTQ *and* ally participants, their friendships with LGBTQ people, and how these friendships relate to LGBTQ community in River City. As I noted in chapter 5, analyzing only LGBTQ participants' perspectives on community in River City provides an incomplete picture of this community, especially given the key role allies have played in forming LGBTQ institutions. First, the *type* of friendship matters in parsing out the relationship between friendship and community. Second, the community *role* participants play is central to understanding how friendship relates to a sense of community. Finally, I return to the definitional questions participants raised when discussing their friends and connection to community to highlight the limits of conventional understandings of community, proposing ambivalence as an alternative approach. Some participants explained, as Teagan did, that their friendships constituted a community wholly distinct from what they saw as an institutionalized LGBTQ community, similar to Brown-Saracino's interviewees in lesbian-friendly Ithaca. Like those in Ithaca, River Citizens identified shared community along lines of shared interests, but variations across participants suggest that friendship should be considered as distinct from, but related to, a sense of community. Participants' friendship and community reflections suggest that the very categories of friendship and community are being renegotiated alongside growing acceptance of LGBTQ people, contributing to the kind of ambivalent community evident in River City.

The Meaning of Friendship in LGBTQ Community

In River City, friendships do not generate a sense of community, at least, not in the way we might expect. While both LGBTQ and ally participants noted that their friends connected them to LGBTQ community, the concept of "friends" held a different meaning in each group. For LGBTQ participants, *acquaintances* were more likely to connect them to a sense of LGBTQ community than close friends. For ally partici-pants, *any* LGBTQ friends, acquaintances or close, connected them with LGBTQ community. Given that an accurate representation of LGBTQ community in River City includes both allies and LGBTQ community members, understanding the meaning of "friendship" in creating com-munity requires analyzing both LGBTQ and allies' friendship networks.

LGBTQ Participants' Friendships and Community

LGBTQ participants explained that their *acquaintances* helped them connect with LGBTQ leisure activities in River City and more well-known gay communities in the region. Participants engaged in "vicarious citizenship" (Greene 2014), claiming membership in dis-tant LGBTQ communities, as Theo Greene found in his research on gay neighborhoods in Washington, DC, and Chicago. For example, for Peter, a white, gay, partnered, and lifelong River Citizen, acquaintances were the explicit connection to LGBTQ community, while he connected to a distinct network of family through his partner. After discussing connections to the "white collar or executive community," he stated, "I might think some of my LGBT acquaintances that I have have [sic] made me more connected to some of the LGBT lifestyle things that I might not directly resonate with because I don't experience it day in and day out." Peter's discussion of LGBT "lifestyle things" included LGBTQ institutions like gay bars, more common in larger cities and nonexis-tent in River City. In another example, Callie, a white, queer woman living in a nearby town, described LGBTQ-friendly leisure activities like trivia nights. After stating that "my community are my friendships," she explained:

> I always say there's always other people that are kind of in that network that I wouldn't necessarily say that are my close friends either. There are people that, like, go to trivia, and do all the activities and they're there, but I wouldn't consider them a close friend. Um, just because we haven't established a friendship between the two of us, but they're at all the activi-ties and they're always there, and so they're part of that network, they're part of that community without them being a close friend.

Greg's initial friendships with other gay men when he was first coming out in River City constituted his community but were not necessarily the long-lasting, close friendships he later developed. I asked him whether any of his friendships made him feel connected to community, and he responded:

> I would say . . . yes. Um, growing up on a farm and growing up in in the Catholic Church where I didn't have any gay friends or any gay folks that I knew, to come to [River City] and meet other gays, it was very, it was basically like that first year and a half, I didn't talk to anybody. I'd talk to them when I needed to, but I really didn't talk to anyone, 'cause that was, my friends had become my new community, my new family, and um, they were, they weren't all deep lasting friendships like I wanted some of them to be, but it's alright with that. I would've been a lot more, I felt more connected then, 'cause it's, like, oh, here is my new home. That's what I felt.

Greg described these new friends as an initial connection to a broader community. Other participants echoed this observation. Both Jack (a trans man) and Janine (a trans woman) noted that acquaintances were, as Jack explained, "a stepping stone to a wider community." Janine elaborated:

> There's, like, so many people that I have been able to meet, have, they're the ones that have, you know, some connections to this and that, and I was able to, um, get to know certain people, like the people that put on things like [River City Trans], and things like that, it's like I was able to get in there and say OK, so this person started this up, and this person over here started this up, and now I got, you know, looking at how I have now, now on Facebook, you know, the Transgender Law Center and all these other things, you know, [a regional Pride organization], and all this stuff on my, um, friends' list it's like, that's how it starts out, with certain things like [Kai], and definitely and from [Kai] it goes to, with [their] mom, and you know, or certain friends of them.

Janine's comments illustrated the "stepping stone" approach to community that such acquaintances enabled.

Karen, a leader and trans community icon in River City, named friends who did not appear on her friendship map as people who connected her with LGBTQ community. She stated:

> I think the people that I work with within the community, the people like [Angela and Elina] and you, things that we try to [do] as a whole for the good of the community. I recently became a commissioner for the city because I wanted to be more connected with the community and make more of an impact. I'm the first transgender person to serve [in an important position in the city] for a town like this, in the size. Maybe I'll be the first mayor, transgender mayor of the town some day. I don't know where my future goes or what people are gonna ask of me, but if they asked me, I'll sure try to be there.

Karen's acquaintances, including me, connected her with LGBTQ community through her work "for the good of the community." In sum, acquaintances connected LGBTQ participants to community institutions for leisure, support, and community development. These more distant friendships demonstrate the power of "weak ties" (Granovetter 1973) to generate LGBTQ communities, in contrast to research emphasizing the centrality of close friends (Jo 1996; Nardi 1999; Weinstock and Rothblum 1996) and intimate relationships (Stacey 2005) to LGBTQ communities.

Allies' Friendships and LGBTQ Community

For allies, *any* friend, close or acquaintance, connected them to LGBTQ community, but close friends were more likely to serve in this role. LGBTQ community to these participants largely meant volunteer activities, with one exception. While ally Drew admitted that he was "not so great at feeling that sense of community" within River City more generally, he explained that his friends motivated him to "make change": "Maybe this is an age thing, that with [my friends] looking toward [their children], it seems like we're looking to make change for them or to make connections for them or both. And that to me that's compelling, right, to say there's, um, there are little reasons, here they are right now and that's why this matters." Drew did not mention specific LGBTQ institutions in which they were engaged, due to his friendship with a lesbian couple, however. Brenda, ally and best friend to Karen, a transgender lesbian, as noted in the previous chapter, mentioned "walks" and other events that Karen encouraged her to attend. She explained that Karen connected her to LGBTQ community, "with her getting more connected to it and to these groups and stuff, it makes me more aware of it."

Paul, a white, straight, male drag queen, became increasingly embedded in LGBTQ community throughout my research in River City. At this time, Paul explained, "I can honestly say I am straight, you know. I, I think I'm on the spectrum that's, you know, between straight and gay than, you know, like I think everyone is." Despite his straight identity, Paul also identified his location "on the spectrum" between straight and gay and explained that he "feel[s] more comfortable around the LGBT community." Paul's connections to LGBTQ community reflected this growing enmeshment in LGBTQ community events and institutions, like the LGBTQ youth group and a new drag group. For Paul, the friendships that connected him to LGBTQ community included both close friends and an acquaintance: "My three LGBT friends, again, because the connections with that and then my [lesbian] friend . . . that [I didn't enter] 'cause she's a little further out. Again, it's because we are connected through volunteer things we do and so that's a big connection to me to my community."

Paul's connection with LGBTQ community was in flux over the course of my research, and I return to his story in the conclusion. Overall, ally participants identified LGBTQ community primarily as volunteer activities in which they participated with and through their close and more distant friends. For ally and LGBTQ participants, not all friendships generated connections to LGBTQ community, and not all functioned in the same way. For LGBTQ people, friendship *distance* mattered, while, for allies, *any* LGBTQ friendship offered a route to community engagement.

Friendship and LGBTQ Community Role

Elina, a straight, cisgender woman of color who was close friends with Mark, a white, gay man, contradicted other allies' approaches to LGBTQ community. She paradoxically noted that being able to say *no* to her

LGBTQ close friends enabled her to feel connected and accepted within the LGBTQ community. Being able to say no demonstrated the depth of trust in her friendship with her gay friend Mark. She explained:

> Constantly in [River City], it's very difficult to say no because that no could be take, seen as rejection or the fact that you're not interested or you're not contributing, so I have to wear a mask of, oh, I can't be myself now. I just need to go or do this or say this. So, um, I think in my close circle, I don't have to do that even in the community. The same goes with my, um, friends that are LGBT. Um, is I can comfortably say no, I don't want to do this. I don't want to go to a drag show. 'Cause. I mean, [Mark] and I went to, the day, we, so we were planning on going to the gay bar in, um, [a city about an hour's drive away]. He normally doesn't drink, right, but we still went. And it was, we had already planned and it was the day the Supreme Court upheld the [*Obergefell v. Hodges*] decision. It was interesting 'cause they were now celebrating, but we were already gonna go there anyway, right? Um, and there was a time when we were, like, oh my God, it's probably gonna be crazy. Let's not go. Like both of us said it, and it was so comfortable to just say it. There are people in my, like, even here where I would just have to go, just do it because I'm afraid of offending them or, um, them taking it differently.

For Elina, an occasional participant in LGBTQ events in River City, her close LGBTQ friends held the *opportunity* to connect with LGBTQ events and institutions, but not the *requirement*. On the surface, Elina's comments signal disengagement from LGBTQ community, the kind of "performative progressiveness" that Amin Ghaziani (2014b:255; see also Brodyn and Ghaziani 2021) discusses as typical of ally behavior in post-gay communities. However, a deeper understanding of Elina's involvement in LGBTQ community as an occasional, and well-connected, ally highlights the need to consider participants' roles in analyzing LGBTQ community and friendship. For example, Elina co-organized a workshop for LGBTQ community members to identify community needs and plan for the future. LGBTQ participants (like Karen) described Elina as a key community ally who was working to change the culture of the city to be more LGBTQ-inclusive. And, yet, Elina did not attend every LGBTQ event in River City, and being able to bow out of such events was a marker of the closeness of her friendship with an LGBTQ community member. Elina's role as an ally in the LGBTQ community is one example of the ways friendships relate to community formation.

In understanding how friendship relates to LGBTQ community, the *role* of community members matters. Previous research has focused on the relationship between LGBTQ *individuals* and community. For example, Wayne Brekhus (2003) identified three types of suburban gay men, typified by their method of engagement with gay community. In Brekhus's research, "peacocks" are gay men who socialize largely in gay networks; "chameleons," like Greene's "vicarious citizens" (2014), live and work in suburbs but connect with gay communities in nearby cities; and "centaurs" minimize their gay identities in their work, leisure, and home lives.

In River City, I identified three community roles that matched participants' involvement in LGBTQ community: leaders, occasionals, and absents. These roles operated differently to connect both LGBTQ and ally individuals to community institutions, events, and action. For example, when I asked participants whether and how their friends connected them to community, two participants and community leaders responded that *they* played that role for their friends. One of these participants was an ally (Angela), while the other was a lesbian (Robin). Angela initially responded no to this question, then added, "I think I feel like I'm in that role. [laughs] In my case, like, hey, did you know about that? Like, I'm trying to connect them." She offered an example of a non-LGBTQ friend who wanted to become more involved in LGBTQ community events and contacted Angela to identify ways to be more engaged. Robin also noted that she thought she was "probably that friend for people," and her vast networks of connections across multiple communities in River City demonstrated her interests and role as a community networker. Both Robin and Angela were what I call leaders, people who played an active role in LGBTQ community institutions like LGBTQ support groups, events like the Pride picnic and educational workshops, and the newly formed LGBTQ nonprofit, River City Collective (RCC). Participants who were less active in LGBTQ community but still occasionally attended events I call occasionals, and participants who did not attend LGBTQ community events at the time I interviewed them and conducted observations are absents. Participants' classifications can

TABLE 6.1. Participants' Roles in LGBTQ Community Institutions

	Leader	Occasional	Absent	Total
LGBTQ	13	18	10	41
Ally	3	2	8	13
Total	16	20	18	54

be found in table 6.1. It's important to note that the largest group of LGBTQ participants are occasionals, while the largest group of ally participants were absents.

Leaders' Community Connections

LGBTQ leaders formed LGBTQ support organizations, created educational workshops and trainings, and provided technical and administrative support for LGBTQ events. Peter, Karen, Robin, Callie, and Kai are good examples of LGBTQ leaders. As discussed in previous chapters, Peter co-organized several Pride picnics, and Karen founded a River City–based transgender support, education, and advocacy organization. Robin offered educational trainings to businesses and organizations aiming to better support LGBTQ people and organized an LGBTQ families group. Callie was a member of the inaugural board of a new GSA (gay-straight alliance) for high school students in a nearby town. Angela and Shelley are ally leaders, exemplified through both Angela's administrative support for a handful of LGBTQ support groups housed at the Center for Multicultural Community (CMC) and Shelley's leadership in River City's former Parents and Friends of Lesbians and Gays (PFLAG) chapter.

Despite their similar leadership and involvement in LGBTQ community institutions and events, leaders' identities affected how they connected with community. LGBTQ leaders tended to connect to LGBTQ community through acquaintances, while ally leaders were connected to LGBTQ community equally through close friends and acquaintances. For example, gay participant Peter's friendship map included a large circle he labeled "acquaintances," where he located most of his LGBTQ friends. Peter has been central to River City community institutions, as a key organizer of the annual Pride events and known networker, and he was often suggested to me as a potential interviewee. At community events, hugs and handshakes from acquaintances were frequent and sincere for Peter, and, yet, he admitted that his closest friends included more family, and his partner's family, than friends, and he was a self-described introvert, even though he acknowledged that "a lot of people" think he is an extrovert.

Angela and Shelley are clear ally leaders who connected to LGBTQ community through close friends, family, and professional LGBTQ contacts. Shelley's involvement in a River City municipal board, an LGBTQ-focused conference, and as a leader in the local PFLAG organization places her squarely in the leader category, and she noted friendships with gay and lesbian friends who, while not close, were coworkers in community events. As discussed in chapter 5, Shelley has been a long-standing LGBTQ community advocate and supporter, but she became involved in PFLAG when her daughter came out as a lesbian, later becoming president of the River City chapter. Close relationships also connected Angela to LGBTQ community, and her leadership role developed through her work at the CMC. Her friendships with gay men when she was living near Chicago's Boystown drew her to gay Pride parades as a source of fun and entertainment, and her life in LGBTQ-friendly communities in the Southwest and on the West Coast developed her "social activist" identity. She returned to River City after the birth of a child and connected with the growing LGBTQ community through her role at the CMC. For both Angela and Shelley, close relationships prompted their leadership and involvement in LGBTQ community in River City.

Occasionals' Community Connections

Occasionals did not play a leadership role in LGBTQ community, although they attended some LGBTQ community events. LGBTQ occasionals tended to be younger than leaders, suggesting a possible generational divide in LGBTQ participants' roles in the River City LGBTQ community, although there certainly were young LGBTQ participants who were leaders as well. LGBTQ occasionals seemed to need LGBTQ community less than leaders did, although they recognized its importance. Marilyn, a Southern transplant to River City who was "white and

Cherokee" and identified as bisexual, is a good example of an LGBTQ occasional. Marilyn was cognizant of both how she was perceived, as someone who could pass as straight, white, and Catholic, and of her distance from LGBTQ community in River City. For example, she hesitated to describe River City's LGBTQ community because "maybe I'm too far on the periphery." Yet Marilyn was close friends with a small "line-up of guys" Marilyn's husband jokingly identified as her "gay boyfriends." She explained that her "husband laughs 'cause if he doesn't wanna go dancing or getting to go get his hair done or go to see the girl movies or whatever," her gay friends will engage in these friendship activities.

LGBTQ occasionals connected to LGBTQ community primarily through close friends, unlike LGBTQ leaders, who connected through acquaintances. Genderqueer participant Leah named one of six close friends on their friendship map as a community connector, a friend who "keeps me connected to community in [a town about an hour's drive away], and they're a pretty big community as well. They have a very big Pride parade down there, and they have gay bars that you can go to, and so I kind of stay connected in that aspect through her." I saw Leah at LGBTQ community events in River City, periodically, usually with a close friend. Leah's friendships, organized around shared interests rather than shared identity, formed the core of their community.

Unlike LGBTQ leaders, LGBTQ occasionals attended LGBTQ community events with close friends, rather than acquaintances, in tow. Marilyn described her close friends, one of whom is Kyle, who helped her "make gay jewelry" she sold at the annual Pride picnic. Marilyn and her husband "really consciously wanted to make sure" they supported the former River City gay bar, Next Level, with their close friends, a gay male couple. Just-out-of-college Maddy, who is white and identified as queer, stated that LGBTQ community is "necessary," and she named specific LGBTQ community organizations she learned about through her close gay friend. Charlie, described above, also attended LGBTQ community events with her close queer friend Callie. Like Marilyn, Charlie consciously patronized Barney's, the gay-owned bar that her friend Callie described as River City's lone "queer bar." LGBTQ occasionals, overall, had close friendship networks that included LGBTQ people but also supported them, the kinds of friendships-as-community that some participants named explicitly. Yet close friends pulled LGBTQ occasionals into community events and institutions in ways that differed from LGBTQ leaders.

There were only two ally occasionals, Brenda and Elina, both of whom were similarly aware that they did not play a central role in LGBTQ community. Like ally leaders, ally occasionals connected to LGBTQ community through their close friends, Karen and Mark, respectively. Brenda, as noted in chapter 5, stated that she "wouldn't go out of [her] way" to connect with LGBTQ community events without her friendship with Karen. Elina valued being able to say no to attending LGBTQ community events as a form of trust within her friendship with Mark. Like LGBTQ occasionals, ally occasionals recognized the need for LGBTQ community, especially for marginalized LGBTQ community members like young LGBTQ people beginning to come out. And like ally leaders, ally occasionals also connected to LGBTQ community through their close friends. Allies, overall, were pulled into LGBTQ community primarily through their close friends.

Absents' Community Connections

Finally, LGBTQ absents tended to connect, at least in theory, to LGBTQ community through acquaintances, and ally absents connected through close friends. While it may seem odd to discuss how community absent participants viewed community, all had reflections about LGBTQ community and how they *would* connect to it, even if they were not connected to LGBTQ community in River City at the time of my research. Vickie, a partnered lesbian and former River Citizen who now lives in a Western state, identified "lesbians in the softball league in wherever I go" as an example of the way acquaintances connected her specifically to lesbian community. Kit, a lesbian-identified River City native and college student at a nearby university, mentioned "knowing some of the people I know who also know each other" and "having friends that are part of the LGBT community" in response to the question about friends and community. Other LGBTQ absents who lived in the River City metro area included bisexual-identified Allyson, agender Arlen, and partnered gay men Derek and Sean. LGBTQ absents, generally speaking, were deeply embedded in family networks, like Allyson, who named "the friend community around [her] family" as important to her. Derek and Sean's social time was similarly spent with their families, very rarely attending LGBTQ community events. For LGBTQ absents, families pulled them away from LGBTQ community and toward integration in family life.

Allies, who were more likely to be absents, explained that close friends were a primary, or exclusive, connector to community events more generally. Married couple Drew and Wendy are good examples, and they identified their close lesbian friends as a primary connector to LGBTQ community in the past. Wendy, for example, responded to the question about whether friendships connected her to community with the following: "I definitely think [our two lesbian friends] do and I think it's definitely because of their engagement, well, and especially when [one friend] was working for the city and even now she still has some relationships. When we're with them and especially with them and we're in [River City] at an event, then I feel more engaged. More so than I would with others."

It is clear in Wendy's comments that her engagement with community is experienced *through* her relationship with her lesbian friends, who, as I argued in chapter 5, operated in some ways as "diversity resources." When I asked whether Wendy was referring specifically to LGBTQ community, she responded that she meant she "was just thinking like [River City] and diversity in general not necessarily just LGBTQ." Allies Rochelle and Lindsay, whose immediate family included gay and lesbian people, and ally Nadine, whose overall community engagement was high, just not in LGBTQ community events and organizations, were other examples of ally absents. Other participants referred to multiple communities in which they were engaged with their friends, but for ally absents, connection to LGBTQ communities occurred through close friends.

Overall, LGBTQ and ally participants' roles in LGBTQ community, whether as absents, occasionals, or leaders, related to their friendships and connection to LGBTQ community. Allies who played all roles connected to LGBTQ community through their close friends, and ally leaders also connected to LGBTQ community through their acquaintances. LGBTQ leaders and absents connected to LGBTQ community primarily through their acquaintances, and LGBTQ occasionals connected to LGBTQ community through their close friends (table 6.2). This additional layer of understanding the social structure of a

TABLE 6.2. Participants' Roles and Connections to Community

	LGBTQ	Ally
Leader	Acquaintance	Acquaintance, close friend
Occasional	Close friend	Close friend
Absent	Acquaintance	Close friend

community helps us better understand the relationship between community and friendship, specifically, how community role matters in community formation through friendships.

Conclusion: Community and Friendship Limitations

Friendships do not universally convey a sense of LGBTQ community for both ally and LGBTQ participants; in fact, different friendships and community roles helped generate the particular ambivalent community present in River City. This finding echoes Brown-Saracino's (2011) discussion of "ambient community" as an affective sense of connection based on shared interests and values, not institutions. However, I have added that the definition of "friendship" must be examined to consider friendship closeness and its relationship to LGBTQ community. Furthermore, I have highlighted the *role* participants played in River City's small LGBTQ community, emphasizing LGBTQ community institutions and events. Participants' roles in River City's LGBTQ community, similar to the suburban gay men Brekhus (2003) describes, affected not just their community involvement but also the *way* they connected to community through their friends.

In other words, not all friendships are created equal in forming community, and these variations affect *how* ambivalent LGBTQ community forms in River City. "Weak ties" (Granovetter 1973) play a greater role in connecting LGBTQ participants to community events and organizations, while stronger ties connect allies to LGBTQ community. More specifically, weak ties connect *all* community leaders and LGBTQ absents to LGBTQ community, while stronger ties serve a community connection function for LGBTQ occasionals and ally leaders, occasionals, *and* absents. This finding raises important questions about the role of close LGBTQ friends, specifically for allies. In chapter 5, I demonstrated the role that allies played in contributing "diversity resources" to sustaining LGBTQ community. We can now ask: would LGBTQ community exist without allies' close LGBTQ friends? For LGBTQ people, will acceptance into families of origin spell the end of LGBTQ community organizations, as more LGBTQ people become absents? And are close LGBTQ friends needed for LGBTQ communities to persist (and, if so, for whom)? Furthermore, these findings raise questions for LGBTQ people seeking close friendships in places like River City. What is the relationship between community engagement and developing close friendships for LGBTQ people seeking those connections? How do LGBTQ people develop close LGBTQ friendships if not through community? Friendship closeness and community role are key elements in LGBTQ communities' ongoing, ambivalent existence.

7

"We Haven't Jumped over the Need for One"

Inclusive, Progressive, and Exclusive Approaches

Toward the end of my interviews, I asked participants to reflect about contemporary LGBTQ life. In their responses, participants shared their hopes for LGBTQ futures (Jones 2013; Muñoz 2009), and these hopes describe the shape of River City as an ambivalent community. In particular, I asked participants to respond to the following statement: "some researchers say that we are living in a post-gay moment where LGBTQ communities are less central to LGBTQ life." Some participants agreed with this statement, but the vast majority of participants disagreed, although not fully. Peter, who had long been involved in LGBTQ community events such as the annual Pride picnic, responded in the most typical way. Recall that, in chapter 3, Peter explained that an LGBTQ community center was no longer needed, a perspective that supports the idea that LGBTQ communities have become integrated into mainstream life. However, Peter's full response to my question about post-gay community demonstrates participants' ambivalence about LGBTQ community:

I think that's true in some aspects, like we were talking about before. I don't think that you necessarily need to have a community center or an advocacy as much as it once was, because society has progressed a lot, and it's kind of second nature. But at the same time, we lose our personal identity or our unification as a broader community when you don't have that forum or that outlet. I think society's come a long way, but I don't think that they are still to the point where everywhere you go you feel comfortable being who you are.

Peter's statement exemplifies a clear sense of ambivalence about the present and future of LGBTQ communities: "society's come along way," but not yet "to the point where everywhere you go you feel comfortable being who you are." Peter suggested that both rural and urban communities still need to change, noting, "But I think then it's kind of twofold, because I hear about a lot more of the bigotry that might be happening in the bigger cities because there's more people there." Describing the problem of post-gay community as a "catch 22," his understanding of progress and the ongoing need for LGBTQ community expresses ambivalent desires for a time when "it doesn't make a difference who you are and who you love" and the realization that River City, and possibly larger cities, has not yet arrived at the doorstep of post-gay community. In fact, as Peter suggests, perhaps larger cities are not yet post-gay either, raising questions about whether smaller communities *could* be post-gay sooner than larger cities. This possibility challenges a linear narrative of gay progress based in urban, gay communities; perhaps communities in cities like Chicago, New York, and San Francisco are ambivalent, too.

Peter's ambivalent response to the post-gay question highlights an ongoing theme in LGBTQ community and identity research, and in identity research more generally: the changing, perhaps declining, relevance of LGBTQ (or at least gay) identities and the decreasing desire for exclusive LGBTQ spaces. Participants expressed a desire for inclusion, for their identities to "not matter," within the larger River City community, even as they identified a need for LGBTQ-specific institutions and fears about assimilation (the idea that "we lose our personal identity," as Peter put it). As noted in the introduction, researchers have long considered the causes and consequences of identity-based differentiation in forming LGBTQ social movements (Armstrong 2002; Bernstein 1997; Ghaziani 2009; Seidman 2003), consequences of discourses of inclusion and diversity (Ahmed 2012; Bell and Hartmann 2007), and resistance to pressures to assimilate (Duggan 2004; Vaid 1995; Ward 2008; Warner 2000). River City LGBTQ community members offered responses to this post-gay question that demonstrated ambivalence about desires to be included, just as they are, into "straight" culture, a process that, some argue (Conrad 2014; Sycamore 2008), constitutes assimilation. In fact, most did not see full inclusion as an achievable goal, at least in the short term. However, their desires for a post-gay *future* differed, as some hoped for a day when identity differences no longer mattered.

Participants' reactions to the idea of post-gay community demonstrate three specific types of ambivalence about post-gay community and its

future, which I call inclusive, progressive, and exclusive. Inclusive participants generally agreed that post-gay community had not yet been realized,
but they hoped it would be some day. Progressive participants saw the arc
of LGBTQ history bending toward inclusion through an iterative, incre-
mental process. They shared the perspective of inclusive participants that
post-gay community did not exist, but, unlike inclusive participants, they
did not express a desire for a post-gay future. While they saw acceptance
of LGBTQ people growing in the future, they were not interested in a
time when LGBTQ identities no longer mattered. Exclusive participants,
although few in number, were more emphatic that post-gay community
should *never* exist, maintaining that distinctive LGBTQ communities are
essential to LGBTQ lives. Participants' responses demonstrate one way
that ambivalence as a theoretical frame might be developed, particularly
in identity-based communities that face the dual pressures of differentiation and assimilation (Garcia 2016). These ambivalent responses may be
specific to River City, and assessing their presence or absence in other
community contexts suggests one way forward in developing a theory of
ambivalent community.

Inclusive: Our Future Is Post-Gay

Inclusive participants recognized that LGBTQ community has not fully
disappeared, but they emphasized an idealized future with minimized
LGBTQ identities. An inclusive response acknowledges the complexity
of the current moment while still expressing a desire for a post-gay,
post-LGBTQ, post-queer (Green 2002; Orne 2017), and, in some cases,
post-racial (Bonilla-Silva 2006) future. This approach should be most
familiar, as it aligns with narratives of assimilation that are common
in American culture. However, even among the two participants who
strongly agreed with the post-gay statement, their responses suggest
a conflicting desire for LGBTQ community. Leah, a queer-identified
River City native, stated clearly that she believed a post-gay moment
had arrived. She said, "I would agree. Like I said, there are our own
cliques within the LGBT community now and so we don't view ourselves as a whole community, but rather cliques inside the community
now. So being seen as a huge force isn't really something we need to do
anymore." While Leah's response to the post-gay statement was clearly

not ambivalent, Leah later noted that she "would like to see that strong community feel come back." Leah recognized value in both "our force of, like, this is the community and we're here to actually support each other" and in connecting with non-LGBTQ-focused subcultures, especially for LGBTQ young people. And, yet, Leah's life did not centrally involve engagement with LGBTQ community events and organizations. Leah's life echoed those of Japonica Brown-Saracino's "ambient community" (2011) members: Leah participated in a music subculture organized around shared aesthetic tastes, not around LGBTQ identities, even as Leah did not hide a queer identity in these groups.

Karen, a local transgender activist who identifies as a lesbian, agreed. In many ways, Karen's and Leah's lives radically differed. While Leah came out as a lesbian in middle school, Karen came out as a trans woman and lesbian later in her life, and she is an active advocate for transgender people in River City. Karen's efforts to generate specifically trans community in River City are well known by those in the LGBTQ community, and she often makes appearances at LGBTQ and other community events, speaking up about her experiences and answering questions from attendees. She founded River City Trans, an organization she created to provide resources and support to transgender River Citizens and education to cisgender allies. When I asked the post-gay question, Karen responded: "I think that's true. I think, you know, no longer are we the closed society that we used to be, and LGBT people hung around [only] with each other." Again, her later comments suggest that perhaps that post-gay moment is not quite realized. She asserted, "I think it's time for history to change it, you know. We were worried for so long that, well, we belong over here. Well, why can't we belong with everybody?" Her reflections on post-gay community demonstrate the desire for an inclusive future echoed by other participants; after listing the groups who should be accepted equally, she asserted, "Let's make it a one world thing, and I say get rid of the individuality that makes us all, you know."

Marilyn's discussion of post-gay community in her previous home, a large Southern city, was tempered by her claim that "we haven't jumped over the need for one here [in River City]." And, yet, she argued that "it'd be nice to think we don't need a gay community because everybody was accepted and it was totally cool to be who you are and to wear it on your sleeve or to hold their hand and kiss and do whatever everywhere, just like heterosexuals do, but I . . . think in [River City], that's not the case." Marilyn, a mixed-race woman who identifies as bisexual, has long been a supporter of LGBTQ community, which she connects closely with her gay friends. For Janine, a white, pansexual-identified trans woman, "it has gotten better in a way speaking, I mean, I can see that. It's just, you know, as long as you're able to get out and about and just be yourself, and hang out with people no matter who they are, it's, like, and just have a good time, you know? . . . It's, like, come on. I'm just, I'm just like anybody else." For Janine, Karen, and Leah, their ambivalence about LGBTQ community emphasizes inclusion, the ultimate goal of being seen as "just like anybody else," although the unnamed "anybody else" also hints at a desire for assimilation into River City's mainstream culture.

An inclusive response was strongly expressed by LGBTQ allies as well. Angela is a straight, married woman whose connections to LGBTQ community have followed in the Western and Southern states in which she has made her home. She returned to her native River City when her child was young and works in the community organization that houses the LGBTQ youth and adult support groups. In Angela's reaction to the post-gay question, she stated: "I guess in a utopian world, we're all a part of one human race and one big community, so why would you need to have a section that, you know, for LGBT, like a LGBT-specific community. And we're all accepting, everyone's all ah, right, you know, or why would you need that? Like . . . I don't think we're there."

Angela's work in an organization that emphasizes multiculturalism, rather than difference, echoes a post-gay approach to community, even as she agrees that "one big community" has not yet arrived. Paul more strongly asserted that a post-gay era had not yet been realized, noting, "I don't think that's true. I do like that idea where we don't have straight community and an LGBT community, there's just community. Um, and so that's the utopia I hope we get to but I think until that happens, I don't think we're there yet." Both Angela and Paul described their "utopia" as one community in which differences are no longer needed, key features of an inclusion model. Paul expressed hope for the future in describing what he had learned from his high school daughter, that "no one cares" about students' LGBTQ identities in River City. Paul said, "I'm, like, that's wonderful, that's how it should be."

Shelley, who moved to River City with her husband from a Southern state, discussed the process of racial desegregation, suggesting that desegregation resulted in fractured Black community institutions and highlighting her desire for a post-racial, uniform community: "I mean we all are just human beings, anyway, it doesn't make any difference in, and I would love to see where, does it need to have a separate community, is what I hope." She also acknowledged that LGBTQ community spaces are still needed, primarily for dating purposes. She said, "There's still definite needs for places for folks to be able to find each other, and be able to, um, mingle and find others that you would possibly want to date or to marry." Finally, Brenda echoed Janine's hopes for inclusion through sameness, even as she argued that "I don't think it's completely true, but I think it's getting better towards that way." She described the lesbians she knew from work and through family, noting that "they're just like you and me."

Notably, the largest proportion of participants who reflected an inclusive approach to post-gay community were white allies like Angela, Paul, Shelley, and Brenda. This finding is not surprising, given that research on the role of allies in LGBTQ communities demonstrates the ways that allies privilege heterosexual norms and identities in these spaces (Burgess and Baunach 2014; Dean 2014; Mathers et al. 2018). Allies' emphasis on inclusion reflects an overarching cultural emphasis on a future in which sexual differences are minimized or deemed irrelevant, which could erase the inequalities LGBTQ people experience. This model of "utopia" is quintessentially post-gay, but it has particular implications in River City. Given the central role of allies in LGBTQ community institutions in River City, discussed more fully in chapter 5, the use of inclusive language that encourages LGBTQ people to minimize their identities because "no one cares" (for example) suggests desires for sameness that may play out in LGBTQ community organizations and spaces.

Hoping for a utopian future in which differences are no longer central to LGBTQ lives is especially imaginable for those outside of LGBTQ community; what is more surprising is that LGBTQ participants shared this inclusive perspective, too. In the context of River City's ambivalent LGBTQ community, we might imagine why a future time when marginalized identities "don't matter" would be appealing, when this context demands that these differences be identified, but not celebrated, and few spaces exist in which to celebrate them. Inclusive LGBTQ participants varied in age, gender expression, class, and education level, but their friendship maps suggested one similarity: close friends who are largely not LGBTQ, and LGBTQ friends who are not deeply engaged or active in LGBTQ community. I discuss LGBTQ participants' friendships in chapters 4 and 6, but evidence from participants' friendship maps generally suggests that inclusive LGBTQ participants were not closely connected with politically active LGBTQ friends. These connections matter in the possibilities that inclusive-oriented LGBTQ people have to access celebratory spaces in the here and now (Jones 2013; Muñoz 2009). In other words, institutional connections and relationships, key elements of community in River City, affected LGBTQ people's perspectives on queer (and LGBTQ, more generally) futures.

Progressive: We're Not Post-Gay, and Some LGBTQ People Still Need Community

Most LGBTQ participants expressed ambivalence about post-gay community with an incrementally progressive, but not fully inclusive, inflection. They rejected the idea of post-gay community but described the arc of history as tending toward inclusion, even as they did not express a strong preference for a future in which gender and sexual identities are minimized or irrelevant. Participants referenced same-sex marriage and legal protections for transgender people as evidence of this progress while also expressing concerns about disappearing community and the ongoing need for LGBTQ community, particularly for the most vulnerable LGBTQ people. Mark, a key LGBTQ community activist, flatly denied the post-gay statement, saying, "Oh, that's such crap. . . . Just because there is gay marriage and there is, you know, no discrimination or zero tolerance for discrimination . . . that doesn't mean that discrimination and people [who] are of that identity don't feel not included." He later acknowledged that some post-gay communities may exist: "So I do think that, I think the overt discrimination in some parts of the country that maybe those communities are past that. But you still need the support, the visibility. The people like, yo where are we here?" Teagan, a young, politically progressive, white woman and River City native who identified as "bisexual or something," shared a similarly frustrated response, stating:

> Post-gay just made me mad. . . . Not mad, but just like . . . it comes down to the idea that like the fight for gay equality is over because we have gay marriage now from the Supreme Court which is being upheld in the states kind of? Not really? Have laws changed? Has very much changed in the states where it wasn't already? I don't know. I forgot the question because I was upset by it, not upset by it but like post-gay made me bristle.

Her sarcasm in this moment, what she described as "making a sarcastic face," suggests both awareness of and frustration with this narrative of progress.

Callie, a queer-identified participant introduced in chapter 2, summarized a progressive perspective when she responded to the post-gay statement, saying, "No, I wouldn't agree. I wouldn't say that we're, um, there's progress, obviously. Um, better, yes. But completely post and everyone's OK, no. No, not everyone is OK." She described her experiences being out in the community with a new partner and "the looks and the feelings" associated with being visibly out. Colby and Nate both explicitly referenced "history"; Colby stated that "obviously being together as a core helped make a lot of progress. So coming back together as a core, make more progress, you know." His plan for making this progress involved symbolic unification of LGBTQ community: "you know, if you push on something from a bunch of different angles, it's not gonna move. But if you push it from one point it will move." Notably, this "progress" did not explicitly involve the erasure of LGBTQ identities. Nate, a reluctant advocate for a post-gay era, referenced the "natural evolution" toward assimilation, even as he acknowledged the ongoing need for community in places like River City, perhaps less so in the larger cities where he has lived. Finally, for Kyle, the arc of gay history now also includes transgender identities, and, while he reluctantly agreed that we may be approaching a post-gay era, "I would say that for certain we are more post-gay than post-trans. I think that trans is the new issue that's up there as it should be but, um, . . . makes us think we're post-gay."

Participants with a progressive reaction to ambivalent community also referenced the vulnerable groups who still need a sense of, or a connection to, LGBTQ community, like young or trans community members, as in Kyle's above quote. Elina, an active ally and woman of color, responded to the post-gay statement by suggesting that "I think that's coming from people that don't need it, and some of the people do. Maybe those are the ones that are not powerful enough to say that they need it. It's the ones that are educated, it's the ones that are in power, it's the ones that are connected to resources so they don't feel the need for it." Elina's comment highlights an implicit, disempowered group that need LGBTQ community.

Greg described a kind of gay "orientation grace period" in which LGBTQ people who are coming out need support from those who share their identities. He explained, "We don't need the gay center so to speak," and he continued, "I think there's a sort of need for them, for when you're first coming out, there's always that, like, orientation grace period." His ambivalence around transitions to post-gay communities especially in Chicago were demonstrated in the following quote:

> I don't think there's the need for having this overly, we need to have rainbow flags everywhere. Like, I'm sad to say what's happened with Boystown in Chicago, for example. Here was a nice, beautiful, gentrified, gay area, and then we let all the straights in. I really get upset with Pride in Chicago. It's, like, really? All these stupid straight people are here. Go the fuck away! This isn't for you; this is for me! Fuck off! Why are you here?

It is unclear whether the need to have rainbow flags is still necessary in Boystown, even as Greg's desires for community for LGBTQ people coming out and for vicarious community (Greene 2014) in Boystown persists. Greg's statement presents a conundrum: without the rainbow flags in "beautiful, gentrified, gay area[s]," how do straights know which spaces are not for them? While Greg and his husband, Steve, explained that they "pass" as straight, they simultaneously resisted "let[ting] all the straights in." In a way, Greg and Steve were engaging in their own process of gentrification in River City, on a tiny scale. Their very lives demonstrated this kind of progressive response to post-gay community:

while they are not visibly gay and claim to not need LGBTQ organizations, they recognize that others might need them, and they value Pride events, as long as they don't involve straight people. They recognized the historical progress that allowed them to live comfortable, if less visible, gay lives, even as they supported LGBTQ organizations and events for those who need them. Greg's comments highlight a tension between two elements of post-gay community: the incorporation of straight people into gay community (Ghaziani 2014b; Hartless 2018), and the desire for gay people like Greg and Steve to participate in straight culture (through processes of gentrification or "passing"). Overall, progressive participants like Greg and Steve asserted that historical progress was central to their sense of ambivalence about post-gay LGBTQ community. These largely LGBTQ participants agreed that, despite this progress, some LGBTQ community organizations would likely be needed in the longer term, especially for the most marginal LGBTQ community members.

Exclusive: Post-Gay? No Way

Some participants projected the need for gay community into the future, an approach that suggests an active resistance to assimilation, even as the pressure to assimilate persists. Participants who shared this exclusive approach emphasized the ongoing need for community, even as they acknowledged the existence of post-gay communities for some. Charlie, for example, described the difference between "culturally queer" people and normative gay, lesbian, and some trans people for whom their "sexuality or gender does not require you now to have this community in order to live a satisfying life." Charlie, a queer woman of color educated in a progressive, small liberal arts college, was not a River City native, and she struggled to find the kind of queer community she valued in River City. While her professional connections afforded her some connection to a thoughtful, if small, group of queer friends, she anticipated a need for nonnormative queer community in the future. For Charlie, queer community "is central to my experience in my life," and she echoed queer theorists like José Esteban Muñoz (2009) in her discussion of essential queer futures. Charlie's response hints at the possibility that a *normative* post-gay future could exist alongside exclusive, transgressive queer community.

Alimah's response to the post-gay statement was emphatic, and she noted, "No, the need for community is always fundamental!" Alimah's experiences as a college student and member of overlapping communities, like the North African family and friends with whom she had grown up, informed her discussion of the importance of community. She extended her understandings of community to her experiences as a newly out lesbian. She referenced a recent TED talk where the speaker claimed:

> We're a world that's, like, we're all experiencing the same world but we're fractured by perspectives and the only way to, like, what do you call it, heal that is by community, and, like, yeah. . . . I think that there's always a need to, like, especially with an oppressed group of people, you need to have a community, that's the only way you can fight it, you know what I mean, or feel less oppressed or, and, like, see yourself as a soul who's, like, who needs to, like, be stronger, like, is by your community, there's no need to not ever have community.

Alimah, like Charlie, expected to connect with "community" throughout her life, although her irritation at the lack of a sense of community among her college peers emerged throughout our interview.

Robin was similarly frustrated by River City LGBTQ community members who take a post-gay approach to community. This frustration was coupled with her own desire to make ongoing connections with LGBTQ people, particularly around families, given her own small family with her partner and children. She stated:

> There are plenty of gay people in [River City] who have been gay forever and not been out. Who have [not] given two squats about gay community. They've been post-gay community since they were out, you know? So I believe that that attitude as well as the attitude of believing that gay community is important, both have always existed, you know? I mean when I came here and I was trying to interest people in being more connected, whatever that meant. There were plenty of people who were, like, that's not how I define myself. No, I'm not interested, leave me alone, you know? . . . And I really want to know same-sex families with children my age. I really want that, desperately, you know? Um, again, we don't have

to be best friends but at least to see each other regularly and to check in and to see what each other is experiencing. And how does that relate, and how is that the same and how is it different from what I'm experiencing. And, you know, like those are the things that I really want. And are difficult to force to happen.

Robin later worked to "force" such community to happen, cofounding a group for LGBTQ parents at the local community center. The group has, unfortunately, met infrequently due to low attendance.

Grey's reflections on post-gay community align with Robin's. Grey noted that "especially for this area . . . since people are secluded, they're looking for the community. Or they're not actively looking for it, but they're wishing it was there." Grey, a white participant who identifies as nonbinary/genderqueer and queer, lives and works as a young professional in small towns in the greater River City metro area but travels to River City to participate in LGBTQ community events. Grey preferred living near River City to living in the South, where they attended college. They explained that they would never have stayed in the South because "one, it was way too hot. Lizards, cockroaches. Um, also, you know, it's a little bit more conservative down there. Gender norms, gender everything, it's really strict and, yeah, that's basically it." Grey described themself as a "nerdy 1950s boy," referring to their interests and gender expression. In Grey's online LGBTQ community, they connected with other LGBTQ people from a "really small town" who stated that "there's nobody gay here and I wish there was." Grey felt an affinity with those similarly "secluded" LGBTQ people, as their friendship network was composed largely of straight and cisgender friends and family members. On the other hand, Grey also knew people whose friends were all gay. When asked where such people live, Grey shared their response: "In a huge city where they can just huddle together and have gay hugs." For Grey, however, such a context is not appealing, despite the hugs; their desires were more separatist: "If we could just have, like, a gay commune out, out in the [laughs] country." Grey anticipated a future need for LGBTQ community, and they described "A-Camp," a summer camp run by Autostraddle, a progressive, feminist, and queer online blog and community, as a possible future queer space they might enjoy, if they could overcome their self-described "fear" of other LGBTQ people.

Grey, Robin, Alimah, and Charlie expressed a desire for exclusive LGBTQ community, even in the face of social pressures toward post-gay community. However, participants who expressed exclusive responses to the post-gay interview question were relatively few. These participants shared one characteristic: a sense of isolation and outsider status, even though each had grown up in the Midwest, if not in a nearby town. It is possible that this low number of LGBTQ people with an exclusive approach to post-gay community is specific to River City, given overall normative pressures within the city's conservative culture. Future research might further specify whether exclusive approaches are as common in larger cities as post-gay researchers suggest (Brown-Saracino 2011, 2015; Ghaziani 2014b).

Conclusion: Uncertain, Ambivalent Futures

Inclusive, progressive, and exclusive responses to the post-gay question demonstrate mixed perspectives about the need for LGBTQ communities, as well as visions for LGBTQ futures. Inclusive and progressive responses suggest movement toward futures that minimize LGBTQ communities in favor of an inclusive, difference-minimizing community, even if such a state is not yet realized in River City. Exclusive approaches acknowledge and resist inclusive pressures. These three responses (inclusive, progressive, and exclusive) demonstrate one way forward in developing a theory of ambivalence as it relates to identity-based communities in a moment of transition (Coser 1966; Garcia 2016). They answer the question: how might ambivalence be measured in these kinds of communities? They offer evidence of how tensions between "sameness and difference" in LGBTQ social movements (Ghaziani et al. 2016) play out in nonactivist LGBTQ people's everyday lives, as they encounter pressures to express or minimize their identities.

Participants' responses to the post-gay question suggest perspectives on the future of LGBTQ communities that may well guide participants' actions. However, in my observations, LGBTQ and ally individuals who demonstrate *each* of these three approaches participate in LGBTQ community-making processes. They share spaces, organize events together, and support each other, even if their ultimate visions for LGBTQ futures differ. Further specifying how types of ambivalence contribute to the cyclical community formation process discussed above is beyond the scope of this chapter, and exploring how inclusive, progressive, and exclusive perspectives connect with powerful narratives in an evolving LGBTQ community context may demonstrate how equality may or may not be achieved. The differences in participants' friendships, however, suggest a key dimension of their approaches that might be further analyzed across a range of urban and rural forms.

An additional open question is whether and how these perspectives may have shifted into following the inequities of the early 2020s, when a global pandemic, increasingly visible racial inequality in the United States, and discourses of political division inform Americans' imagined futures. It is possible, on the one hand, that LGBTQ and ally participants will seek ways to experience and establish queer utopias in the current moment (Jones 2013; Muñoz 2009), as the socially distanced Pride event described in chapter 3 suggests. On the other hand, it is also possible, and perhaps likely, that possibilities for connection among LGBTQ people in River City have been sharply curtailed by these forces, as participants have hunkered down to protect their community, families, and themselves from COVID-19. The political context following the 2016 Trump election might have affected how participants understood a narrative of progress; hints about this political context appeared in my interviews, as participants reflected on the then-upcoming 2016 presidential election. For the majority of my participants, I suspect that this narrative feels stalled, and asking a similar question in the early 2020s might yield a very different range of responses, even as the inclusive, progressive, and exclusive framework likely persists.

Conclusion

Charlie, a higher education professional in her early 30s, whom we met in previous chapters, sat at my dining room table one fall weekend, gamely answering my questions about her plans to eventually leave River City. She sketched the broader outlines of her adult life, describing her experiences in graduate school and persistent desires to plan ahead for her next move. Charlie was not from River City; she grew up in a Chicago suburb; had attended college and graduate school; and worked throughout the Midwest and South. Charlie explained that she "always [had] plans to be someplace else" and struggled to stay in one place for more than a few years at a time. She held this desire to move in tension with a wish to be well grounded in a sense of community, explaining, "I see other people's lives, where they put down roots and they have really strong attachments to community and I want that. At the time . . . if it doesn't happen after a couple years, I just feel, like, well, let's find another place and see if it happens." After I asked what was appealing about putting down roots, she stated:

> I sort of create the analogy of college, or even grad school. Like, just the idea that, like, you have a really good lay of the land socially, and so, like, you have your friends over here for this, and it's funny, like, thinking about, like, 'cause grad school was where I felt like I had the most, like, social connection even though I was only there for two years. 'Cause I had, like, my straight-straight friends, my straight-queer friends, my queer-queer friends, um, and so, like, I felt like all of my needs were really met in very particular ways. So, like, whereas here, I feel like I have a single set of friends, and then I have individual people, um, but I don't have, like, friend groups, and I think I would have more of that if I lived in a place, or, like, the fact that, like, in grad school, we had, like, our bar. Um, it was, like, our place. And so, you know, I don't have, I have some, I have things resembling that here, but it still doesn't make me wanna stay here.

During Charlie's time in River City, she participated in a variety of community events, both LGBTQ and not, and she had friends through her workplace and in the larger River City community. Charlie felt some desire to return to the Chicago area, although, in Charlie's case, that big city was where she grew up. Charlie could imagine other communities throughout the United States where she might live, and River City was not one of them, despite her connections to some elements of LGBTQ community. Callie was one of Charlie's close friends, and Callie and Charlie often patronized what Callie described as River City's "queer bar," usually with other friends. And, yet, she tearfully described what was lacking:

> And so I feel really lonely sometimes amongst the friends that I have now. And I realize there are times when I just don't need to hang out with them. Like, there are times when I'm lonely, and so I think of, like, I should go hang out with them, and [I] hang out with them and I'm, like, they don't, no, this is not hitting the spot. Um, and it's because I don't have, like, other sets of friends to, like, offset that feeling.

For Charlie, participation in River City LGBTQ community did not provide the friendships she needed to sustain her, to develop "really strong attachments to community." Conversely, her friendships did not create the sense of deep-rooted community she wanted to attain. Even though Charlie's friendships with LGBTQ people in the River City area connected her to community institutions, she still felt lonely and, ultimately, left River City for a job in a nearby state.

Mark, whom I introduced in chapter 3, also felt this sense of loneliness, and he explained that he did not see how he could stay in River City. He stated:

> I'm too young I feel, like, to retire here in a way. Like, to be, like, yup, this is going to be home. Like, no. There are bigger, I want to live in a bigger city to see how that's going to affect me as a person. Um, and also, I just can't see myself right now raising a family here and feeling comfortable and feeling welcomed and included, and not stared at, and maybe even said to somethings [sic], you know? Because when I see how the community, some community members treat people of color and other people

who are different than them, you know it's a signifier for me. And I just can't, I don't think I want to deal with it.

Mark foresaw a time when River City's larger community would be too hostile for him and a future family to tolerate. His comments were prophetic, as he left River City for a much larger city on the East Coast not long after our interview.

Mark's and Charlie's experiences align with stories of gay migration (Carrillo 2017; Weston 1995) in which LGBTQ people have moved from smaller towns and cities throughout the United States to the larger cities on the coast in order to participate more deeply in an imagined gay community. Yet, in River City, *elements* of this imagined gay community existed in the form of LGBTQ support organizations, events, and small, if disconnected, groups of friends. Charlie and Mark *had* LGBTQ friends, as well as connections to family in the area (in the case of Mark) and favorite queer spaces like Barney's. In theory, friendships should have connected Charlie and Mark to a feeling of LGBTQ community in River City, but these connections ultimately failed. If we read Charlie's and Mark's experiences alongside those of Kai, whom we met in the introduction, a theme of queer loneliness emerges, one experienced particularly for single, young LGBTQ adults.

Each of these three participants resolved ambivalent feelings about LGBTQ community in River City in different ways: two have subsequently left River City (Charlie and Mark), and one has committed to staying (Kai). The difference has much to do with identities, friendships, families, institutions, and the larger social context of River City as a small, rural, Midwestern city. And, yet, leaving (or staying) introduces new ambivalences, highlighting the ways shifting communities continue to inform and shape individuals' experiences within them.

With some exceptions, sociologists of LGBTQ community usually focus on institutions and their relationships to individuals, while sociologists of friendship analyze personal relationships without their community contexts. Charlie's, Mark's, and Kai's interwoven stories of community and friendship failure highlight the need to consider not just LGBTQ community institutions, and not just friendships, but how each of these elements of community connect. Peter Nardi's groundbreaking book on gay men's friendships describes this connection as an "ongoing dialectic" between friendship and community: "Friendship networks, thus, become the primary site where the daily lives of gay men and lesbians are carried out and shaped. . . . Networks of friendships, often reconceptualized as kinships of choice, become the source for developing communities of identity and inequality" (1999:192). Friendships create community, and community develops friendships, at least sometimes. For Charlie and Mark, this dialectic is revealed in its failure: their friendships did not create a sense of community, and community participation did not lead to the development of friendships (with LGBTQ *or* non-LGBTQ people) that felt sustaining or supportive.

For Mark and Charlie, the failure to connect to community through friends in some ways grew from a sense that better options were available, and accessible, in other communities. And this sense proved to be accurate. Charlie's experiences in college and graduate school, for example, offered a template of what her ideal queer community might be, and Mark's perspective after actually "going through war" taught him that discrimination was not tolerable in his future life. This story is one of class, in some ways, as middle-class, if not especially well-paying, jobs enabled them to imagine a move to another part of the United States as possible and have the means to carry it out. It's also a story of race and culture, as River City's white supremacist and American Midwestern context meant that Charlie's and Mark's identities would not, and perhaps could not, be fully celebrated in their everyday lives.[1] Despite their efforts to establish and connect to LGBTQ community, Charlie's friendships and activities in River City's LGBTQ community did not align with her imagined queer community, and Mark's friendships and work as an LGBTQ community leader did not suggest that community change was likely to occur at the speed he needed to feel connected and safe.

Charlie's, Mark's, and Kai's stories reveal a set of tensions I have explored throughout this book: between community coalescence and diffusion, between friendship and community, and between community and individuals' lives. Urban-based LGBTQ community research focused on gay neighborhoods has generally responded to these tensions by identifying a linear narrative of community progress and acceptance, and by conflating friendship and community as part of this teleological process. My research challenges this framing in two ways: first, these linear narratives of progress miss everyday ambivalences experienced in LGBTQ communities. Ambivalence is not an extraneous part of a progress narrative in which communities will ultimately dissolve under assimilative pressures; analysis of River City's LGBTQ community reveals that ambivalence is *central* to LGBTQ community formation and change. Second, explorations of friendship have remained underexplored and underspecified with studies of community. A focus on friendship demonstrates community formation and dissolution processes and challenges community definitions that focus on institutions at the expense of relationships. Below I discuss the challenges my research offers both to LGBTQ community research and sociological research more broadly, and I suggest future possible research oriented toward these findings.

Ambivalence in Nonurban LGBTQ Spaces

Researchers focused on urban gay communities have described a linear process of community change (Ghaziani 2014b), one that locates friendships as the starting point of gay community (Nardi 1999). Proponents of these theories argue that, for example, post-gay approaches to community are beginning to, in a sense, "trickle down" to suburban, small-town, and rural LGBTQ communities as acceptance of LGBTQ people grows. Other theorists of nonurban LGBTQ communities have offered alternative frameworks that challenge this approach (Brown-Saracino 2015; Gray et al. 2016), while still others have critiqued the prioritization of urban gay life over LGBTQ lives in other communities (Forstie 2020; Gray 2009; Halberstam 2005; Stone 2018). While the critique of the centrality of urban gay communities is not new, analyses of the 2016 US presidential election and calls for racial justice following the 2020 murder of George Floyd suggest a need to engage deeply with what has been called "flyover country," the rural Midwest, in particular.

I suggest that we might benefit from instead considering the ways that our theory making about LGBTQ communities might "trickle up" from more peripheral LGBTQ spaces (Connell 2008), changing the ways we think about LGBTQ communities even in those urban contexts (Manalansan et al. 2014). In other words, a dominant focus on urban contexts has meant that analyses of urban LGBTQ communities may have missed the kinds of ambivalences that suburban and rural communities manage every day—and ones that are already present in urban spaces. Indeed, recent research examining queer pop-ups (Stillwagon and Ghaziani 2019) and clusters of LGBTQ subcultures (Ghaziani 2019) examines community phenomena that have long existed in small cities and rural places (Gray 2009). Indeed, given that *urban* LGBTQ communities, as well as other marginalized urban communities, are likely subject to similar kinds of local, national, and global dynamics as those in smaller places, perhaps these similarities are not surprising. And, yet, there are likely some differences between ambivalent communities in small Midwestern cities like River City and large Midwestern cities like Chicago, and also among other small cities in the United States. Because River City is a small city in the middle of a primarily rural part of the country, evidence from my research highlights the need to maintain a sense of ambivalence about LGBTQ communities and ongoing change in both rural *and* urban contexts.

Ambivalence and Linear Narratives of Progress

I want to be specific about what is missed in the focus on linear narratives of progress based in urban centers. As my research shows, the overlap between assimilation and differentiation is substantial in River City, as the case of Barney's suggests. While Barney's might well be seen as an inclusive, post-gay space, it could also easily be seen as closeted, given the absence of visible indicators of gay community. A linear narrative of gay community progress misses this overlap, while ambivalent community makes space for multiple, even conflicting experiences of LGBTQ community. Indeed, there is space for ambivalence within post-gay narratives of community progress; these narratives of progress are meaningful to my participants, if only as a source of critique that they are truly reflective of LGBTQ lives.

Some researchers have signaled that such ambivalences exist; Nardi describes the fracturing of gay community, as discourse shifted to relationship dyads and fewer friendships (1999:193), and Amin Ghaziani (2014b) notes that LGBTQ communities may shift between closet, post-gay, and coming-out phases. Theo Greene's research on "vicarious citizenship" (2014) offers a number of examples of the ways LGBTQ people of color ambivalently navigate access to communities that do, and do not, offer a sense of connection. My research in River City reveals that ambivalence is central to LGBTQ communities, particularly in an era of "post" ideologies that, community members in my research seem to agree, are not an accurate reflection of how marginalized people negotiate lived realities. Future research should explore whether this finding is borne out in other community contexts. Perhaps rather than understanding communities as closeted, coming out, or post-gay, or as more or less hostile, understanding communities as normative, queer, queernormative, or post-queer (Green 2002; Orne 2017) might offer a way to distinguish between communities of similar sizes, with similar dynamics, in multiple regions across the United States. River City might be one example of a normative LGBTQ community, one marked by pressures to conform to particular gendered, racialized, sexual, and relationship (e.g., family) models, while other, similar-sized cities might be seen as queer inasmuch as their LGBTQ communities encourage deviance over conformance. Finally, perhaps some cities might be seen as post-queer, or perhaps queernormative; as Jay Orne's (2017) research suggests, gay neighborhoods may be increasingly de-radicalized, and perhaps small-city LGBTQ communities are following. While I remain skeptical of linear narratives of progress, a queer analytic dimension of LGBTQ communities might reveal key differences in how such communities cohere or disperse.

Ambivalence must also be explored in other identity-based communities, as discourses of "post" become increasingly common, at least among community outsiders. How do communities of color navigate American cultural ambivalence around race, given colorblind ideologies (Bonilla-Silva 2006), for example? How might working-class Americans navigate meritocratic expectations as they access middle-class institutions (Allan 1998)? As the meanings of identities shift at a broader, cultural level, their local effects on identity-based communities should be assessed in terms of ambivalence, alongside narratives of progress.

The Role of Friendship in LGBTQ Community

My research highlights a second challenge to LGBTQ community research: the missing friendships in LGBTQ community literature and the ongoing, if sometimes contradictory, centrality of friendships in

LGBTQ community. LGBTQ community researchers have referenced friendships as an aspect of communities, but it is unclear what "friendship" means (Brown-Saracino 2011; Ghaziani 2014b). Conversely, those who study LGBTQ friendships typically leave out community contexts entirely or miss the ways different communities might affect friendship formation (Adams and Allan 1999; Muraco 2012). While individual and dyadic friendships have been extensively analyzed, the role of friendships in constituting, or limiting, LGBTQ community has previously remained underspecified. However, for participants in my research, such as Charlie, their connections to, and exit from, LGBTQ community in River City cannot be understood without knowing about and considering the landscape of their friendships.

In other words, my research suggests that we cannot understand LGBTQ community as a whole without analyzing the central role of friendships. For example, we cannot assume that friendships universally constitute community, or that all friendships lead to community in the same ways. "Friendship," as an analytic category, applies to a range of relationships (Fischer 1982b), some of which generate LGBTQ community, and others that do not. Some friendships cause people to show up at LGBTQ institutions, while others draw people away. I thus propose that an in-depth understanding of friends' *identities*, friendship *closeness*, and friends' *roles* in LGBTQ community can help us operationalize how friendship can be central to the formation of LGBTQ communities. Rather than assume that friendships necessarily and automatically generate community, an alternative question might be: *Which* friendships generate community, and under what conditions? In my research, identities mattered, even as *both* LGBTQ and ally participants played a crucial role in the formation and maintenance of LGBTQ communities. My research showed that acquaintances connected LGBTQ participants to community, while close friends connected allies to community, and families played a role in community dis/connection.

Furthermore, friendships cause us to question the definition of LGBTQ community, one that lies at the heart of a research trajectory that flows from urban centers. Must LGBTQ community always revolve around the growing, or declining, visibility of LGBTQ institutions (Thomsen 2021)? In other words, as my research has demonstrated, studying friendship should be central to community research. In rural towns of just a few hundred, for example, like those that represent "home" to many of my participants, perhaps friendships *are* community, full stop. This possibility echoes research about LGBTQ "care networks" constructed around sick or aging LGBTQ community members (Aronson 1998; D'Augelli and Hart 1987; Dykewomon 2018; Roseneil and Budgeon 2004; Vries and Megathlin 2009). We can further imagine how friendships coalesce in rural contexts, where groups of friends make temporary communities in public spaces (Gray 2009) or in their own homes (Hall and Fine 2005). As in Allyson's case, in these smaller towns, families may be increasingly embedded in friendships and may constitute families for LGBTQ people, a possibility that suggests a shift in the chosenness of families. Even (some) rural families welcome their LGBTQ children home for the holidays, in other words. However, no matter how accepting, families also ran the risk of pulling LGBTQ participants away from engagement with LGBTQ community institutions, although not in all cases.

Components of Community: Friendships and the Decline of LGBTQ Institutions

Friendships are a central answer to the question: how do we measure community in places with few LGBTQ institutions? In small cities like River City, the range of community that friendship generates is quite visible, from communities centered around groups of friends to those located in LGBTQ institutions like gay bars. For example, I observed clusters of LGBTQ friends at non-LGBTQ community events like a local storytelling forum. In another example, one lesbian-identified participant created a Facebook group for informal LGBTQ activities, and small groups of newly met LGBTQ people and allies gathered to walk with dogs and children through local parks on sunny summer days. In some cases, these clusters of friends generated new organizations, which spawned additional subgroups that remained active, at least for a time (one produced a monthly magazine, for example). In one aforementioned instance, River City Collective (RCC), an LGBTQ-focused nonprofit, was created by a group of friends, several of whom were new to River City and looking to create a centralized place to "catalyze" LGBTQ community, as their website suggested. While RCC and

River City Pride (RCP), a nonprofit that emerged after RCC disbanded, remain focused on social activities and fundraising for RCC and other support organizations, their role in River City's politics is minimal. This gap in more vocal political activity is being filled by Kai, a newly out, trans community member, along with others who see a need to organize something beyond socializing. New LGBTQ and ally leaders are emerging, with the support of close friends and acquaintances, and I am curious about the shape of political organizing given anti-trans legislation proposed in River City's home state and neighboring states. Not all LGBTQ institutions, in other words, are equally political or equally likely to mobilize should the need arise (Stein 2002), and their relative politicization depends in part on the networks of friends such leaders employ (as described in chapter 6). Whether and how these organizations actively change the overall culture of River City remains an open question, especially as the leadership of organizations like RCC and RCP remains uncertain. Similar organizations may be forming in other LGBTQ communities like those of River City, especially given the bump in anti-LGBTQ legislation following the 2016 US election, and understanding the role of LGBTQ people, allies, and their acquaintances and close friends will be crucial to understanding how social change occurs in the coming years.

Similar to urban gay communities, River City's gay community also gathered in a traditional gay institution: a new gay bar, the Underground, described briefly in chapter 1. Extended networks of gay friends had connected through their attendance at Next Level, a visible gay bar replete with rainbow flags that closed in recent years. These friendship networks emerged again at the Underground, a new word-of-mouth gay bar that is more muted in its gay visibility. The "queer pop-up" bar events organized in the Underground (also discussed in chapter 1) suggested an overlapping network of largely new-to-River City, largely white, lesbian, queer, and trans community members. Friendship circles, especially divisions between gay and lesbian, queer, and trans community members, partially explain how and why a queer pop-up bar appeared within the space of an (implicitly) gay bar (Stillwagon and Ghaziani 2019).

The queer pop-up bar within the less visibly gay bar is a good example of how friendship networks mobilized small communities of friends in River City. River City's size made it an ideal location to observe the range of manifestations of community through friendship, sometimes in smaller groups unconnected to institutions and, at other times, more recognizably urban and gay. And, yet, the size of the city is not the only indicator of friendship-community relationship. A comparison with other small cities across the United States could be instructive, for example, in the case of lesbian-friendly cities (Brown-Saracino 2017). If we take seriously the possibility that post-gay communities centrally feature the disappearance of gay institutions, friendships constitute new community formations (Ghaziani 2019) or, at the very least, relationships that should be examined for their ambivalent post-gayness and, possibly, post-queerness (Orne 2017).

Communities are not static, nor are participants, and a number of changes suggest avenues for possible future research. Especially in smaller cities like River City, individual-level changes, relationship break-ups, and friendship shifts can have sizable effects on broader friendship networks and community coherence. Two participants "came out," one as gay and the other as transgender. Paul, the straight drag queen discussed in chapter 2, publicly came out as gay near the end of my time in River City, soon began spending more time with gay friends, and started dating a man from a nearby town. Paul's already-in-place friendship networks, established in part through his involvement in a drag group and the LGBTQ youth group, supported him as his life shifted from one of a straight, middle-class, married man to that of a single, middle-class, gay man. Furthermore, more than one couple in which I interviewed at least one participant ended their relationships, causing ripples in organizations and social events. In one case, such a breakup pulled a participant further into LGBTQ community events while pushing a second participant away. Participants' roles in community have changed, in some cases quite rapidly, as their romantic, family, and friend relationships have shifted, especially following the 2016 election season and 2020 COVID-19 pandemic. Friendship networks are snapshots at one moment in time (Muraco 2012), as are communities, and a longitudinal study of LGBTQ friendship networks in coming years would offer a more complete picture of how friendships do or do not constitute community, and how these relationships change as national and local discourses, policies, and legislation affect LGBTQ people's everyday lives in River City.

The Role of Origin Stories in LGBTQ Community

One element of friendship and community that I have not explored is community of origin. Participants' birthplaces and where they grew up affected their friendships, migration in and out of River City, and participation in LGBTQ community events. Some have moved from River City, particularly single participants who were not River City natives, while others who self-identify as "from" River City have doubled down on their commitment to changing River City to be more inclusive of LGBTQ folks. Some have refocused their activism on antiracist and other political work, while others have withdrawn from LGBTQ engagement. Being "from" River City or a nearby town affects social networks, connections to family, and the ways friendships are constituted (including families of origin, for example). Participants' communities of origin affected their expectations for acceptance, for the contours of gay community, for what a good life for an LGBTQ person looks like (one free from violence, and one of tolerance, but not necessarily full acceptance). Those who were "from" River City, on the whole, were not interested in queer identities or communities, and some were openly critical of LGBTQ people they perceived as too queer. Some, too, were implicitly, if not openly, racist. These normative perspectives meant that queer-identified, or less normative, participants, and especially queer-identified Black, Indigenous, and People of Color (BIPOC) participants, like Charlie, felt lonely, alienated, and less able to connect with a sense of community.

Race, Gender, and LGBTQ Friendship Networks

I have only scratched the surface of the racialized, classed, and gendered friendship networks of River Citizens. As many have suggested (Gillespie et al. 2015; McPherson et al. 2001; Ueno et al. 2012), friendship homophily is an especially sticky characteristic of personal relationships. Homophily is the tendency for "birds of a feather to flock together" (McPherson et al. 2001), or people to form friendships primarily with those who share their identities and backgrounds, a social phenomenon that persists despite claims that we are living in a post-identitarian moment. However, friendships do indeed form across identity lines, although race and class lines remain less permeable than sexuality and gender lines (Goins 2011; Korgen 2002; Muraco 2012; Wimmer and Lewis 2010). White participants often shamefacedly told me that they had no close friends who were people of color, even as they enthusiastically described their white LGBTQ friends, although participants of color tended to have more friends who crossed race, gender, and sexuality identity lines. While I did not explicitly ask about friendships that crossed lines of class, markers of class (like college attendance, types of social activities, foci of discussion) suggested that most friendships were within-class. Given a central role of friendships in LGBTQ community, my research indicates that friendship homophily may have consequences for LGBTQ community formation processes. In River City, friendship homophily left LGBTQ people of color and working-class LGBTQ people disconnected from the most active LGBTQ community institutions, and these participants found other communities that required that they travel (to Chicago, for example) or further minimize their identities (in substance abuse recovery organizations, for example). Friendship homophily cost the most marginalized LGBTQ people in River City time, money, and the ability to fully be themselves.

River City includes (if not supports) growing communities of color, as especially Black social, political, and support organizations are becoming increasingly visible, although white River Citizens have been actively fighting integration for decades. White supremacy and racism remain endemic to River City, in explicit ways, like a 2016 cross burning, to implicit ways, like the language of "from Chicago" that white participants used to refer disparagingly to Black River Citizens. The power of racial segregation in River City seems too strong an institutionalized force to overcome within LGBTQ community, and one participant suggested that distinct LGBTQ communities of color might form around their shared identities, rather than attend largely white LGBTQ spaces and organizations. On the other hand, there is some preliminary evidence that LGBTQ community in River City may be increasingly welcoming to LGBTQ people of color. A night at the newly opened Underground featured a small, and surprisingly diverse, crowd, while events like drag shows have often included both performers and participants of color. Indeed, the newly formed River City Pride is headed by two BIPOC LGBTQ people, as noted in chapter 3. Yet participants of color were more likely to connect with communities of color in nearby cities like Chicago, engaging in the kind of "vicarious citizenship" Greene describes (2014). The relationship between LGBTQ people of color and predominantly white LGBTQ community institutions and events should be explored further, especially as friendships across lines of race are uncommon, especially in River City. Other similarly sized cities might enable cross-race friendships, and a comparison case with such a city would further develop our understanding of how more intersectional, just, and equitable LGBTQ communities are possible.

When friendships across lines of race did occur, they often put LGBTQ people of color in an awkward position as a token friend of color (Korgen 2002). Charlie, who identified as a Black American "cisgender woman with gender queer leanings," identified race as a barrier to friendships in River City. She noted, "I don't feel as close to my friends here because I do feel like I'm their only Black friend." She described the effects of being the "only Black friend" on her friendships and experience of LGBTQ community in River City:

> There's a sense of which, like, if I'm your only Black friend, I feel like I'm not just, I'm not [Charlie]. I'm your Black friend. Whereas if you have at least one other Black friend that I know, like, OK. So you have a point of reference. So everything I do is now not reflective on all Black people 'cause you have a point of reference. Um, and so, and so there's that as well. Um, yeah. I don't know. Like I—I do think that the experience of race is very big for me when it comes to queerness, 'cause I also feel like I just miss diversity. Like it just is not a thing here. Um, and again, because my experience with queerness is so related to race, like, that also makes me feel like it's just not a very queer place, um, if I can't connect to, you know, queer Latinos and, like, queer Filipinas and, like, all these things, all these people who've, like, kind of enriched my experience of my sexuality.

River City's lack of racial diversity and potential for white friends to see her as a "token" Black friend clearly influenced Charlie's ability to make friends and connect with LGBTQ community. Charlie's comments here also tell us something about the experiences of BIPOC people in River City more generally, and the ways racial diversity make life possible specifically for BIPOC River Citizens.

Yet white LGBTQ participants also seemed to be making little effort to support communities of color. The absence of white, gay participants in particular in events supporting River Citizens of color should also be elaborated in future research, as events like local Juneteenth celebrations, film screenings, and protest marches and vigils were attended *only* by white lesbians, queer women, and trans men (with the exception of the Pulse massacre vigil). While white LGBTQ participants decried their lack of friends of color, they also did not, on the whole, publicly engage with communities of color to build those friendships. The limitations of River City's racist history and current racial dynamics play out in friendships, which affect LGBTQ community and contribute to its overwhelming whiteness. This process demonstrates the limitations of friendship, particularly as a utopian institution (Eng 2010), and exploring the dynamics of race, gender, and sexuality within friendships and community institutions in River City would help us understand how segregation and racial inequality persist in LGBTQ communities more generally.

Gendered elements of friendship and community networks deeply affected LGBTQ institutions, organizations, and events, and while my focus was largely on LGBTQ community members and allies, a gendered analysis of friendship and community should be central to understandings of community going forward. For example, while gay men and transgender women most visibly led LGBTQ organizations, social events, and drag shows, transgender men and cisgender lesbian and queer women were less visible overall but more visible as activists. Cisgender lesbians, queer women, and trans men were involved in a variety of organizations, showing up at marches and protests, carrying signs, leading ally trainings, and, importantly, caring for families and friends of their own. While gay men, trans women, and non-LGBTQ allies remain the most visible LGBTQ community representatives, with some exceptions, cisgender lesbians, queer women, and trans men may be more numerous in the community, in line with Emily Kazyak's (2012) research on lesbian and queer women in the rural Midwest. Kai described this hidden community as "introverts," but I suspect that the reality is much more gendered and reveals an avenue for further research, as well as a bifurcation in the literature focused largely on urban, gay communities.

A second dimension of gender, noted briefly above, should be explored as central to friendship and community. While research on trans friendships is a small, but growing, field (Galupo et al. 2014), the relationship between friendship and community specifically for transgender men and women, and agender, genderqueer, and nonbinary people, should be analyzed more fully. While comparisons between a possible transgender community and gay community are not fully accurate, there are hints of a growing trans community in River City that echo gay community institutions. A trans-specific community organization emerged to share information about, and to support, trans River Citizens. And, yet, trans friendship networks differ widely by gender. Recall that trans men mapped the largest group of friends of any group of participants, while trans women had relatively small circles of friends. Research on transgender people's friendships and their relationship to LGBTQ communities should not treat all trans identities as equivalent.

The Conceptual Limits of Community and Friendship

My research raises two set of definitional questions for future consideration: the limits of "community" and the limits of "friendship." First, LGBTQ participants across community roles also noted that their friends *were* their community; in other words, they did not initially connect their friendships to LGBTQ institutions. While some allies stated that their friends are their community, proportionally more LGBTQ participants made this claim. Teagan's quote at the start of chapter 6 is a good example, as she stated that "most of my friendships are kind of interconnected and are their own community." For some LGBTQ participants, *all* of their friendships "counted" as community, while, for others, their LGBTQ friends constituted a community. Fia, a performance artist, River City native, and white trans woman, for example, described a specific party from 2006, complete with a list of friends and a sense of "synchronicity" that generated a feeling of community. Thoughtful, transgender college student Colby focused on LGBTQ friends, and he stated that

so, like, where, I feel like community is wherever these friends are. And so when I have LGBTQ friends, it's like I feel a sense of that community in and out of the contacts or in and out of the LGBTQ contacts. Like, if I have LGBTQ friends, I feel like I feel that community. I feel other communities. I feel like a belonging to other things. I feel like friendships are communities in themselves almost.

These examples should give us pause in considering the definition of community and the role of friendship therein. In River City's LGBTQ community, described as "cliquey" and disconnected, some LGBTQ participants see their friendship circles as more authentic community than the kind of community observed in institutions and events. This observation is not new, as Mary Gray (2009) observed similar patterns in her analysis of a rural LGBTQ community and its temporary communities formed in the aisles of Wal-Mart, for example. However, I suggest that friendship-based communities offer a new way to consider how LGBTQ communities are more durable than recent post-gay (Ghaziani 2014b), and now post-queer (Green 2002; Orne 2017), literatures suggest. Locating, and analyzing, friendships at the center of LGBTQ community helps us understand how these communities change, and persist, even in contexts that seem to lack LGBTQ institutions. And, yet, the limits of these friendship-based communities should be analyzed in future research. Do friendship-based communities mobilize action and resources in the same way that LGBTQ institutions do? And, critically, will friends be aware of, or vote in favor of, LGBTQ-supportive legislation and speak out against anti-LGBTQ legislation?

Second, what was striking for LGBTQ participants is how many participants included family as central both to their friendship networks *and* to their sense of community. Allyson, who was in her early 20s, for example, described her family as the linchpin in her sense of community:

Um, I guess for, like, [my town], a lot of it is the family and friends that have formed a community. I guess the friend community around my family is important to me. Both my parents have, um, just a mass . . . a huge collection of friends over the years. My mom has a lot of very close friends. And they're always doing stuff and they're always inviting us and, um, we definitely go to things and, um, it's important to me to maintain that friendship. Because these people, when I'm not around they look after my mom. If we're all at work or something and my mom needs the driveway plowed or something, like it will be done before she even wakes up in the morning. Like, I really appreciate the close-knit community that she has. And I try to be a part of it. I'm not quite as much as I probably should be but, um, I guess that's the one that matters most to me in [my town]. Not necessarily having my own close-knit community. It's probably my mom's.

Allyson, who identified as bisexual, connected to some degree with her mom's "close-knit community," a network of people who engage in onerous, wintertime labor like driveway plowing. Yet it was unclear whether Allyson's non-LGBTQ family would be transformed into ally occasionals or leaders, or whether her family would attend LGBTQ community events with her. Peter, mentioned above, is close especially to his partner's family and is an extrovert-seeming introvert. He acknowledged that his closest relationships are with his partner's immediate family, who accepted Peter and his relationship with his partner. Some research has shown the ways that families constitute LGBTQ communities (Moore 2011), and others have demonstrated the ways family and friendships generate LGBTQ support (Broad et al. 2008; Duhigg et al. 2010; Fingerhut 2011). However, future research should examine how growing acceptance in families might be pulling LGBTQ people away from community engagement.

And Robin's comments about the importance of family in her identity highlight the changing role of multiple generations of families in LGBTQ community. After the values of "living simply, and valuing people over things, and equity" as core elements of her "culturally Catholic" identity, she stated: "It's what I aspire to and what I would call a part of being culturally Catholic. Family being very important. And family is an interesting part of my identity. Because it's now two families, it's my family of origin and now it's the family that I've created with my wife, you know?"

These participants' perspectives on family acceptance echo research that highlights the overlap between family and friendship (Carrillo 2017; Spencer and Pahl 2006). While participants like Peter and Robin included family on their friendship maps, it was clear that their families saw them, and their partners, *as family themselves*, not as friends, euphemistically (Carrillo 2017). In other words, LGBTQ participants saw their families as their close friends, a phenomenon Liz Spencer and Raymond Pahl call "suffusion" (2006). This phenomenon should be explored further especially within LGBTQ communities, as families increasingly comprise LGBTQ people's social networks, perhaps asserting family relationships as normatively superior to friendships.

And, yet, the sense of "chosen family" (Weston 1991) has not completely disappeared among LGBTQ participants. Nate, who grew up in River City but has since left for the West Coast, identified his four closest friends as "yadeed [sic]" which, he explained, is

a Hebrew word. It means a friend that's closer than a brother. . . . And so I would say these guys are, the four of these guys are my yadeed. So closer than brothers, I could call them at any time and completely be accepted and they'll be behind me no matter what decision I ever make, you know. And they love me enough to yell at me when I'm doing something stupid. But even if I decide to keep on doing stupid, they'll be right behind me.

Nate's description of his yadeed resonates with the concept of chosen family, and these relationships are central to his life outside River City, one in which he is estranged from much of his family of origin.

The concept of chosen family has also been adopted by allies who are themselves estranged from their families. Paul, for example, explained:

I just, I'm not, I really don't have anything to do with them [my family]. And it saddens me sometimes. . . . So, um, I think I look to my community as kind of my family and my friends. I mean I, you know, there are some friends that I have and I'm, like, you're my family. And I think that's another way I relate to the LGBT community 'cause you often hear, LGBT community, you know, these are my family because a lot of time their families reject them, um, or, you know, they can't deal with them. And so this has become, and so I'm, I'm kind of like that, too. Um, and I think that's another way that I kind of relate to the LGBT community that I choose my family for the most part.

Paul's discussion of his chosen family highlights the need to explore how such a framework for family manifests in a variety of community contexts (Moore 2011).

A key question here is whether and how families—either through suffusion or chosen families—create or contribute to community. At this point, families of origin and homonormative (Van Eeden-Moorefield et al. 2011) nuclear families centered around a queer couple seem to draw LGBTQ participants away from community (Carrington 1999; Lehr 1999), while chosen and extended families connect them to community (Moore 2011; Weeks et al. 2001). Yet research also suggests that LGBTQ family members connect allies to LGBTQ events, institutions, and, in some cases, activism (Broad 2011; Broad et al. 2008; Johnson and Best 2012). Whether and how families generate communities, or pull people away from them, remains an open question, one that is dependent to some degree on definitional overlaps with friendship. While my research demonstrates the need to specify the relationship between friendship and community, it also highlights definitional challenges in a changing cultural context of growing LGBTQ acceptance.

Friendships and the Future of LGBTQ Communities

River City's LGBTQ community remains in flux, although some have noted a growing queer nightlife (Adeyemi et al. 2021), for example, coalescence around drag shows and the newly active Pride organization. In early 2017, rumors that a new gay bar was on the cusp of opening began to circulate among LGBTQ community members. In early April, a Facebook page appeared in which it was described as an "all-lifestyles" bar, and its owner is a gay man well known in River City's gay community. This new bar, the Underground, represented the culmination of the gay social events that had exploded in 2016–17, spurred by the leaders of RCC, and the bar was a kind of coalescing force: a space for a benefit drag show, for example, and the site of the aforementioned "queer pop-up bar." Yet community outsiders would not know that Underground is a "gay bar." Like Barney's, at the time of my research, the Underground had no gay iconography, beyond what patrons bring on their bodies; the bar was lit by an array of colorful, vertical lights, but no rainbow flags were visible, and the music, largely catchy, contemporary pop, did not reference LGBTQ culture in any noticeable way. For all the excitement about a new gay bar in town, ambivalence persists in River City, as the "new gay bar" was not obviously gay.

Perhaps what made the Underground gay was its bartenders and clientele, who were more visibly gay than in other, nearby bars. I have a hard time imagining non-LGBTQ River Citizens feeling wholly unaware of the Underground's implicit gayness, although it was not signaled by any concrete element of the bar's decoration. From the street, it looked like any other bar in River City's downtown, windows lit by fluorescent beer signage. Rather, the Underground's gayness was made evident in and through *friendships*: in the ways patrons laugh and touch each other's arms, in the cluster of short-haired lesbians perched around the table closest to the front window, in the ways everyone watches to see if they know the person who just entered, or left, via the front door, to see if hugs are forthcoming. If the Underground was to offer a successful challenge to the "post-gay" era, it would do so through those friendships, acquaintances and close, homophilous or heterogenous. Yet the Underground's potential as a *queer* or *trans* community space remains unrealized, given River City's overarching normative pressures, as well as economic pressures in the 2020 pandemic year, which may have led to its closing. In any case, the future of *any* fully inclusive LGBTQ space in River City depends in part on the friendships that form within and across identity lines in the coming politically fraught years.

Indeed, LGBTQ people in River City have weathered the 2020 pandemic, political polarization, and growing visibility of racism and racial inequalities in ways that will likely affect the shape of LGBTQ ambivalent community for years to come. Deep community divisions and long-existing marginalization have been exacerbated and made visible through social media, for example, and an increasingly hostile political climate may well cause more LGBTQ people, especially BIPOC LGBTQ people, to leave. However, a mass exodus of LGBTQ people from River City is not a foregone conclusion, as these pressures might also catalyze a newly visible, newly insistent, and nonapologetic (if small) LGBTQ community interested in, frankly, the ambivalent processes of survival and joy. There is some evidence that these processes have already occurred in other small cities (Allen 2020; Mattson 2020) and, yet, ambivalences remain. Those who stay in River City, LGBTQ and ally alike, like Kai, Karen, Robin and Keri, and Angela and Brenda, will continue to live and shape community, alongside temporary community members like Charlie, Mark, and Callie. Understanding how ambivalent community is generated by, and shapes the lives of, community insiders and outsiders will remain central to understanding the possibilities (and failures) of LGBTQ communities to come.

ACKNOWLEDGMENTS

Knowing that I cannot fully acknowledge all of the contributions to this project, I am going to make an awkward attempt! Most importantly, this book would not exist without the stories of my River City participants— LGBTQ and ally alike. I am humbly grateful for your generosity in sharing your lives, stories, joys, and challenges, and I appreciate your kindness and willingness to be open with a stranger to your cities.

The seed of this project began back in Portland, Maine, when I became frustrated by the limitations of current thinking about LGBTQ community loss as a local lesbian bar was closing (one of many that have subsequently disappeared). At that time, I was encouraged by three colleagues who supported my research (Ardis Cameron) and my preliminary inkling that perhaps graduate school to pursue a PhD was possible (Wendy Chapkis, along with my undergraduate advisor and friend, Nancy Riley). Many thanks for your early, and ongoing, support and friendship.

After arriving at Northwestern, I found myself surrounded by a wonderfully warm, kindly critical, and at-times hilarious group of colleagues, both graduate students and faculty. My cohort and subsequent cohort grad-school friends kept me sane over many cappuccinos, and a special thanks to (in no particular order) Lisa-Jo van den Scott, Joseph Guisti, Justin Louie, Savina Balasubramanian, Josh Kaiser, Derek Burk, Stefan Vogler, Theo Greene, and Jeff Kosbie. My superstar dissertation committee cheerfully challenged me as this project developed: many thanks to Héctor Carrillo, Kristen Schilt, Gary Fine, and Al Hunter. And thank goodness for Héctor, my committee chair, whose helpfully critical feedback, gentle encouragement, and supportive mentorship both shaped this project and helped me to survive graduate school with my humanity intact.

I worked on what started as a dissertation, then became a manuscript, across several institutions: Northwestern University, the University of

Wisconsin–Platteville, Farmingdale State College, and, now, the University of Minnesota. Along the way, these institutions have supported a number of components of this project. Many thanks to the Department of Sociology at Northwestern University, the Sexualities Project at Northwestern, the University Fellows program at the University of Wisconsin–Platteville, and the Sociology and Anthropology Department at Farmingdale State College for providing funding (and time and mentorship) to develop this project and to attend conferences to share my findings.

Many colleagues along the way have made this manuscript possible. Thanks to my multiple writing groups, especially stef shuster and Ellen Lamont, for feedback, guidance, and encouragement; to Platteville colleagues Jen DeCoste, AC Stokes, Jon Brown, and Emily Stier for their mentorship and enthusiastic friendship; to Farmingdale colleague Angela Jones for publication (and overall survival) support; and to Greggor Mattson and Brandy Simula for the frequent reality checks and helpful professional perspective. Anonymous reviewers offered significant support in polishing this book as it moved forward from its very roughest state; I thank you for your kindly critical feedback. And a special thanks to my editor at New York University Press, Ilene Kalish, for belief in my project and support in moving it forward.

Finally, I remain indebted to my family for their ongoing support and curiosity about this project. Many thanks to my parents; to my brilliant and funny sister, Ann; and wry, hardworking brother, Adam. This work would not have been possible without the (mostly) silent support of my furry family members, Kitchen, Molly, and Bailey, one of whom reclines on my lap as I type these very words. To my partner, Mel, all of my gratitude and love. I remain grateful for your encouragement and support—material, emotional, and otherwise. Our partnership has long enabled my work, and your influence on LGBTQ communities continues. A final, small thank-you to our kiddo, Kai, who really has no idea what I'm working on, but who has gamely visited me with snacks and hugs while I'm "working." These little supports, too, have helped to move this project forward.

APPENDIX A

Interview Script

INTRODUCTION

Hello! Thanks for taking the time to participate in this interview. I'm Clare Forstie, and I'm a researcher at Northwestern University studying lesbian, gay, bisexual, transgender, and queer (or LGBTQ) friendships. We're going to talk today about your friendships and what they mean to you, and I'll ask you questions related to your friendships and where you spend time with your friends. Please note that there are no right or wrong answers to these questions, and I want to encourage you to share your honest responses.

This interview will be audio recorded, but you can ask me to pause the audio recording. I'll take notes throughout the interview, but I won't include your name in my notes. Please use your first name only during the interview, and, if you're uncomfortable using your first name, choose a pseudonym to use in the interview. If you're referring to friends in our discussion, please also only use their first names and try to avoid sharing information about them that would identify them. You can also choose to end the interview at any time. Are you ready to proceed?

Great! Thanks. I will now start the audio recording.

INTERVIEW QUESTIONS

Identity
1. First, tell me a little about you. Where are you from? Where do you live now? How long have you lived there? Do you have plans to stay or do you intend to move?
2. How would you describe yourself?
3. What parts of your identity are most important to you?

4. How would you define your sexuality? Your gender? How did you come to understand them in the way you do now?

5. Are there parts of your identity we haven't addressed that you'd like to discuss?

Friendship

1. Please take a few minutes to draw a diagram of your friends (see friendship diagram sheet).

2. Tell me about the friends you noted in your diagram.

   a. Who are they? How do you know them? Where did you meet them? How long have you known each other? When did you know that they had become a friend?

   b. How would you describe them? Are they LGBTQ? Are most of your friends LGBTQ? Why or why not?

   c. How important is it to you to have LGBTQ friends? Why?

   d. Are your friends generally similar to you? Different from you? In what ways?

   e. Do your friends acknowledge or support the parts of your identity that are most important to you? If so, how so? If not, what do you think about that?

   f. Would you put your family on this diagram? Would you put a romantic or sexual partner here? Why or why not?

   g. Have your friendships changed at all in recent years? If so, how? Why? Thinking longer term, have your friendships changed over time? If so, how and why?

3. What kinds of things do you do together with your friends? Why?

   a. Do you find yourself socializing in a primarily LGBTQ or straight environment when you're with your friends? How do you feel about that?

   b. Do you attend LGBTQ events? If so, why? If not, why not? Do you attend with your friends? Do you see your friends there? If so, or if not, how do you feel about that?

   c. If you have LGBTQ friends, are there things you do with them that you don't do with your other friends? Are there things you do with your other friends that you don't do with your LGBTQ friends? Why?

d. Have there been any changes in what you do together? If so, why?

e. Do you feel any pressure to be romantically involved with your friends? Have you been romantically involved with any of your friends?

4. Where do you primarily socialize?

a. How often do you go to these places/that place?

b. If you like it, why? What is it you like about it?

c. If not, why not? What do you not like about it?

d. Have you changed places you socialize at all in recent years? Or over time? If so, how and why?

e. Are there any activities you do, or do differently, just because of your friends? Are there any organizations, groups, businesses, volunteer work, or anything else you've done because of them?

5. Who is your closest friend in this group? How do you know them? Why are they your closest friend?

a. Do you think your friend's identity affects your friendship at all? In positive ways? In negative ways?

b. How does this friend get along with your other friends? Do you have a romantic partner? If so, how does this friend get along with them?

c. Do you feel any pressure to be romantically involved with this friend? Do others have this expectation of your relationship?

d. Has your friendship given you experiences that you would not have had otherwise? Has your friendship given you contact with groups or ideas you would not have had otherwise? Can you give me an example or two?

e. Has this friendship changed over time? If so, how? How do you feel about those changes?

f. Have you lost any friends recently? How? What happened? Is there anything that would cause you to end a friendship?

6. How do you interact with your friends? How often do you interact with them and how? What about your closest friend?

a. Have the ways you interact changed over time? If so, how? How do you feel about those changes?

7. Thinking generally, is there anything you wish was different about your friendships?

8. Is there anything you'd like to tell me about your friendships that I haven't already asked?

Community

9. Shifting gears, tell me a little about [River City]. How would you describe it? Has it changed at all in the time you've been here? If so, how so?

10. Do you feel that [River City] is a welcoming place for you? A comfortable place? What makes for a welcoming place to live, work, socialize? Comfortable? What makes for an uncomfortable or unwelcoming place?

11. Is participating in a community important to you? Why or why not?
    a. If so, how would you describe your community? Who is included in this community?
    b. Are all of your friends part of this community, or no?
    c. How do you participate in this community? What do you do? Are there things you don't do that you wish you did? Is it easy or hard to connect with your community?
    d. Has this community changed at all in the time you've been here? If so, how, and how do you feel about these changes?

12. Are there other communities that are important to you? Please describe them.

13. Thinking about LGBTQ community more generally, would you say there is an LGBTQ community here? Why or why not, do you think? If so, how would you describe LGBTQ community in [River City]? How do you know it exists?
    a. How important is LGBTQ community to you? Why?
    b. Do you participate in an LGBTQ community in [River City]? If so, why, and how? If not, why not?
    c. Are there times you've felt that you really should participate in LGBTQ community, but you didn't? When? Why?
    d. Where do LGBTQ people go to meet friends in [River City]? Where do they go to find romantic or sexual partners? How do LGBTQ people connect with other LGBTQ people?
    e. How unified is LGBTQ community in [River City]? Can you explain?

14. Thinking about what you know of LGBTQ people generally, how important do you think LGBTQ community is to LGBTQ people these days in [River City]? Why?
15. Some researchers say that we are now living in a post-gay moment in which LGBTQ communities are less central to LGBTQ life. What are your thoughts on that?
16. Is there anything about LGBTQ community or community in [River City] that you'd like to share with me that I haven't asked about?

Concluding Questions
17. Are there any of your friendships that make you feel more connected to your community? To LGBTQ community? If so, how so? If not, what do you think about that?
18. Are there any aspects of your friendships, your community, or your life that I haven't asked you about that you think I should know?
19. Do you have any questions for me?
20. May I contact any of your friends for an interview?
21. Do you consent to being observed in one or two friendship interactions? This portion of the project is optional.
22. Please complete the demographic questionnaire.

APPENDIX B

Terminology

My students constantly educate me about new LGBTQ terminology, as new gender and sexual identity terms emerge seemingly on a daily basis. At the time of my research, they referenced tumblr as their primary, online, and hyperdynamic encyclopedia of evolving terminology *and* frameworks in which to locate new terms. As just one example, one tumblr page proposes a matrix of "six types of attraction" to which more than 70 terms can be added as prefixes and suffixes (Genderfluid Support n.d.). This list of terms, and its organizational matrix, is likely already outdated. In the more than 15 Safe Zone trainings I conducted with groups of students, staff, faculty, and community members (notably, not part of my research), this proliferation of terminology was a source of anxiety and frustration, especially for those new to LGBTQ terminology. Academics, even those who study gender and sexuality, share these anxieties. In one example, a new call for proposals from the *Journal of Homosexuality* (a title the latter portion of which would no doubt make my students wince) for a special issue on terminology notes that, "for some, the ongoing proliferation of previously unnamed sex, gender, and sexuality categories may feel like just a bit 'too much,' while for others it may feel like finally 'almost enough'" (*Journal of Homosexuality* 2017).

As we might expect, sociologists have been considering the question of LGBTQ terminology for some time, exploring, for example, the best approaches to using sex, gender, and sexuality terminology in survey research (Bauer et al. 2017; Westbrook and Saperstein 2015). Some of the best, meaning most inclusive, approaches allow for maximum flexibility, enabling participants to name the terms they feel best describe their identities. While such an approach may not be feasible for larger-scale studies, my sample was small enough to allow open-ended demographic questions. Wherever possible, I used the terms that participants wrote on their demographic surveys or stated over the course of our interviews in order to remain faithful to participants' self-understandings.

This process was imperfect, and, as quickly as terms become outdated on the internet, many I've used in this book are already outdated, as categorical terms I've used to describe some participants are already changing, and participants' own identities have changed, as I explained in the conclusion. In this moment of terminology flux, however, I wanted to explain how I've used some terms that may seem unclear, or grammatically incorrect, or simply confusing to the LGBTQ terminology novice. My aim in this appendix is also to share some of the perhaps overly simplistic tools I use in teaching about gender and sexuality and explain why I believe we need to continually reexamine how we connect these two types of identity.

I note in my teaching that gender and sexuality are not the same thing. This is an obvious claim that quickly becomes confusing to students and training participants alike when I state that a person can be transgender and straight. I initially used "The Genderbread Person" (Killerman 2020) as a helpful, if cartoonish, shorthand way of distinguishing sex, sexuality ("attraction" in this diagram), gender identity, and gender expression. This approach is not unproblematic, as some have suggested that this diagram is plagiarized (cisnormativity 2016), but it's a useful first step. As sociologists, we, too, need to grow more accustomed to thinking of gender and sexuality as separate, but related, concepts. This is not a new claim; researchers have been arguing for this conceptual distinction at least since the 1960s, but this line of thinking poses challenges for sociologists.

For example, in counting the number of "LGBTQ friends," a question about how to count individuals with multiple identities within the acronym emerges. How should I "count" a friend who is both a transgender woman and a lesbian? Should I count cisgender gay men and lesbians as allies for transgender and genderqueer or nonbinary participants? In my context, I avoid these questions by discussing non-LGBTQ allies only, in the interest of simplicity (and, to be frank, a small sample), but I also highlight research that challenges this oversimplification.

I use the term "transgender" to refer to people whose present gender identity does not align with their gender assigned at birth. However, it seems to me that the term "transgender" is also shifting, meaning that it's increasingly being used by people who are interested in transitioning in some way (surgically, hormonally, or aesthetically). Although I have little evidence to back this up beyond my own observations in my social networks, I suspect that terms like "nonbinary" and "genderqueer" are becoming increasingly popular, especially among young people who identify under the very broad, but still constricting LGBTQ umbrella. The term "nonbinary" generally refers to people whose gender identity does not adhere to a strict female/male or feminine/masculine binary, while "genderqueer" is a broader term encompassing a range of non-normative gender identities and expressions. In this book, I have used them somewhat interchangeably, but I acknowledge here that this is not fully accurate.

The term "cisgender" is often experienced as quite shocking to my students and training participants, many of whom are learning that such a term applies to them for the first time. Cisgender refers to people whose present gender identity aligns with their gender assigned at birth. Statistically, most people in the world are cisgender, and it is a useful concept because it describes a previously unnamed "norm," much like the relationship between the terms heterosexual/straight and homosexual/gay/lesbian.

I use the gender-neutral pronoun "they" and related versions like "themself" to refer to some participants, a usage that is becoming increasingly common, even accepted by major publications (Brooks 2017; Hess 2016). Other gender-neutral pronouns have been proposed, and are occasionally used, even on the most rural college campuses (like the one at which I taught during my research). One tool I often suggest to students and training participants who are unfamiliar with how to use gender-neutral pronouns is the aptly named practicewithpronouns.com, a website that allows users to practice filling in sentences pulled from the fictional podcast series *Welcome to Night Vale* with a small sample of such pronouns.

"Queer" should be distinguished from "genderqueer" in that the latter term refers to gender identity and expression, while the former primarily (although not exclusively) refers to sexual orientation, at least in the way my participants used it. Queer is a surprisingly gendered term, among my participants, as those who used it tended to be cisgender women. I wonder whether "queer" is shifting as a distinctly gendered term to be used by women more than men. Perhaps, in some ways, "queer" is actually the new "lesbian." On the other hand, there is some debate about the meaning of queer as a term that signals critique of overarching systems and structures, as it was intended when it was first used by groups like Queer Nation in the 1990s. Some argue that the term queer is an all-purpose, generally inclusive term that may, at its extremes, actually include straight people, a usage that seems more normative than transgressive (Orne 2017; Ryan 2016; Wortham 2016).

One final note: it behooves us, as researchers, as sociologists, and, critically, as teachers, to engage with this evolving terminology in an ongoing way. It matters to our students, and it affects their ability to connect and learn in the classroom. It also affects the accuracy and long-term impact of our research. I will share two final bits of advice I offer in my trainings, specifically for those who teach. First, *ask* your students about their names and pronouns, not publicly, because that practice can effectively "out" students on the first day of classes. I use a short first-day survey to ask students to share their names and pronouns privately, which even non-LGBTQ students use to provide preferred names like nicknames. I also ask in my survey what students want me to do if someone uses the wrong pronoun to refer to them, effectively misgendering them. This question serves a dual purpose: it allows students a bit more control over how their pronouns are used (and corrected) in the classroom, and my hope is that it provides a moment of pause and, perhaps, education for those who are not often misgendered in day-to-day life. Finally, be curious about your students' lives, and become accustomed to the idea of being wrong. I find that demonstrating this open curiosity, without putting marginalized students on the spot to explain their identities, and modeling how to shift my thinking in a moment of new information (about terminology, for example) are excellent ways to illustrate sociological thinking and, more generally, just good teaching.

APPENDIX C

Participants' Descriptive Statistics

TABLE C.1A

	n	% of Sample
Gender		
Cisgender women	27	50.0%
Cisgender men	16	29.6%
Genderqueer/nonbinary persons	5	9.3%
Transgender women	4	7.4%
Transgender men	2	3.7%
Sexual orientation		
Straight	15	27.8%
Gay	14	25.9%
Lesbian	10	18.5%
Queer	8	14.8%
Bisexual	6	11.1%
Asexual	1	1.9%
Race		
White	46	85.2%
Multiracial	3	5.6%
Asian American	2	3.7%
Black	2	3.7%
Hispanic	1	1.9%
Age		
18–20	5	9.3%
21–25	10	18.5%
26–30	8	14.8%
31–35	7	13.0%

TABLE C.1A. *Continued*

	n	% of Sample
Age		
36–40	7	13.0%
41–45	2	3.7%
46–50	9	16.7%
51–55	3	5.6%
56–60	3	5.6%

TABLE C.1B

Residence	n	% of Sample
River City	43	79.6%
Nearby town	9	16.7%
Distant state	2	3.7%
Length of time at residence (years)		
<1	10	18.5%
1–5	10	18.5%
6–10	8	14.8%
11–15	6	11.1%
16–20	4	7.4%
21–25	8	14.8%
26+	8	14.8%
Partnered?		
Yes	28	51.9%
No	26	48.1%

TABLE C.1C

	n	% of Sample
Education level		
High school	7	13.0%
Some college	11	20.4%
Associate's degree	1	1.9%
Bachelor's degree	16	29.6%
Master's degree	14	25.9%
Law degree	1	1.9%
Doctorate	3	5.6%
(blank)	1	1.9%
Employed?		
Yes	46	85.2%
No	7	13.0%
(blank)	1	1.9%
Salary		
1–10K	9	16.7%
10K–20K	8	14.8%
20K–30K	8	14.8%
30K–40K	6	11.1%
40K–50K	3	5.6%
50K–75K	10	18.5%
75K+	3	5.6%
(blank)	7	13.0%

APPENDIX D

Reflections on Methodology

It seems fitting that I have been thinking ambivalently about my research methods and about my connection to River City, as a temporary community member. There are some ways I might be seen as a community insider, and, by some measures, I am clearly an outsider. I hold both of these feelings in tension.

First, along the dimension of nationality and sovereignty, I, along with the vast majority of River Citizens, am an outsider in the Midwest and in the nation we call the United States. We are all products of settler colonialism, and we occupy lands stolen from, yet still shaped by, Indigenous people. I share others' skepticism that this kind of simple "land acknowledgment" is especially useful in generating broad-based social change (Asher et al. 2018), and writing about land acknowledgments, especially in higher education settings (Red Shirt-Shaw 2020), highlights the kinds of institutional shifts that are essential to work toward more just futures for Indigenous people. While I cannot disclose the specific histories of Native Midwesterners in and around River City without breaking anonymity, I can encourage readers and researchers to take specific actions to support "land back" initiatives, to examine their research methods in relation to the lands they and their participants occupy, and to learn about their communities' Indigenous histories.

Other dimensions of community and identity mark me as a River City outsider as well. I did not grow up in River City, and my middle-class family was not employed in the industries that generated its economic success and decline in the mid-20th to 21st century. While I grew to know and love its landscapes, I did not grow up within them, and I do not share everyday experiences of marginalization felt by my Black, Indigenous, and People of Color (BIPOC) and working-class participants. Perhaps most damningly, I left River City, departing for a job opportunity in another state. I feel this difference quite acutely, especially when reviewing Karen's description of River City's LGBTQ community and the need for people to *stay*.

As an insider, my Midwestern parents shaped my (in some ways) culturally Midwestern childhood, even as I grew up in a small town on the East Coast. I am an LGBTQ community member, a queer person on the nonbinary spectrum, and someone whose gender and sexual identities do not fall neatly into the binaries that also constricted my participants' lives. I lived in River City for three years and, along with my partner and, eventually, tiny son, became integrated into professional, nonprofit, and activist networks there. I developed dear friendships I maintain probably not as well as I would like. My partner and I fit somewhat neatly into River City's local norms, especially in regard to race (we're both white), partnership status, class, and at least knowledge of the predominant religion.

This ambivalent status has shaped how I view River City and, thus, my research findings. This reality is unavoidable, and, in my view, working toward researcher objectivity is neither a possible nor a desirable task. Debates within sociology about the purported objectivity of ethnographic and interview research are ongoing, and I often find myself wondering how to approach these debates with a framework of ambivalence, rather than resolution (Brim and Ghaziani 2016; Compton, Meadow, and Schilt 2018). Indeed, all research with humans requires an ambivalent approach. Throughout the research process, I have aimed to both honestly represent my participants' perspectives and, sometimes painfully, locate these perspectives within broader systems of inequality. As a former mentor suggested, perhaps this approach has made me "too nice" to my participants, but I hope that I have been, more accurately, ambivalently kind.

I approached River City's LGBTQ community with a sense of curiosity and interest in the everyday lives of my participants. As I noted in the introduction, and in line with other researchers (Abelson 2019; Brown-Saracino 2017; Gray 2009), traditional methods of recruitment were challenging in a community context that relies on relationships and word-of-mouth. I was initially uncertain about whether community members would want to talk to someone like me, an obvious blue-haired outsider. These fears were informed by both my learned stereotypes and my lived experience having grown up in a small town and having spent many months living in rural Midwestern towns as a child. My first surprise was how warmly I felt welcomed into LGBTQ communities and how generous community members were in sharing their stories. I tried to offer what is inadequately described as "compensation" for this work, and for these stories, both by paying participants for their time and by volunteering at LGBTQ events in various capacities. At the end of the day, if a participant asked me to support them or their work within LGBTQ community, I did my best to make it happen. A question remains, for me, about whether I've offered as much to participants, and to River City, as they have offered to me.

A final note about my participant sample: snowball sampling is limited in important ways (Brown-Saracino 2017) and, yet, I aimed to talk with, and to observe, a broad range of people with identities that might capture the range of LGBTQ people (and allies) in River City. I am certain I did not fully achieve this task, nor is such a task necessarily achievable, even in a small city like River City. And for reasons explained in the introduction and chapter 1, arriving at a truly "representative sample" of LGBTQ River Citizens is neither possible nor desirable. I could have chosen to focus specifically on a subpopulation of LGBTQ people in River City, for example, gay men, or trans youth, or queer women and nonbinary people. Had I focused on one of these groups, I might have been able to respond in more depth to some of the research generated recently by my excellent colleagues (for example, exploring the emerging "sexy community" [Orne 2017] among queer women and nonbinary people, an area of research I believe should be more deeply explored). Given the dearth of research on LGBTQ communities in small cities, sampling for range felt like a better starting point. Yet the insights I've gained (and, by now, hopefully you have, too) from this research raise questions stemming from a range of experiences shared by LGBTQ people, questions about River City as a "case" (Small 2009), and questions that might be applied to similar (and different) small cities as well as larger cities and smaller towns.

NOTES

INTRODUCTION

1 Kai uses the gender-neutral pronouns "they" and "them." I use pseudonyms, such
as "River City," for place-names in order to protect participants' identities.

2 I use the term "allies" here to refer to straight and/or cisgender River Citizens
who support their LGBTQ family and friends. I used the language "allies"
while recruiting participants, and allies who responded to my calls for participation were clear about the ways they engaged in that support, which I detail
further, along with its limitations, in chapter 5. However, it is important to
note that, as with all identity terms, "allies" refers to an identity claimed in a
particular moment; at least one of my participants who identified as an ally at
the time of our interview has subsequently come out as an LGBTQ community
member.

3 As I note in appendix B, gender terminology is perpetually changing, and
"Latinx" was considered a marginally more inclusive (gender-neutral) term than
"Latino" and "Latin@" at the time of my research. More recently, activists and
scholars have debated the limitations of the term "Latinx" and have proposed
terms more concretely grounded in Spanish grammar, such as "Latine." Editorials
on this debate abound, and I'd recommend Blas (2019), Mochkofsky (2020), and
Pereira (2021).

4 Although not directly addressed here, research on people who engage in same-sex
sexual behavior but refuse gay or lesbian identities further examines the LGBQ
boundary-making process. Most relevant to the context of River City is Silva's
(2021) work on sexual flexibility, including "bud-sex," among self-identified
straight men in rural communities and Budnick's (2016) research on same-gender
sexuality among working-class women. See also Bridges (2014), Carrillo and
Hoffman (2018), Duffin (2016), and Silva (2017, 2019).

5 The county that encompasses River City is designated as a Metropolitan Statistical
Area (Office of Management and Budget 2010), and River City is the main Urban-
ized Area within it (US Census Bureau 2019). However, as researchers note (Johnson and Lichter 2020; Lichter and Brown 2011; Woods 2009), distinctions between
rural, urban, suburban, exurban, and other designations are increasingly blurry,
especially as rural and urban areas are increasingly interconnected. Furthermore,
there is no clear consensus about what constitutes "small cities," especially in
relation to size, cultural context, and proximity to larger urban centers (Forstie

2020). In my research, River City represents a type of small city that, by statistical and symbolic measures, resides at the boundary between rural and urban, distinct from small cities that are folded into urban agglomerations. For example, River City County receives the smallest urban designation according to two key measures of rurality; these measures are helpfully summarized in Vanderboom and Madigan (2007). Four of its six neighboring counties are designated by Office of Management and Budget measures as "nonmetropolitan" (one is micropolitan and one is metropolitan). River City's urban and rural characteristics are further discussed in chapter 1.

6 The term "cisgender" means that one's current gender identity matches their gender assigned at birth.

7 Some participants belong to multiple categories, as in, for example, a transgender woman who identifies as a lesbian.

CHAPTER 1. RIVER CITY

1 Social scientists often define community formations like "rural" and "urban" based on characteristics like population density and proximity to other cities. For more on the boundaries of what "counts" as rural, see Gray et al. (2016); Johnson and Lichter (2020); Lichter and Brown (2011); and Woods (2009).

2 "Farm and fleet" stores are big-box retail stores that sell a mix of farm equipment, farm animal and pet supplies, home supplies, clothes, boots, snacks, and other sundries. They are typically found in cities and towns located in rural areas, and there may be more than one competing chain in any given city.

3 All participants' names and business names are pseudonyms.

CHAPTER 2. SHOULD I STAY OR SHOULD I GO?

1 While I cannot directly cite it without identifying River City, one book written by a sociologist examines precisely this kind of discourse in River City in the 1990s, and this author's analysis rings true to my research a quarter of a century later. A challenge with keeping River City anonymous is that I can't directly cite relevant data and analyses that would reveal River City's location, and a drawback with this approach is that underappreciated sociological research (as in the book I've described here) remains in shadow.

2 "Stealth" or "going stealth" refers to the ongoing process of not revealing one's transgender identity, for example, in the workplace (Schilt 2011).

CHAPTER 3. OUT, BUT NOT TOO OUT

1 I use pseudonyms for place-names to protect participants' identities.

2 The second organization is River City Trans, which, unlike River City Collective, names the identity it supports in the organization title. River City Trans is an organization staffed entirely by Karen, a transgender woman who has become the most visible face of transgender River Citizens in local, regional, and national contexts.

3 In contrast, newly formed River City Pride's general description is focused on "LGBTQ+ individuals" and does not mention allies, although membership is explicitly open to allies who meet membership criteria (like attending an educational training, as noted in the "About" page on their website).

4 I attended six drag shows in four separate venues during my time in River City.

CHAPTER 4. WHAT DO YOU MEAN YOUR GAY FRIEND?

1 It is important to note here that the term "friendship" was intentionally undefined in this friendship mapping exercise, and, as a result, maps varied in terms of friends' closeness to participants. Findings from friendship mapping should be seen as tentative, although it is also worth noting that participants generally did distinguish between close and more distant friends on their maps. Additional research is needed to further refine these preliminary results.

2 While the focus of my research is shared gender and sexual identities, the friendship talk and friendship maps of participants suggest that friendship homophily—the idea that "birds of a feather flock together" (McPherson, Smith-Lovin, and Cook 2001)—was evident in terms of race and class.

3 For more on LGBTQ compartmentalization within friendship networks, see Ueno et al. (2012).

4 The sample examined in these tables is small, but noteworthy, and is meant to prompt examination of these trends at a larger scale, or in a comparative context (Small 2009).

5 While I do not address LGBTQ participants' likelihood of having friendships that cross lines of race in this chapter, my data from friendship mapping suggest a number of questions about friendship and identity intersections in a largely white, fairly conservative city. In brief, racial homophily is maintained in friendships even for LGBTQ participants, some of who shared, somewhat shamefacedly, that they had no friends of color.

6 Here, too, I use "they" as a gender-neutral pronoun. Kai identified as a lesbian at the time of this interview, and they later identified as a trans man, shifting to "he," "him," and "his" pronouns. Kai is beginning to use "they," "them," and "their" pronouns at the time of this writing, and I use the pronoun "they" to more accurately represent the complexity of their identity, as someone who can identify as both a trans man and as a lesbian.

7 As I indicated before, the term "cisgender" means that one's gender identity matches the gender assigned at birth. In this chapter, following my participants' identities, I distinguish gender from sexual orientation. For example, some participants identified as transgender and straight and were explicitly critical of being included in the LGBTQ acronym or LGBTQ community. In another example, not all lesbian-identified participants were cisgender women; Karen, for example, is a transgender woman who identifies as a lesbian. The complexity of this research suggests a need to more carefully unpack the LGBTQ acronym and its uses and limitations in research on gender and sexuality.

CHAPTER 5. STRAIGHT WOMAN IN A GAY MAN'S WORLD
1 For other analyses of diversity talk in practice, see Ahmed (2012) and Brink-Danan (2015).
2 *Obergefell v. Hodges* is the 2015 US Supreme Court decision guaranteeing the right to marry for same-sex couples.
3 Center for Multicultural Community website, accessed May 29, 2017.
4 There is some evidence to suggest that activism supporting lesbians and trans men is relatively invisible, in River City. For example, River City Collective was led by gay men and one transgender woman, and social events have been attended almost exclusively by gay men.

CHAPTER 6. "THERE'S VARYING DEGREES OF FRIENDSHIP IN HERE"
1 An important caveat here is that a change in tumblr's policies about what kinds of sexuality-related content can be shared on the platform has significantly curtailed the kinds of communities that are possible within and across the platform.
2 While participants referred to a range of communities in their discussions of friendships and community, my focus in this chapter is on participants' discussion of LGBTQ community specifically.

CONCLUSION
1 As noted in the introduction and chapters 1 and 2, there is evidence to suggest that River City is white supremacist in at least two ways. First, River City is uniquely white supremacist, demonstrated in the kinds of rhetoric, events, and experiences documented in this book, part of a longer history of white supremacism that is specific to River City's history. This fact is further documented in research that cannot be named in this book without revealing River City's location. Second, River City's white supremacy is part of a larger project of settler colonialism and white supremacy that researchers have identified in similar small cities and rural contexts (Abelson 2019; Eaves 2017).

REFERENCES

Abelson, Miriam. 2019. *Men in Place: Trans Masculinity, Race, and Sexuality in America*. Minneapolis: University of Minnesota Press.

Adams, Rebecca G., and Graham Allan, eds. 1999. *Placing Friendship in Context*. New York: Cambridge University Press.

Adeyemi, Kemi, Kareem Khubchandani, and Ramon Rivera-Servera. 2021. *Queer Nightlife*. Ann Arbor: University of Michigan Press.

Ahmed, Sara. 2012. *On Being Included: Racism and Diversity in Institutional Life*. Durham, NC: Duke University Press.

Allan, Graham. 1979. *A Sociology of Friendship and Kinship*. London: Unwin Hyman.

———. 1990. *Friendship: Developing a Sociological Perspective*. Boulder, CO: Westview.

———. 1998. "Friendship, Sociology and Social Structure." *Journal of Social and Personal Relationships* 15(5):685–702.

———. 2008. "Flexibility, Friendship, and Family." *Personal Relationships* 15(1):1–16.

———. 2009. "Review Essay: Research on Friendship." *Journal of Family Theory and Review* 1(4):223–27.

Allen, Samantha. 2020. *Real Queer America: LGBT Stories from Red States*. New York: Back Bay Books.

Anderson, Benedict. 2006. *Imagined Communities: Reflections on the Origin and Spread of Nationalism*. London: Verso.

Anthony, Amanda Koontz, and Janice McCabe. 2015. "Friendship Talk as Identity Work: Defining the Self through Friend Relationships." *Symbolic Interaction* 38(1):64–82.

Anzaldúa, Gloria. 1999. *Borderlands/La Frontera: The New Mestiza*. San Francisco: Aunt Lute Books.

Armstrong, Elizabeth A. 2002. *Forging Gay Identities: Organizing Sexuality in San Francisco, 1950–1994*. Chicago: University of Chicago Press.

Armstrong, Elizabeth A., and Suzanna M. Crage. 2006. "Movements and Memory: The Making of the Stonewall Myth." *American Sociological Review* 71(5):724–51.

Aronson, Jane. 1998. "Lesbians Giving and Receiving Care: Stretching Conceptualizations of Caring and Community." *Women's Studies International Forum* 21(5):505–19.

Asher, Lila, Joe Curnow, and Amil Davis. 2018. "The Limits of Settlers' Territorial Acknowledgments." *Curriculum Inquiry* 48(3):316–34.

Bailey, Marlon M., and Rashad Shabazz. 2014. "Gender and Sexual Geographies of Blackness: New Black Cartographies of Resistance and Survival (Part 2)." *Gender, Place and Culture* 21(4):449–52.

Barth, Jay, L. Marvin Overby, and Scott H. Huffmon. 2009. "Community Context, Personal Contact, and Support for an Anti–Gay Rights Referendum." *Political Research Quarterly* 62(2):355–65.

Battle, Juan, and Colin Ashley. 2008. "Intersectionality, Heteronormativity, and Black Lesbian, Gay, Bisexual, and Transgender (LGBT) Families." *Black Women, Gender + Families* 2(1):1–24.

Battle, Juan, Robert B. Peterson, Nicole Lucas, and Sheldon Applewhite. 2017. "Their Own Received Them Not: Black LGBT Feelings of Connectedness." *Journal of Black Sexuality and Relationships* 4(2):45–72.

Bauer, Greta R., Jessica Braimoh, Ayden I. Scheim, and Christoffer Dharma. 2017. "Transgender-Inclusive Measures of Sex/Gender for Population Surveys: Mixed-Methods Evaluation and Recommendations." *PLOS ONE* 12(5):e0178043.

Baumle, Amanda K., D'Lane Compton, and Dudley L. Poston Jr. 2009. *Same-Sex Partners: The Social Demography of Sexual Orientation.* Albany: State University of New York Press.

Beauchamp, Toby. 2018. *Going Stealth: Transgender Politics and US Surveillance Practices.* Durham, NC: Duke University Press.

Becker, Howard S. 1963. *Outsiders: Studies in the Sociology of Deviance.* Oxford: Free Press Glencoe.

Bell, David, and Gill Valentine. 1995. "Queer Country: Rural Lesbian and Gay Lives." *Journal of Rural Studies* 11(2):113–22.

Bell, Joyce M., and Douglas Hartmann. 2007. "Diversity in Everyday Discourse: The Cultural Ambiguities and Consequences of 'Happy Talk.'" *American Sociological Review* 72(6):895–914.

Bell, Wendell, and Marion D. Boat. 1957. "Urban Neighborhoods and Informal Social Relations." *American Journal of Sociology* 62(4):391–98.

Bernstein, Mary. 1997. "Celebration and Suppression: The Strategic Uses of Identity by the Lesbian and Gay Movement." *American Journal of Sociology* 103(3):531–65.

Bernstein, Mary, and Verta A. Taylor. 2013. *The Marrying Kind? Debating Same-Sex Marriage within the Lesbian and Gay Movement.* Minneapolis: University of Minnesota Press.

Blas, Terry. 2019. "'Latinx' Is Growing in Popularity. I Made a Comic to Help You Understand Why." *Vox.* Retrieved July 15, 2021. www.vox.com.

Blatterer, H. 2015. *Everyday Friendships: Intimacy as Freedom in a Complex World.* New York: Palgrave Macmillan.

Bondi, Liz. 2004. "10th Anniversary Address for a Feminist Geography of Ambivalence." *Gender, Place and Culture* 11(1):3–15.

Bonilla-Silva, Eduardo. 2006. *Racism without Racists: Color-Blind Racism and the Persistence of Racial Inequality in the United States.* Lanham, MD: Rowman and Littlefield.

Bourdieu, Pierre. 1986. *Distinction: A Social Critique of the Judgement of Taste.* London: Routledge.

Brekhus, Wayne. 2003. *Peacocks, Chameleons, Centaurs: Gay Suburbia and the Grammar of Social Identity.* Chicago: University of Chicago Press.

Brennan, Niall, and David Gudelunas, eds. 2017. *RuPaul's Drag Race and the Shifting Visibility of Drag Culture: The Boundaries of Reality TV*. New York: Palgrave Macmillan.

Bridges, Tristan. 2010. "Men Just Weren't Made to Do This: Performances of Drag at 'Walk a Mile in Her Shoes' Marches." *Gender and Society* 24(1):5–30.

———. 2014. "A Very 'Gay' Straight? Hybrid Masculinities, Sexual Aesthetics, and the Changing Relationship between Masculinity and Homophobia." *Gender and Society* 28(1):58–82.

Brim, Matt, and Amin Ghaziani. 2016. "Introduction: Queer Methods." *WSQ: Women's Studies Quarterly* 44(3):14–27.

Brink-Danan, Marcy. 2015. "Value and Meaning: Paradoxes of Religious Diversity Talk as Globalized Expertise." *Language and Communication* 44:44–58.

Broad, K. L. 2002. "GLB + T? Gender/Sexuality Movements and Transgender Collective Identity (De)Constructions." *International Journal of Sexuality and Gender Studies* 7(4):241–64.

———. 2011. "Coming out for Parents, Families and Friends of Lesbians and Gays: From Support Group Grieving to Love Advocacy." *Sexualities* 14(4):399–415.

Broad, K. L., Helena Alden, Dana Berkowitz, and Maura Ryan. 2008. "Activist Parenting and GLBTQ Families." *Journal of GLBT Family Studies* 4(4):499–520.

Brodyn, Adriana, and Amin Ghaziani. 2021. "Performative Progressiveness: Accounting for New Forms of Inequality in the Gayborhood." Pp. 15–44 in *The Gayborhood: From Sexual Liberation to Cosmopolitan Spectacle*. Lanham, MD: Lexington Books.

Brooks, Raillan. 2017. "'He,' 'She,' 'They' and Us." *New York Times*, April 5. Retrieved May 31, 2017. www.nytimes.com.

Browne, Kath. 2009. "Imagining Cities, Living the Other: Between the Gay Urban Idyll and Rural Lesbian Lives." *Open Geography Journal* 1(1):25–32.

Brown-Saracino, Japonica. 2011. "From the Lesbian Ghetto to Ambient Community: The Perceived Costs and Benefits of Integration for Community." *Social Problems* 58(3):361–88.

———. 2015. "How Places Shape Identity: The Origins of Distinctive LBQ Identities in Four Small US Cities." *American Journal of Sociology* 121(1):1–63.

———. 2017. *How Places Make Us: Novel LBQ Identities in Four Small Cities*. Chicago: University of Chicago Press.

Budnick, Jamie. 2016. "'Straight Girls Kissing'? Understanding Same-Gender Sexuality beyond the Elite College Campus." *Gender and Society* 30(5):745–68.

Burgess, Elisabeth O., and Dawn M. Baunach. 2014. "Heterosexual Allies? Understanding Heterosexuals' Alliance with the Gay Community." *Sexuality and Culture* 18(4):936–58.

Butler, Judith. 2002. *Antigone's Claim*. New York: Columbia University Press.

Carrillo, Héctor. 2017. *Pathways of Desire: The Sexual Migration of Mexican Gay Men*. Chicago: University of Chicago Press.

Carrillo, Héctor, and Amanda Hoffman. 2018. "'Straight with a Pinch of Bi': The Construction of Heterosexuality as an Elastic Category among Adult US Men." *Sexualities* 21(1–2):90–108.

Carrington, Christopher. 1999. *No Place like Home: Relationships and Family Life among Lesbians and Gay Men*. Chicago: University of Chicago Press.

Casey, Mark. 2004. "De-dyking Queer Space(s): Heterosexual Female Visibility in Gay and Lesbian Spaces." *Sexualities* 7(4):446–61.

Center for Multicultural Community. 2016. "Center for Multicultural Community: About Us." Website accessed July 31, 2016.

Chauncey, George. 1995. *Gay New York: Gender, Urban Culture, and the Making of the Gay Male World, 1890–1940*. New York: Basic Books.

cisnormativity. 2016. "The Genderbread Plagiarist." Retrieved January 25, 2016. https://storify.com/cisnormativity/the-genderbread-plagiarist.

Collard, James. 1998. "Leaving the Gay Ghetto." *Newsweek*, August 17, 53.

Collins, Randall. 2004. *Interaction Ritual Chains*. Princeton, NJ: Princeton University Press.

Comerford, Susan A., M. Maxwell Henson-Stroud, Corbett Sionainn, and Elizabeth Wheeler. 2004. "Crone Songs: Voices of Lesbian Elders on Aging in a Rural Environment." *Affilia* 19(4):418–36.

Compton, D'Lane R., Tey Meadow, and Kristen Schilt, eds. 2018. *Other, Please Specify: Queer Methods in Sociology*. Berkeley: University of California Press.

Connell, Raewyn. 2008. *Southern Theory: The Global Dynamics of Knowledge in Social Science*. London: Allen and Unwin.

Connidis, Ingrid Arnet, and Julie Ann McMullin. 2002. "Sociological Ambivalence and Family Ties: A Critical Perspective." *Journal of Marriage and Family* 64(3):558–67.

Conrad, Ryan. 2014. *Against Equality: Queer Revolution, Not Mere Inclusion*. Edinburgh, UK: AK Press.

Coser, Rose Laub. 1966. "Role Distance, Sociological Ambivalence, and Transitional Status Systems." *American Journal of Sociology* 72(2):173–87.

Cramer, Katherine J. 2017. "The Grievances of the White Working Class." *Contexts* 16(2):20–22.

Crenshaw, Kimberlé. 1995. "Mapping the Margins: Intersectionality, Identity Politics and Violence against Women of Color." Pp. 357–83 in *Critical Race Theory: The Key Writings That Formed the Movement*, edited by K. Crenshaw, N. Gotanda, G. Peller, and K. Thomas. New York: New Press.

Cronin, Anne M. 2015. "Gendering Friendship: Couple Culture, Heteronormativity and the Production of Gender." *Sociology* 49(6):1167–82.

D'Augelli, Anthony R., and Mary M. Hart. 1987. "Gay Women, Men, and Families in Rural Settings: Toward the Development of Helping Communities." *American Journal of Community Psychology* 15(1):79–93.

Dean, James Joseph. 2014. *Straights: Heterosexuality in Post-Closeted Culture*. New York: New York University Press.

DeFilippis, Joseph, Michael W. Yarbrough, and Angela Jones, eds. 2018. *Queer Activism after Marriage Equality*. New York: Routledge.

D'Emilio, John. 1998. *Sexual Politics, Sexual Communities: The Making of a Homosexual Minority in the United States, 1940–1970*. Chicago: University of Chicago Press.

Doan, Long, Annalise Loehr, and Lisa R. Miller. 2014. "Formal Rights and Informal Privileges for Same-Sex Couples: Evidence from a National Survey Experiment." *American Sociological Review* 79(6):1172–95.

Doan, Petra L. 2007. "Queers in the American City: Transgendered Perceptions of Urban Space." *Gender, Place and Culture* 14(1):57–74.

———. 2010. "The Tyranny of Gendered Spaces—Reflections from beyond the Gender Dichotomy." *Gender, Place and Culture* 17(5):635–54.

Duck, Steve W. 1994. *Meaningful Relationships: Talking, Sense, and Relating.* Thousand Oaks, CA: SAGE.

Duffin, Thomas P. 2016. "The Lowdown on the Down Low: Why Some Bisexually Active Men Choose to Self-Identify as Straight." *Journal of Bisexuality* 16(4):484–506.

Duggan, Lisa. 2004. "Equality, Inc." Pp. 43–66 in *The Twilight of Equality? Neoliberalism, Cultural Politics, and the Attack on Democracy.* New York: Beacon.

Duhigg, Julie M., Sharon S. Rostosky, Barry E. Gray, and Mary K. Wimsatt. 2010. "Development of Heterosexuals into Sexual-Minority Allies: A Qualitative Exploration." *Sexuality Research and Social Policy* 7(1):2–14.

Dykewomon, Elana. 2018. "The Caregiver and Her Friends." *Journal of Lesbian Studies* 22(1):94–101.

Easterbrook, Adam, Richard M. Carpiano, Brian C. Kelly, and Jeffrey T. Parsons. 2013. "The Personal Experience of Community among Urban Gay Men, Lesbians, and Bisexuals: Melting Pot or Mosaic?" *Social Science Quarterly* 95(3):682–700.

Eaves, LaToya E. 2017. "Black Geographic Possibilities: On a Queer Black South." *Southeastern Geographer* 57(1):80–95.

Eliasoph, Nina, and Paul Lichterman. 2003. "Culture in Interaction." *American Journal of Sociology* 108(4):735–94.

Eng, David L. 2010. *The Feeling of Kinship: Queer Liberalism and the Racialization of Intimacy.* Durham, NC: Duke University Press.

Esterberg, Kristin G. 1997. *Lesbian and Bisexual Identities: Constructing Communities, Constructing Selves.* Philadelphia: Temple University Press.

Eve, Michael. 2002. "Is Friendship a Sociological Topic?" *European Journal of Sociology / Archives Européennes de Sociologie / Europäisches Archiv Für Soziologie* 43(3):386–409.

Faderman, Lillian. 1991. *Odd Girls and Twilight Lovers: A History of Lesbian Life in Twentieth-Century America.* New York: Columbia University Press.

———. 2015. *The Gay Revolution: The Story of the Struggle.* New York: Simon and Schuster.

Fassinger, Ruth E., and Julie R. Arseneau. 2007. "'I'd Rather Get Wet Than Be under That Umbrella': Differentiating the Experiences and Identities of Lesbian, Gay, Bisexual, and Transgender People." Pp. 19–49 in *Handbook of Counseling and Psychotherapy with Lesbian, Gay, Bisexual, and Transgender Clients,* 2nd edition, edited by K. J. Bieschke, R. M. Perez, and K. A. DeBord. Washington, DC: American Psychological Association.

Ferguson, Roderick A. 2003. *Aberrations in Black: Toward a Queer of Color Critique.* Minneapolis: University of Minnesota Press.

Fine, Gary Alan. 2001. *Difficult Reputations: Collective Memories of the Evil, Inept, and Controversial*. Chicago: University of Chicago Press.

Fingerhut, Adam W. 2011. "Straight Allies: What Predicts Heterosexuals' Alliance with the LGBT Community?" *Journal of Applied Social Psychology* 41(9):2230–48.

Fischer, Claude S. 1982a. *To Dwell among Friends: Personal Networks in Town and City*. Chicago: University of Chicago Press.

———. 1982b. "What Do We Mean by 'Friend'? An Inductive Study." *Social Networks* 3(4):287–306.

Forstie, Clare. 2018. "Ambivalently Post-lesbian: LBQ Friendships in the Rural Midwest." *Journal of Lesbian Studies* 22(1):54–66.

———. 2020. "Theory Making from the Middle: Researching LGBTQ Communities in Small Cities." *City and Community* 19(1):153–68.

Fuist, Todd Nicholas. 2017. "'It Just Always Seemed Like It Wasn't a Big Deal, Yet I Know for Some People They Really Struggle with It': LGBT Religious Identities in Context." *Journal for the Scientific Study of Religion* 55(4):770–86.

Galupo, M. Paz. 2007. "Friendship Patterns of Sexual Minority Individuals in Adulthood." *Journal of Social and Personal Relationships* 24(1):139–51.

Galupo, M. Paz, et al. 2014. "Transgender Friendship Experiences: Benefits and Barriers of Friendships across Gender Identity and Sexual Orientation." *Feminism and Psychology* 24(2):193–215.

García, Dalia I., Jennifer Gray-Stanley, and Jesus Ramirez-Valles. 2008. "'The Priest Obviously Doesn't Know That I'm Gay': The Religious and Spiritual Journeys of Latino Gay Men." *Journal of Homosexuality* 55(3):411–36.

Garcia, Jesus A. 2016. "Resisting Assimilation and Other Forms of Integration." *Sociology Compass* 10(6):468–76.

Gates, Gary J. 2013. "Geography of the LGBT Population." Pp. 229–42 in *International Handbook on the Demography of Sexuality*, International Handbooks of Population, edited by Amanda K. Baumle. Dordrecht, Netherlands: Springer.

Geertz, Clifford. 2002. "Thick Description: Toward an Interpretive Theory of Culture." Pp. 63–68 in *Cultural Sociology*, edited by L. Spillman. Hoboken, NJ: Wiley-Blackwell.

Genderfluid Support. n.d. "Orientation Master List." Retrieved May 31, 2017. http://genderfluidsupport.tumblr.com/orientations/.

Ghaziani, Amin. 2009. "An 'Amorphous Mist'? The Problem of Measurement in the Study of Culture." *Theory and Society* 38(6):581–612.

———. 2011. "Post-gay Collective Identity Construction." *Social Problems* 58(1):99–125.

———. 2014a. "Measuring Urban Sexual Cultures." *Theory and Society* 43(3):371–93.

———. 2014b. *There Goes the Gayborhood?* Princeton, NJ: Princeton University Press.

———. 2015. "Lesbian Geographies." *Contexts* 14(1):62–64.

———. 2019. "Cultural Archipelagos: New Directions in the Study of Sexuality and Space." *City and Community* 18(1):4–22.

Ghaziani, Amin, Verta Taylor, and Amy Stone. 2016. "Cycles of Sameness and Difference in LGBT Social Movements." *Annual Review of Sociology* 42(1):165–83.

Gillespie, Brian Joseph, David Frederick, Lexi Harari, and Christian Grov. 2015. "Homophily, Close Friendship, and Life Satisfaction among Gay, Lesbian, Heterosexual, and Bisexual Men and Women." *PLoS ONE* 10(6):1–16.

Goins, Marnel Niles. 2011. "Playing with Dialectics: Black Female Friendship Groups as a Homeplace." *Communication Studies* 62(5):531–46.

Gould, Deborah. 2001. "Rock the Boat, Don't Rock the Boat, Baby: Ambivalence and the Emergence of Militant AIDS Activism." Pp. 135–57 in *Passionate Politics: Emotions and Social Movements*, edited by J. Goodwin, J. M. Jasper, and F. Polletta. Chicago: University of Chicago Press.

Granovetter, Mark S. 1973. "The Strength of Weak Ties." *American Journal of Sociology* 78(6):1360–80.

Gray, Mary L. 2009. *Out in the Country: Youth, Media, and Queer Visibility in Rural America*. New York: New York University Press.

Gray, Mary L., Colin R. Johnson, and Brian J. Gilley, eds. 2016. *Queering the Countryside: New Frontiers in Rural Queer Studies*. New York: New York University Press.

Green, Adam Isaiah. 2002. "Gay but Not Queer: Toward a Post-queer Study of Sexuality." *Theory and Society* 31(4):521–45.

———. 2013. *Sexual Fields: Toward a Sociology of Collective Sexual Life*. Chicago: University of Chicago Press.

Greenberg, Daniel, Maxine Najle, Oyindamola Bola, and Robert P. Jones. 2019. "Fifty Years after Stonewall: Widespread Support for LGBT Issues—Findings from American Values Atlas 2018." Washington, DC.

Greene, Theodore. 2014. "Gay Neighborhoods and the Rights of the Vicarious Citizen." *City and Community* 13(2):99–118.

———. 2018. "Queer Street Families: Place-Making and Community among LGBT Youth of Color in Iconic Gay Neighborhoods." Pp. 168–81 in *Queer Families and Relationships after Marriage Equality*, edited by M. Yarbrough, A. Jones, and J. DeFilippis. New York: Routledge.

———. 2021. "The Whiteness of Queer Urban Placemaking." Pp. 143–60 in *The Gayborhood: From Sexual Liberation to Cosmopolitan Spectacle*. Lanham, MD: Lexington Books.

Griswold, Wendy. 2013. *Cultures and Societies in a Changing World*. Los Angeles: SAGE.

Halberstam, Judith. 2005. *In a Queer Time and Place: Transgender Bodies, Subcultural Lives*. New York: New York University Press.

Hall, Ruth L., and Michelle Fine. 2005. "The Stories We Tell: The Lives and Friendship of Two Older Black Lesbians." *Psychology of Women Quarterly* 29(2):177–87.

Hartless, Jaime. 2018. "Questionably Queer: Understanding Straight Presence in the Post-gay Bar." *Journal of Homosexuality* 66(8):1035–57.

Hess, Amanda. 2016. "Who's 'They'?" *New York Times*, March 29. Retrieved January 18, 2017. www.nytimes.com.

Hochschild, Arlie, and Anne Machung. 2003. *The Second Shift*. New York: Penguin.

Hochschild, Arlie Russell. 1979. "Emotion Work, Feeling Rules, and Social Structure." *American Journal of Sociology* 85(3):551–75.

hooks, bell. 2000. *Feminist Theory: From Margin to Center.* 2nd edition. Cambridge, MA: South End Press.

Hulko, Wendy, and Jessica Hovanes. 2018. "Intersectionality in the Lives of LGBTQ Youth: Identifying as LGBTQ and Finding Community in Small Cities and Rural Towns." *Journal of Homosexuality* 65(4):427–55.

Hunter, Albert. 1974. *Symbolic Communities: The Persistence and Change of Chicago's Local Communities.* Chicago: University of Chicago Press.

———. 1975. "The Loss of Community: An Empirical Test through Replication." *American Sociological Review* 40(5):537–52.

———. 2006. "Contemporary Conceptions of Community." Pp. 20–33 in *Handbook of Community Movements and Local Organizations,* edited by R. Cnaan and C. Milofsky. Hoboken, NJ: Blackwell.

Hunter, Marcus Anthony, and Zandria F. Robinson. 2018. *Chocolate Cities: The Black Map of American Life.* Berkeley: University of California Press.

Ingram, Gordon Brent, Anne-Marie Bouthillette, and Yolanda Retter. 1997. *Queers in Space: Communities, Public Places, Sites of Resistance.* Seattle, WA: Bay Press.

Izienicki, Hubert. 2017. "Catholics and Atheists: A Cross-Cultural Qualitative Analysis of Religious Identities among Gay Men." *Sociology of Religion* 78(3):263–88.

Jerolmack, Colin, and Shamus Khan. 2014. "Talk Is Cheap: Ethnography and the Attitudinal Fallacy." *Sociological Methods and Research* 43(2):178–209.

Jo, Bev. 1996. "Lesbian Friendships Create Lesbian Community." Pp. 288–91 in *Lesbian Friendships: For Ourselves and Each Other,* edited by J. S. Weinstock and E. Rothblum. New York: New York University Press.

Johnson, Colin R. 2013. *Just Queer Folks: Gender and Sexuality in Rural America.* Philadelphia: Temple University Press.

Johnson, J. L., and Amy L. Best. 2012. "Radical Normals: The Moral Career of Straight Parents as Public Advocates for Their Gay Children." *Symbolic Interaction* 35(3):321–39.

Johnson, Kenneth M., and Daniel T. Lichter. 2020. "Metropolitan Reclassification and the Urbanization of Rural America." *Demography* 57:1929–50.

Jones, Angela. 2013. "Introduction: Queer Utopias, Queer Futurity, and Potentiality in Quotidian Practice." Pp. 1–17 in *A Critical Inquiry into Queer Utopias, Palgrave Macmillan's Critical Studies in Gender, Sexuality, and Culture,* edited by A. Jones. New York: Palgrave Macmillan.

Joseph, Miranda. 2002. *Against the Romance of Community.* Minneapolis: University of Minnesota Press.

Journal of Homosexuality. 2017. "Submit Your Papers to This Special Issue on 'What's in a Name?'" Retrieved December 4, 2017. http://explore.tandfonline.com/cfp/ah/journal-of-homosexuality-call-for-paper.

Kampler, Benjamin, and Catherine Connell. 2018. "The Post-gay Debates: Competing Visions of the Future of Homosexualities." *Sociology Compass* 12(12):e12646.

Kazyak, Emily. 2012. "Midwest or Lesbian? Gender, Rurality, and Sexuality." *Gender and Society* 26(6):825–48.

Kennedy, Elizabeth Lapovsky, and Madeline D. Davis. 1993. *Boots of Leather, Slippers of Gold: The History of a Lesbian Community*. New York: Routledge.

Killerman, Sam. 2020. "The Genderbread Person version 3." Retrieved December 18, 2020. https://www.itspronouncedmetrosexual.com/2015/03/the-genderbread-person-v3/#sthash.nViuJa9E.dpbs.

Kirkey, Kenneth, and Ann Forsyth. 2001. "Men in the Valley: Gay Male Life on the Suburban-Rural Fringe." *Journal of Rural Studies* 17(4):421–41.

Korgen, Kathleen Odell. 2002. *Crossing the Racial Divide: Close Friendships between Black and White Americans*. Westport, CT: Praeger.

Lamont, Michèle, and Ann Swidler. 2014. "Methodological Pluralism and the Possibilities and Limits of Interviewing." *Qualitative Sociology* 37(2):153–71.

La Pelle, Nancy. 2004. "Simplifying Qualitative Data Analysis Using General Purpose Software Tools." *Field Methods* 16(1):85–108.

Lehr, Valerie. 1999. *Queer Family Values: Rethinking the Myth of the Nuclear Family*. Philadelphia: Temple University Press.

Levine, Martin P. 1979. "Gay Ghetto." *Journal of Homosexuality* 4(4):363–77.

Lichter, Daniel, and David Brown. 2011. "Rural America in an Urban Society: Changing Spatial and Social Boundaries." *Annual Review of Sociology* 37:565–92.

Logan, Laura S. 2013. "Status Homophily, Sexual Identity, and Lesbian Social Ties." *Journal of Homosexuality* 60(10):1494–519.

Love, Heather. 2009. *Feeling Backward: Loss and the Politics of Queer History*. Cambridge, MA: Harvard University Press.

Lüscher, Kurt. 2002. "Intergenerational Ambivalence: Further Steps in Theory and Research." *Journal of Marriage and Family* 64(3):585–93.

Lüscher, Kurt, and Andreas Hoff. 2013. "Intergenerational Ambivalence: Beyond Solidarity and Conflict." Pp. 39–63 in *Intergenerational Relations: European Perspectives on Family and Society*, edited by I. Albert and D. Ferring. Bristol, UK: Policy Press.

Lüscher, Kurt, and Karl Pillemer. 1998. "Intergenerational Ambivalence: A New Approach to the Study of Parent-Child Relations in Later Life." *Journal of Marriage and the Family* 60(2):413.

Manalansan, Martin F., IV, Chantal Nadeau, Richard T. Rodríguez, and Siobhan B. Somerville. 2014. "Queering the Middle: Race, Region, and a Queer Midwest." *GLQ: A Journal of Lesbian and Gay Studies* 20(1–2):1–12.

Mathers, Lain A. B., J. Edward Sumerau, and Koji Ueno. 2018. "'This Isn't Just Another Gay Group': Privileging Heterosexuality in a Mixed-Sexuality LGBTQ Advocacy Group." *Journal of Contemporary Ethnography* 47(6):834–64.

Mattson, Greggor. 2020. "Small-City Gay Bars, Big-City Urbanism." *City and Community* 19(1):76–97.

McCabe, Janice. 2016. "Friends with Academic Benefits." *Contexts* 15(3):22–29.

McNaron, Toni A. H. 2007. "Post-Lesbian? Not Yet." *Journal of Lesbian Studies* 11(1/2):145–51.

McPherson, Miller, Lynn Smith-Lovin, and James M. Cook. 2001. "Birds of a Feather: Homophily in Social Networks." *Annual Review of Sociology* 27:415–44.

McQueeney, Krista. 2009. "'We Are God's Children, Y'all:' Race, Gender, and Sexuality in Lesbian- and Gay-Affirming Congregations." *Social Problems* 56(1):151–73.

Merton, Robert K. 1976. *Sociological Ambivalence and Other Essays*. New York: Free Press.

Merton, Robert K., and Elinor Barber. 1963. "Sociological Ambivalence." Pp. 91–120 in *Sociological Theory, Values, and Sociocultural Change: Essays in Honor of Pitirim A. Sorokin*, edited by E. A. Tiryakian. New York: Free Press.

Mitchell, Gregory. 2015. *Tourist Attractions: Performing Race and Masculinity in Brazil's Sexual Economy*. Chicago: University of Chicago Press.

Mochkofsky, Graciela. 2020. "Who Are You Calling Latinx?" *New Yorker*. Retrieved July 15, 2021. www.newyorker.com.

Monsour, Michael. 2002. *Women and Men as Friends: Relationships across the Life Span in the 21st Century*. Mahwah, NJ: Lawrence Erlbaum.

Moore, Mignon R. 2010. "'Black and Gay in L.A.': The Relationships Black Lesbians and Gay Men Have with Their Racial and Religious Communities." Pp. 188–213 in *Black Los Angeles: American Dreams and Racial Realities*, edited by D. M. Hunt and A.-C. Ramón. New York: New York University Press.

———. 2011. *Invisible Families: Gay Identities, Relationships, and Motherhood among Black Women*. Berkeley: University of California Press.

Morris, Max. 2018. "'Gay Capital' in Gay Student Friendship Networks: An Intersectional Analysis of Class, Masculinity, and Decreased Homophobia." *Journal of Social and Personal Relationships* 35(9):1183–204.

Moussawi, Ghassan, and Salvador Vidal-Ortiz. 2020. "A Queer Sociology: On Power, Race, and Decentering Whiteness." *Sociological Forum* 35(4):1272–89.

Muñoz, José Esteban. 2009. *Cruising Utopia: The Then and There of Queer Futurity*. New York: New York University Press.

Muraco, Anna. 2012. *Odd Couples: Friendships at the Intersection of Gender and Sexual Orientation*. Durham, NC: Duke University Press.

Myers, Daniel J. 2008. "Ally Identity: The Politically Gay." Pp. 167–87 in *Identity Work in Social Movements*, edited by J. Reger, D. J. Myers, and R. L. Einwohner. Minneapolis: University of Minnesota Press.

Myrdahl, Tiffany Muller. 2013. "Ordinary (Small) Cities and LGBQ Lives." *ACME* 12(2):279–304.

Nardi, Peter M. 1999. *Gay Men's Friendships: Invincible Communities*. Chicago: University of Chicago Press.

Ocobock, Abigail. 2013. "The Power and Limits of Marriage: Married Gay Men's Family Relationships." *Journal of Marriage and Family* 75(1):191–205.

———. 2018. "Status or Access? The Impact of Marriage on Lesbian, Gay, Bisexual, and Queer Community Change." *Journal of Marriage and Family* 80(2):367–82.

Office of Management and Budget. 2010. "2010 Standards for Delineating Metropolitan and Micropolitan Statistical Areas; Notice." *Federal Register* 75(123):37245–52.

Orne, Jason. 2017. *Boystown: Sex and Community in Chicago*. Chicago: University of Chicago Press.

Parker, Richard G. 1991. *Bodies, Pleasures, and Passions: Sexual Culture in Contemporary Brazil, Second Edition*. Nashville, TN: Vanderbilt University Press.

Pereira, Evan Odegard. 2021. "For Most Latinos, Latinx Does Not Mark the Spot." *New York Times*, June 15.

Pfeffer, Carla A. 2016. *Queering Families: The Postmodern Partnerships of Cisgender Women and Transgender Men*. New York: Oxford University Press.

Pidduck, Julianne. 2009. "Queer Kinship and Ambivalence: Video Autoethnographies by Jean Carlomusto and Richard Fung." *GLQ: A Journal of Lesbian and Gay Studies* 15(3):441–68.

Puar, Jasbir K. 2007. *Terrorist Assemblages: Homonationalism in Queer Times*. Durham, NC: Duke University Press.

———. 2020. "'I Would Rather Be a Cyborg Than a Goddess.'" Pp. 405–15 in *Feminist Theory Reader*, edited by C. McCann, S. Kim, and E. Ergun. New York: Routledge.

Rawlins, William K. 2008. *The Compass of Friendship: Narratives, Identities, and Dialogues*. Thousand Oaks, CA: SAGE.

Red Shirt-Shaw, Megan. 2020. *Beyond the Land Acknowledgement: College "LAND BACK" or Free Tuition for Native Students*. https://hackthegates.org/wp-content/uploads/2020/08/Redshirt-Shaw_Landback_HTGreport.pdf.

Reid, Helen M., and Gary Alan Fine. 1992. "Self-Disclosure in Men's Friendships." Pp. 132–52 in *Men's Friendships*, edited by P. M. Nardi. London: SAGE.

Rich, Adrienne. 1993. "Compulsory Heterosexuality and Lesbian Existence." Pp. 227–54 in *The Lesbian and Gay Studies Reader*, edited by H. Abelove, M. A. Barale, and D. M. Halperin. New York: Routledge.

Richards, Bedelia Nicola. 2020. "When Class Is Colorblind: A Race-Conscious Model for Cultural Capital Research in Education." *Sociology Compass* 14(7):e12789.

River City Collective. 2016. "River City Collective." Website accessed July 31, 2016.

Robinson, Jennifer. 2006. *Ordinary Cities: Between Modernity and Development*. New York: Routledge.

Rogers, Baker A. 2018. "Drag as a Resource: Trans* and Nonbinary Individuals in the Southeastern United States." *Gender and Society* 32(6):889–910.

Roseneil, Sasha, and Shelley Budgeon. 2004. "Cultures of Intimacy and Care beyond 'the Family': Personal Life and Social Change in the Early 21st Century." *Current Sociology* 52(2):135–59.

Rothblum, Esther D., and Penny Sablove. 2005. *Lesbian Communities: Festivals, RVs, and the Internet*. Binghamton, NY: Routledge.

Rupp, Leila J., and Verta Taylor. 2003. *Drag Queens at the 801 Cabaret*. Chicago: University of Chicago Press.

Ryan, Hugh. 2016. "Why Everyone Can't Be Queer." *Slate.com*, July 14. Retrieved July 30, 2016. www.slate.com.

Schilt, Kristen. 2011. *Just One of the Guys? Transgender Men and the Persistence of Gender Inequality*. Chicago: University of Chicago Press.

Seidman, Steven. 1996. *Queer Theory Sociology*. Hoboken, NJ: Wiley-Blackwell.

———. 2003. *Beyond the Closet: The Transformation of Gay and Lesbian Life.* New York: Routledge.

Silva, Tony. 2017. "Bud-Sex: Constructing Normative Masculinity among Rural Straight Men That Have Sex with Men." *Gender and Society* 31(1):51–73.

———. 2019. "Straight Identity and Same-Sex Desire: Conservatism, Homophobia, and Straight Culture." *Social Forces* 97(3):1067–94.

———. 2021. *Still Straight: Sexual Flexibility among White Men in Rural America.* New York: New York University Press.

Simmel, Georg. 1917. "The Stranger." Pp. 143–49 in *On Individuality and Social Forms: Selected Writings.* Chicago: University of Chicago Press.

Small, Mario Luis. 2009. "'How Many Cases Do I Need?' On Science and the Logic of Case Selection in Field-Based Research." *Ethnography* 10(1):5–38.

———. 2013. "Weak Ties and the Core Discussion Network: Why People Regularly Discuss Important Matters with Unimportant Alters." *Social Networks* 35(3):470–83.

Smelser, Neil J. 1998. "The Rational and the Ambivalent in the Social Sciences: 1997 Presidential Address." *American Sociological Review* 63(1):1–16.

Spencer, Liz, and Raymond Edward Pahl. 2006. *Rethinking Friendship: Hidden Solidarities Today.* Princeton, NJ: Princeton University Press.

Stacey, Judith. 2004. "Cruising to Familyland: Gay Hypergamy and Rainbow Kinship." *Current Sociology* 52(2):181–97.

———. 2005. "The Families of Man: Gay Male Intimacy and Kinship in a Global Metropolis." *Signs* 30(3):1911–35.

Stein, Arlene. 2002. *The Stranger Next Door: The Story of a Small Community's Battle over Sex, Faith, and Civil Rights.* Boston: Beacon.

———. 2010. "The Incredible Shrinking Lesbian World and Other Queer Conundra." *Sexualities* 13(1):21–32.

Stillwagon, Ryan, and Amin Ghaziani. 2019. "Queer Pop-Ups: A Cultural Innovation in Urban Life." *City and Community* 18(3):874–95.

Stone, Amy L. 2009. "More Than Adding a T: American Lesbian and Gay Activists' Attitudes towards Transgender Inclusion." *Sexualities* 12(3):334–54.

———. 2018. "The Geography of Research on LGBTQ Life: Why Sociologists Should Study the South, Rural Queers, and Ordinary Cities." *Sociology Compass* 12(11):e12638.

Swidler, Ann. 1986. "Culture in Action: Symbols and Strategies." *American Sociological Review* 51(2):273–86.

Sycamore, Mattilda Bernstein. 2008. *That's Revolting! Queer Strategies for Resisting Assimilation.* Berkeley, CA: Soft Skull Press.

Thomsen, Carly. 2021. *Visibility Interrupted: Rural Queer Life and the Politics of Unbecoming.* Minneapolis: University of Minnesota Press.

Thorpe, Rochella. 1996. " 'A House Where Queers Go': African American Lesbian Nightlife in Detroit, 1940–1975." Pp. 40–61 in *Inventing Lesbian Cultures in America*, edited by E. Lewin. Boston: Beacon.

Tillmann, Lisa. 2014. *In Solidarity: Friendship, Family, and Activism beyond Gay and Straight.* New York: Routledge.

Tompkins, Avery. 2011. "Intimate Allies: Identity, Community, and Everyday Activism among Cisgender People with Trans-identified Partners." Dissertation, Syracuse University. http://surface.syr.edu/soc_etd/67.

———. 2013. "'There's No Chasing Involved': Cis/Trans Relationships, 'Tranny Chasers,' and the Future of a Sex-Positive Trans Politics." *Journal of Homosexuality* 61(5):766–80.

Tongson, Karen. 2011. *Relocations: Queer Suburban Imaginaries*. New York: New York University Press.

Ueno, Koji, and Haley Gentile. 2015a. "Construction of Status Equality in Friendships between Gay, Lesbian, and Bisexual Students and Straight Students in College." *Sociological Perspectives* 58(3):402–21.

———. 2015b. "Moral Identity in Friendships between Gay, Lesbian, and Bisexual Students and Straight Students in College." *Symbolic Interaction* 38(1):83–102.

Ueno, Koji, Eric R. Wright, Mathew D. Gayman, and Janice M. McCabe. 2012. "Segregation in Gay, Lesbian and Bisexual Youth's Personal Networks: Testing Structural Constraint, Choice Homophily and Compartmentalization Hypotheses." *Social Forces* 90(3):971–91.

US Census Bureau. 2010. "American FactFinder." Retrieved July 31, 2016. http://factfinder.census.gov/faces/nav/jsf/pages/index.xhtml.

———. 2019. "2010 Census Urban and Rural Classification and Urban Area Criteria." Retrieved July 19, 2021. www.census.gov.

Vaid, Urvashi. 1995. *Virtual Equality: The Mainstreaming of Gay and Lesbian Liberation*. New York: Anchor Books.

Van Eeden-Moorefield, Brad, Christopher R. Martell, Mark Williams, and Marilyn Preston. 2011. "Same-Sex Relationships and Dissolution: The Connection between Heteronormativity and Homonormativity." *Family Relations* 60(5):562–71.

Vanderboom, Catherine Prouty, and Elizabeth A. Madigan. 2007. "Federal Definitions of Rurality and the Impact on Nursing Research." *Research in Nursing and Health* 30(2):175–84.

Vries, Brian de, and David Megathlin. 2009. "The Meaning of Friendship for Gay Men and Lesbians in the Second Half of Life." *Journal of GLBT Family Studies* 5(1–2):82–98.

Ward, Jane. 2008. *Respectably Queer: Diversity Culture in LGBT Activist Organizations*. Nashville, TN: Vanderbilt University Press.

Warner, Michael. 1993. *Fear of a Queer Planet: Queer Politics and Social Theory*. Minneapolis: University of Minnesota Press.

———. 2000. *The Trouble with Normal: Sex, Politics, and the Ethics of Queer Life*. Cambridge, MA: Harvard University Press.

Wedow, Robbee, Landon Schnabel, Lindsey K. D. Wedow, and Mary Ellen Konieczny. 2017. "'I'm Gay and I'm Catholic': Negotiating Two Complex Identities at a Catholic University." *Sociology of Religion* 78(3):289–317.

Weeks, Jeffrey, Brian Heaphy, and Catherine Donovan. 2001. *Same Sex Intimacies: Families of Choice and Other Life Experiments*. New York: Routledge.

Weinstock, Jacqueline S., and Esther Rothblum, eds. 1996. *Lesbian Friendships: For Ourselves and Each Other*. New York: New York University Press.

Weiss, Jillian Todd. 2003. "GL vs. BT." *Journal of Bisexuality* 3(3–4):25–55.

Westbrook, Laurel, and Aliya Saperstein. 2015. "New Categories Are Not Enough: Rethinking the Measurement of Sex and Gender in Social Surveys." *Gender and Society* 29(4):534–60.

Weston, Kath. 1991. *Families We Choose: Lesbians, Gays, Kinship*. New York: Columbia University Press.

———. 1995. "Get Thee to a Big City: Sexual Imaginary and the Great Gay Migration." *GLQ: A Journal of Lesbian and Gay Studies* 2(3):253–77.

Wilkinson, Eleanor. 2014. "Single People's Geographies of Home: Intimacy and Friendship beyond 'the Family.'" *Environment and Planning A* 46(10):2452–68.

Williams Institute. 2016. *Same-Sex Couple and LGBT Demographic Data Interactive*. UCLA School of Law. Los Angeles: Williams Institute. Retrieved July 31, 2016. http://williamsinstitute.law.ucla.edu/visualization/lgbt-stats/#density.

Wimmer, Andreas, and Kevin Lewis. 2010. "Beyond and Below Racial Homophily: ERG Models of a Friendship Network Documented on Facebook." *American Journal of Sociology* 116(2):583–642.

Woods, Michael. 2009. "Rural Geography: Blurring Boundaries and Making Connections." *Progress in Human Geography* 33(6):849–58.

Wortham, Jenna. 2016. "When Everyone Can Be 'Queer,' Is Anyone?" *New York Times*, July 12. Retrieved July 30, 2016. www.nytimes.com.

INDEX

Pages numbers in *italics* indicate tables

script, 179–83
segregation, 37
services, 110
setting, 20–24
sexuality terminology, 186
sexual orientation, 86, 87–88, 88, 189
shared-identity friendship: Charlie on, 78–79; in coming out, 76; community generated by, 126; culture and, 83; friendship mapping revealing, 72; friendship talk in, 71–72; gender impacting, 88; need for, 77; of participant, 80–81, 93–94; relationship discussed in, 76–77; Robin on, 85
Shelley, 64, 101, 104–5, 146
similarity, 104–5
small city: ambivalence in, 32; ambivalent community in, 15; inclusion in, 9; inequality in, 65–66; large city contrasted with, 3, 8–9, 29; LGBTQ community in, 1, 27–33; River City as, 1, 21, 28, 197n5
small town, 20–21, 39, 82, 194–95
Smelser, Neil J., 11
social change: activism for, 68–69; ambivalence to, 5; diversity resource for, 118–19; Kai generating, 2–3; Karen influencing, 120
social context, 11, 33–48
sociologists: friendship defined in, 17–18; on LGBTQ community, 157–58; terminology considered by, 185–86, 188
the South, 30–41, 67, 152
Spencer, Liz, 18, 172
state, 31
stealth, 42–43, 198n2 (chap. 2)
straight people, 59–60
suffusion, 18, 172–73
support: activism and, 111, 120; in coming out, 149; for community, 169; emotional, 107–11; for friends, 107, 109; material, 107–11; same-sex

marriage creating, 101–2; services included in, 110
symbol, 6, 28

Teagan: on friendship, 82; friendship mapping of, 124–25; on identity, 124; post-gayness frustrating, 148; in River City, 90–91
terminology: for allies, 197n2; in friendship mapping, 199n1 (chap. 4); Latinx in, 197n3; participant described by, 186; sociologists considering, 185–86, 188; of transgender people, 186–87
tokenism, 168
transgender people: coming out by, 89; hostility toward, 61; identity of, 74; in River City, 169–70; terminology of, 186–87. See also Lesbian, Gay, Bisexual, Transgender, and Queer (LGBTQ) community
Trump, Donald, 60, 65–66, 123
tumblr, 90, 124, 185, 200n1 (chap. 6)

Ueno, Koji, 110
Underground, 31–32, 164, 174–75
urban context, 198n1 (chap. 1); friendship in, 73, 159; LGBTQ community in, 17, 159–60, 162–63; toward post-gayness, 8; River City compared with, 40; River City foiling, 28–29, 96–97; rural context contrasted with, 67

Vanderboom, Catherine Prouty, 197n5
Vickie, 79–80
Vidal-Ortiz, Salvador, 13
vigil, in Orlando, 7, 47, 66
visibility, 119, 147, 164, 175
volunteers, 66–67

Warehouse, 59–60
Wendy, 102, 104, 107, 138
Weston, Kath, 6, 18
white supremacist, 200n1 (conc.)
word of mouth, 21, 27, 50, 55

ABOUT THE AUTHOR

CLARE FORSTIE is a teaching consultant at the Center for Educational Innovation at the University of Minnesota.